A Guide to

Parking

If you own a car, use public transportation, go to work or school, use health care, shop or dine out, or are part of a metropolitan community, parking affects you, probably in more ways than you've thought about. Because parking has such a huge effect on what happens in cities and towns and how the greater transportation system functions, decision-makers are beginning to realize that it's critical to employ parking expertise at the beginning of the planning process. Designing and implementing an effective, professionally managed parking strategy can mean the difference between frustrating and costly traffic congestion and efficient, time-saving traffic flow. *A Guide to Parking* provides information on the current state of parking, providing professionals and students with an overview on major areas of parking and the transportation and mobility industry, punctuated by brief program examples.

The **International Parking Institute (IPI)** is the world's largest and leading association of professionals in parking. Members include everyone from garage owners and operators to architects to city managers to government agencies, health care centers, universities, airports, and convention centers.

"The nation's leading experts have given us a virtual Encyclopedia of Parking that answers almost any question about parking anyone may have. Parking seems simple but it isn't. *A Guide to Parking* shows how good parking management can improve cities, the economy, and the environment."

—**Donald Shoup**, Distinguished Research Professor
of Urban Planning, UCLA, USA

"*A Guide to Parking* is a very easy read; headings make it easy to find what you're looking for. The guide provides information to a wide range of parking professionals and contains targeted ideas and recommendations. It also includes supporting background information that provides context and depth to the discussion, so, not only do you know what to do, you also know why and how to explain your actions."

—**Timothy J. Lomax**, Regents Fellow, Texas
A&M Transportation Institute, USA

A Guide to

Parking

Edited by
International Parking Institute
Kim Fernandez and
Rachel Yoka, CAPP

Routledge
Taylor & Francis Group

NEW YORK AND LONDON

First published 2018
by Routledge
711 Third Avenue, New York, NY 10017

and by Routledge
2 Park Square, Milton Park, Abingdon, Oxon, OX14 4RN

Routledge is an imprint of the Taylor & Francis Group, an informa business

Library of Congress Cataloging-in-Publication Data
A catalog record for this title has been requested

ISBN: 978-1-138-59593-4 (hbk)
ISBN: 978-1-138-59594-1 (pbk)
ISBN: 978-0-429-48808-5 (ebk)

Typeset in Sabon and Helvetica Neue
by Florence Production Ltd, Stoodleigh, Devon, UK

Contents

Contributors

Dave Albersman is an Associate and Senior Planner with Kimley-Horn and Associates. He has 34 years of parking and urban planning experience and holds a bachelor's degree in architecture from the University of Minnesota and a master's degree in public policy from Harvard University. His parking planning experience includes both physical and economic planning, focused primarily on large U.S. airports. His expertise includes landside master planning, parking structure functional design, consolidated rental car facility planning and design, supply/demand analysis, parking rate studies, and parking management analysis. He has provided landside planning consulting services at more than 40 domestic and international airports.

Mike App, AIA, LEED AP, is Director of Architecture at Timothy Haahs & Associates, Inc. He is a registered architect with extensive experience in all phases of building design, from programming and design through documentation and construction administration. For more than 20 years, he has served a variety of clients, ranging from private developers, to educational institutions, to corporate entities, to healthcare networks, assisting with the development of new construction and renovation/adaptive reuse projects, including parking facility design. He holds a master's degree in architecture from Virginia Polytechnic Institute and State University, and is actively involved with the American Institute of Architects. As a LEED Accredited Professional, he is also a strong believer in the importance of the architect's role in the stewardship of our planet's resources and serves as a Parksmart Advisor.

Michael J. Ash, Esq. is a partner in the New Jersey office of DeCotiis, FitzPatrick, Cole & Giblin, LLP. His areas of practice include redevelopment law, real estate, and municipal law specializing in parking matters. The majority of his practice focuses on infrastructure planning and implementation, where his work includes the coordination of property assemblage for right-of-way corridors, utility projects, and parking facilities. He has counseled public and private clients in the development of mixed-use projects with structured parking facilities and the redevelopment of surface parking lots for transit-oriented development projects.

Leonard T Bier, CAPP, JD, is Principal of Bier Associates, an urban redevelopment, mobility, and parking consulting firm. He works extensively in the area of urban redevelopment and specifically consults and advises on the role of parking as the catalyst for public private partnerships (P3) and mixed-use development. He is a co-author of *Parking Matters* "Designing, Operating, and Financing Structured Parking in Smart-Growth Communities". He is Director of both the City of Rahway Redevelopment Agency and Parking Authority. Bier Associates along with teammates received the 2008 NJ Future Smart Growth Award for the Rahway, NJ Town Center Master Plan. Bier lectures extensively around the world on topics such as P3, parking asset monetization, and urban mixed-use redevelopment planning. He is the legal columnist for *The Parking Professional* magazine, published by the International Parking Institute.

L. Dennis Burns, CAPP, is a Senior Practice Builder and Regional Vice President for Kimley-Horn and Associates, Inc. and has more than 30 years of parking operations, management, and consulting experience. He has led national and international research and analysis efforts in the areas of parking system strategic planning and smart parking system development. A leader in sustainable parking and transportation policy development, he recently worked with a team of colleagues at the International Parking Institute to develop the Accredited Parking Organization (APO) program. In 2010, he was honored as the International Parking Institute's Parking Professional of the Year. He provided the keynote at the International Transport Futures conference in Toronto; the Symposium for Urban Space Management in Maringa, Brazil; and the Towns and Cities Conference in Wellington, New Zealand.

Ryan A. Carris is a registered professional engineer in Illinois with 17 years of experience in investigation and repair of distressed facilities. Past projects have included parking structures, stadiums, bridges, and plazas. He is a member of ACI Committee 364 Rehabilitation.

Michael Drow, CAPP, PMP is Senior Vice President, Corporate Development at T2 Systems, one of the largest parking technology providers in North America. In his role, he establishes and manages technology partnerships and acquisitions to align with the long-term strategic goals of T2 Systems. During his career, he has led the development and rollout of several new technology-based business groups and services. He has direct experience in online marketing and permitting, pricing analytics, mobile payments, central command operating services, mobility services, and providing consulting services on technology. He is co-chair of the International Parking Institute's Technology Committee and is certified as a Project Management Professional and CAPP.

Kim Fernandez is Director of Publications for the International Parking Institute, where she serves as Editor of *The Parking Professional* and oversees the *Parking Matters Blog*, the Forum online member community, social media strategy, and special publications. Prior to joining IPI in 2011, she wrote for, edited, and managed consumer, association, and alumni publications. She is a graduate of Loyola University Maryland and member of its Green & Grey Society, holds a graduate certificate in social media marketing from Rutgers University, and has won multiple awards for writing and editing.

Todd Helmer, PE, is Vice President for TimHaahs' Philadelphia office, leading the office's operations, project development, financial management, and business development efforts. TimHaahs is a multi-disciplined engineering and architectural firm that specializes in the planning, design, and restoration of mixed-use parking structures. His recent experience includes parking and mixed-use projects for the Philadelphia Zoo, Temple University, New Jersey Transit, Cooper University Hospital, Seton Hall University, the Camden County Improvement Authority, and other downtown development projects. He provides leadership for TimHaahs University, the firm's in-house professional development program. A civil engineering graduate of The Georgia Institute of Technology, he is a licensed professional engineer in numerous states. He is an active member of many organizations, including the American Society of Civil Engineers, American Concrete Institute, Delaware Valley Association of Structural Engineers, International Concrete Restoration Institute, International Parking Institute, and the Urban Land Institute.

Kim Jackson, CAPP, has served as Director, Transportation & Parking Services at Princeton University since 2008. She provides leadership, expertise, and management for university transportation and parking operations, services, facilities, and programs. She previously worked at the International Parking Institute as Executive Director. Prior to IPI, she served as Director of Parking & Transportation at Rutgers University in New Jersey and was responsible for the university's parking and transportation programs, and management of daily operations of a multi-faceted program for five New Brunswick campuses, including contracted bus and handicap transport. A class-of-2000 CAPP graduate, she is a former chair of IPI's Board of Directors.

Casey Jones, CAPP, has more than two decades of parking and transportation experience and is Vice President at Timothy Haahs & Associates, Inc. Before becoming an access and mobility consultant, he oversaw parking programs in Seattle, Portland, and Spokane, and at the University of Colorado and Boise State University. He has led award-winning programs recognized for superior customer service, technological innovation, and sustainability. He is past Chair of the International Parking Institute Board of Directors and serves on the Accredited Parking Organization (APO) board of directors and the California Public Parking Association board of directors. He is the founding president of the Pacific Intermountain Parking and Transportation Association. He holds a master of public administration degree, a bachelor's degree in political science, and a graduate certificate in sustainability leadership. He is also a CAPP. He and his wife and two boys reside in Boise, Idaho.

William F. Kavanagh, AIA, is a licensed architect with more than 20 years of experience in the design of parking garages and mixed-use buildings. He is Director of Parking Planning and Design for the Harman Group, a structural engineering and parking consultancy firm with offices in Philadelphia and New York. He has designed more than 150 parking garage projects. A graduate of the University of Pennsylvania and the Syracuse University School of Architecture, he is a Parksmart Advisor and active in the American Institute of Architects, International Parking Institute, and the Pennsylvania Parking Association.

Blake Laufer, CAPP, is an entrepreneur and technology investor with a long history in parking. He started his first company in the 1990s, building management software for permits and enforcement, and later merged with T2 Systems. He remained at T2 where he led product development and held other technology-related roles. In 2017, he returned to his entrepreneurial roots with a new start-up providing parking space detection and analytics, founding MiStall Insight Inc. He is the author of numerous parking technology articles and presentations, a CAPP graduate, and co-chair of the International Parking Institute's Technology Committee.

Casey Leedom, PE, an engineer with Kimley-Horn and Associates, joined the firm in 2014 after finishing her master's degree in structural/earthquake engineering from UCLA. Since then, she has been involved in the planning and design of new parking facilities as well as the structural evaluation of existing parking structures. In addition, she has worked on a variety of site-related structural design and analysis projects for local municipalities and private developers.

Shawn McCormick has 19 years of enforcement management and operations experience, and is currently Director of Parking Enforcement and Traffic for the San Francisco Municipal Transportation Agency. He has managed parking enforcement programs in the City of Beverly Hills and the City of Los Angeles. He has international enforcement experience as Director of Operations for the ATVAM traffic enforcement program in Riyadh, Saudi Arabia. He was named Parking Professional of the Year by the California Public Parking Association in 2009 and has a Lean Six Sigma Black Belt certification. He is married to Tracie McCormick and has two adult children, Jonathan and Nicole, and two step-children, Michael and Russell.

Gary A. Means, CAPP, is Executive Director of the Lexington Parking Authority and a CAPP with a bachelor's degree in broadcasting from Eastern Kentucky University. He serves on the International Parking Institute Board of Directors and as Secretary on its Executive Committee. In the past, he co-chaired IPI's *Parking Matters*(r) Committee and Professional Recognition Awards Committee. He has also served on the Mid-South Transportation & Parking Association board as well as boards and committees, including the High Street YMCA board, the Downtown Lexington Management District board, and the advisory committee for the Downtown Lexington Partnership. In 2000, he received Downtown Lexington Corporation's Outstanding Individual Award. After 12 years of parking management experience with one of the nation's largest parking operators, he moved from private to public parking as executive director of the LPA. He and his wife, Melissa, have two children and two grandchildren.

Isaiah Mouw, CAPP, LEED GA, has worked in the parking industry for more than 10 years and directed nearly every facet of parking management in a municipal setting. In his role as Vice President of Municipal Operations for Citizens Parking, he works with his firm's regional and local operating teams to enhance Citizens Parking's existing public-sector parking operations across the country, including municipal, airport, and university. He serves on the International Parking Institute's Technology Committee and the Board of Directors for IPI's CAPP Board. In 2014, he was awarded the Chairman's Award from IPI.

Colleen M. Niese, with more than 20 years' experience in the human resources industry, partners with Marlyn Group clients to assess their internal scope of services in the areas of strategic human resources, employee career development, and talent acquisition. With that insight, she identifies with internal stakeholders those opportunities and subsequent deliverables for improved performance, at the individual, team, and company levels. She is the past Chairperson for the Women in Parking Association and is an active member of IPI, WELD (Women For Economic Leadership Development), SHRM, and ASA.

Sanjay Pandya, PE, is an Associate and Senior Project Manager with Kimley-Horn and Associates. He has more than 30 years of project management and structural engineering experience. For more than 20 years, he has been involved in the planning and design of new parking facilities and condition appraisals, repair, and retrofit of existing building structures. He has led teams in the design of new parking structures for a variety of clients, including municipalities, private developers, hospitals, and universities. He also has directed numerous parking consulting projects, including parking supply/demand, parking structure site feasibility studies, and parking structure functional design development. He is a registered professional engineer in four states and a structural engineer in three states.

Vicki Pero is well-balanced in operational leadership and support; as Principal of The Marlyn Group, she zeros in on employee training, recruitment, and organizational development programs to improve outcomes, putting people first. Twenty years of experience in the parking industry has cross-trained her to manage challenges from the inside out. During her career, she has managed a regional territory comprised of 80 locations, led a company's field audit function, and designed training solutions for all levels of employees. She is an active member of the International Parking Institute and serves on its Education Development Committee.

Stephen J. Rebora, RA, is President of DESMAN. He is a licensed architect and has been an integral part of the parking design and planning industry for more than 30 years. His works have been published by many parking publications, The Urban Land Institute, and Architectural Record. His experience within the architectural field includes master planning, green building design, project management, and field coordination. Through his involvement in parking structure design, he has developed a wide range of capabilities pertaining to parking structure planning, sustainability, and innovation. During his tenure with DESMAN, he has been involved with hundreds of parking projects throughout the U.S. and abroad.

Charles D. Reedstrom, CAPP, has been a nationally renowned parking planner and technologies consultant for almost 30 years. He is known for his expertise with the development of projects involving technology systems, strategic/master planning, and the design and implementation of parking revenue control systems and parking guidance systems. Many of his projects include parking management and operations audit and assessment; parking rate analysis; parking guidance and wayfinding systems design and implementation; parking supply/demand analysis; and the design and implementation of parking revenue control systems.

Brian Shaw, CAPP, is Executive Director of Parking and Transportation Services at Stanford University. He is a specialist in the area of sustainable transportation, and created new programs at Stanford, the University of Pennsylvania, the University of Chicago, and Emory that fostered carpooling, biking, walking, and riding public transit to campus. Under his leadership, Stanford has been able to keep its peak hour trips under a cap established in 2000, while the campus has continued to grow and thrive. He has served on the International Parking Institute's Board of Directors since 2014, co-chairing the association's Sustainability Committee while serving on the Education Development Committee. He recently developed a TDM course for IPI and Green Business Certification, Inc., to help educate non-practitioners. He is a CAPP and a frequent contributor to *The Parking Professional* magazine.

Alexander Smith, CM, is Operations Manager with the Phoenix-Mesa Gateway Airport Authority in Mesa, Ariz. His areas of expertise include airfield management, aviation security, landside operations, and parking management. He has been published on the International Parking Institute's *Parking Matters* blog. He holds a bachelor's degree (magna cum laude) in air traffic management and a master's degree in criminal justice, both from Arizona State University. He is credentialed as a Certified Member with the American Association of Airport Executives.

Vanessa K. Solesbee, CAPP, is President of The Solesbee Group, a management consulting firm founded in 2013 and based in Denver, Colo. The Solesbee Group provides parking and mobility management consulting for municipalities and universities. She carefully curates project-based teams whose members are passionate about creating world-class communities by elevating the parking and transportation experience of residents and visitors. Previously, she was a consulting planner for Kimley-Horn and Associates. She has served on parking expert advisory panels in Colorado, Montana, Texas, New Jersey, and Utah, and presented the keynote address for the 2016 Parking Australia Conference in Perth. She was the youngest recipient of the Corridor's Most Influential Women award for her post-flood recovery work in Cedar Rapids, Iowa. She and her husband, John, live in Denver with their two daughters.

Torrey L. Thompson serves as Director of Restoration at Carl Walker, a division of WGI. He has more than 23 years of restoration project experience focused mainly on the evaluation and restoration of existing parking facilities, plaza systems, and building facades. He is active in the International Concrete Repair Institute and the American Concrete Institute.

Mark A. Vergenes is President of MIRUS Financial Partners. The firm was founded with the goal of assisting its clients in every aspect of their financial lives. His clients are individuals, families, nonprofits, and small business owners. His practice focuses on the advantages of asset management and wrap fee programs through Cetera Advisor Networks LLC. Knowledge and experience play key roles in helping clients more effectively work toward their financial goals. A longtime resident of Lancaster, Pa., Vergenes is active in the community. He served as Chairman of the Board for the Lancaster City Parking Authority, from 2006 to 2018, and he is President of the Pennsylvania Parking Association.

Patrick Wells is a leading consultant in marketing and new business development for DESMAN. With nearly 20 years of experience in heavy commercial construction and through a progression of positions with two leading regional firms, he has developed technical and management skills covering field operations, cost control, estimating, marketing, proposal writing, and sales. As Regional Director of Business Development, he is responsible for the company's success in the Ohio and Pennsylvania region. He reports directly to the president of the company and is the primary interface between DESMAN and the client. He holds a bachelor's degree in communications from The Ohio State University.

Paul Wessel is the USGBC Market Development Director responsible for the global rollout of the Parksmart parking and transportation certification program. Paul led the 2014 launch of Parksmart's precursor, Green Garage Certification, and developed partnerships with BOMA, IFMA, DOE, and the USGBC to further the mission of high-performance parking. He has presented on sustainable parking to the American Planning Association, the Better Buildings Alliance, CBRE, Colliers, the National Governors Association, and the Urban Land Institute. He was previously Deputy Economic Development Administrator and Director of Traffic & Parking for the City of New Haven, Conn., and served on the boards of the New Haven Parking Authority, Greater New Haven Transit District and Greater New Haven Clean Cities. He has a bachelor's degree in history from Wesleyan University and a master's degree in urban policy analysis and management, Milano School of International Affairs, Management, and Urban Policy, The New School.

Richard W. Willson, PhD, FAICP, is a professor in the Department of Urban and Regional Planning at Cal Poly Pomona. He is an expert on transportation planning, parking supply and management, and climate change planning. His 2013 book, *Parking Reform Made Easy*, provides a method for reforming minimum parking requirements. *Parking Management for Smart Growth* (2015) provides a strategic approach to parking management in the context of a sharing economy. Recent research papers address new ways of measuring parking occupancy and evaluations of dynamic pricing pilot projects. He consults on parking issues with regional and local agencies such as the Bay Area Rapid Transit District, local cities, and developers of urban infill projects. He holds a PhD in urban planning from UCLA and is a Fellow of the American Institute of Certified Planners.

Brett Wood, PE, CAPP, is the Director for Kimley-Horn's national parking planning practice, helping define creative parking management solutions throughout the U.S. He leads a team of 15 practice builders whose mission is to help their clients think beyond the parking space and search for solutions that integrate shared mobility, transportation demand management, and right-sized parking. The Kimley-Horn parking team is widely recognized for its mindset on parking management and reduction of parking demand as communities and campuses adapt to changing transportation conditions.

Rachel Yoka, CAPP, LEED AP BD+C, is Vice President of Program Development for the International Parking Institute, leading the organization in technology, research, data analytics, and industry accreditation and certification. She was editor of *Sustainable Parking Design and Management: A Practitioner's Handbook*. Prior to joining IPI staff in 2014, she was selected as the Parking Professional of the Year. She has spearheaded the sustainability movement in the parking industry, leading the development of the first industry-specific rating system for sustainability in parking structures, now Parksmart. In 2016 she was appointed USGBC faculty. She was previously vice president for an architecture firm specializing in the planning, design, and rehabilitation of parking and mixed-use structures, as well as a member of the IPI Board of Directors. A frequent speaker and author for a variety of publications, she is a graduate of the Georgetown University School of Foreign Service.

CHAPTER 1

Introduction

Kim Jackson, CAPP and
Charles Reedstrom, CAPP

Introduction to Parking

Everyone who owns a car knows the importance of the availability, and access to, sufficient parking supply. One UCLA study found that there are between two and six parking spaces available for every car in the U.S. [1] Parking has been and will continue to be recognized as a critical resource, even with advances on the horizon that include greater transportation demand management strategies, the rise of transportation network companies (TNCs), and the development of autonomous vehicles.

Overview of the Parking Industry

The parking industry is conservatively estimated to be in the range of a $25 to $30 billion[2] industry employing more than 1 million parking professionals[3] and with more than 40,000 parking facilities operating within the United States.[4]

The parking industry may be separated into various industry sectors, each with its own unique characteristics, users, and challenges. This list is not comprehensive but is designed to provide a broad perspective on the industry as a whole.

Airports

Typically, revenue generated from the parking facilities represents the second largest revenue generator within an airport, second only to landing fees.[5] One critical characteristic for airport parking is that patrons can quickly find parking and have plenty of time to proceed through security, arrive at the gate, and board their flight. An adequate parking supply with appropriate wayfinding is necessary for any airport.

Airport master planning is based upon the number of annual enplanements—that is, the number of patrons boarding aircrafts. Basing the parking supply on the number of annual enplanements allows an airport to balance the amount of parking supply with the demand.

Many airports have implemented special programs designed to provide enhanced parking services and customer experiences at the airport. Some of these include premium parking services, such as a reserved parking program, offered at additional costs. These include reserved parking close to the terminal at a premium price, frequent-parking areas with private entry and exit lanes and a loyalty-points program, and valet parking. Some airports have joined with local transit agencies to provide transit service directly to the airport, and many provide areas for taxis, shuttle services, and TNCs such as Uber or Lyft.

Hospitals and Major Medical Centers

Hospital parking services tend to have several customer-specific goals, with the highest priority provided to patients. Hospitals must also provide parking for visitors and employees; frequently, employee parking is restricted to specific areas or provided at remote locations to reserve more convenient parking for patients.

A common challenge is providing parking during shift changes, which normally happen twice a day. Having two shifts of employees onsite at once can create a bottleneck at facilities without careful planning and assignment of parking facilities. Many hospitals allow patients to park without incurring a parking fee. Additionally, hospitals sometimes provide a validation program that provides for reduced or free parking.

Municipalities

Municipalities must provide parking to ensure convenient, economical, and user-friendly access for customers, commuters, residents, and visitors to the downtown area. This is usually achieved with a mix of on- and off-street parking facilities. Municipal parking goals include providing adequate parking without impeding traffic flow throughout the city and offering efficient parking for patrons of local establishments.

On-street parking spaces are usually restricted and enforced by the amount of time a patron may park, and based on location and intended use of the parking space, this can vary from 10 to 20 minutes up to 10 hours. Enforcement is typically performed by parking enforcement officers (PEOs) who patrol and issue citations for vehicles parked in violation of posted limits. Additional enforcement measures might include booting or towing the vehicles, particularly those that have multiple outstanding violations/citations.

Some cities regulate parking for residents with a residential permitting system. These permitting systems restrict the parking in residential areas, with priority given to the residents.

Retail and Mixed-Use Facilities

Retail and mixed-use facilities have unique parking requirements. They typically experience high parking turnover as many visitors patronize restaurants, shops, or bars. The mix of parkers includes users of the establishments, employees and staff, and sometimes residents. Establishing rules for employee parking is critical to ensure there's enough parking for the users of the facilities.

Parking convenience is vitally important in mixed-use areas. Therefore, management of these facilities provide flexible parking systems that include a time-based parking fee, valet parking, and validations that offer free or reduced parking to patrons of the establishments. These facilities develop programs to entice patrons to drive to their establishments.

Transit and Multi-Model Facilities

Transit agencies offer low-cost parking at remote locations where a park-and-ride or transit station facility is located to encourage patrons to leave their vehicles outside the city, to reduce vehicular traffic and congestion. The challenge is to offer this parking at a substantially reduced cost from what parking costs in the downtown core. Sometimes the price of parking is included in the price of riding the bus or train.

Many agencies offer a permitting process in which patrons can sign up and manage their parking accounts over a secure internet link. Additionally, transit agencies can team up with pay-by-cell providers to let patrons use their smartphones to pay for parking. Enforcement requires a high-tech application, usually with a mobile or stationary license plate recognition (LPR) application that captures a vehicle's license plate and verifies that the vehicle is either a valid permit holder or has paid by phone. Enforcement activity might include the issuance of a warning, issuance of a full citation, or booting or towing the vehicle.

Universities and Major Campus Facilities

Managing university parking can be challenging and requires the ability to balance varying and opposing customer demands. Users are faculty, staff, students, visitors, and strategic partners, who affect the same supply on a daily basis. Organizations try to meet all customer needs through technology solutions, flexible permit types, reservation systems, and even valet services that offer a mix of options, price ranges, and services.

> "There are competing goals between using parking lots as a placeholder of land use for future development. Parking is pushed to the perimeter where land is less expensive."
> Becca White,
> University of Virginia

College campuses typically offer a variety of parking options, from large, multi-story parking structures to small surface lots containing 15 to 20z permitted parking spaces. Many campuses offer a variety of parking permit types, all the way from annual and semester permits to a half-day or visitor permit good for a few hours. Enforcement of these programs is generally a large, concerted effort that can be facilitated by real-time computerized permitting systems and the ability to compare that information to a database of valid permits and identify vehicles without valid permits.

Campus development also affects parking revenue sources. On many campuses, surface parking is a placeholder and will eventually be developed. Surface parking tends to be pushed to the outer edge of the campus footprint. As development takes surface parking supply away, organizations must implement more transportation demand management (TDM) policies or build more parking, typically farther away from the central campus.

Universities are major contributors to alternative transportation initiatives that include such items as individual or group bike lockers, bus or transit passes, on-demand vehicle rental programs, and ride share programs such as carpools and vanpools.

Universities are also responsible for the management of game-day or special events that require a substantial amount of parking for a short period of time. University parking management groups must gear up for these major events with special policies and systems designed to support them, as well as extra personnel, equipment, and many detailed pieces of information and equipment.

Corporate Campuses

Many major corporations have developed significant and sprawling campuses. These campuses provide parking for employees and staff primarily through permit programs, and may be at low or no cost to employees. They also must accommodate visitors.

One of the primary challenges for corporate campuses is accommodating an influx of employees during a short window in the morning and then getting everyone out during a short time period in the late afternoon or evening. Parking facilities and associated roadways must be designed to empty quickly and efficiently without adversely affecting or inundating the surrounding roadways. Many larger campuses also offer TDM strategies for employees such as shuttle service to transit and shared-ride programs to encourage carpools and vanpools.

Commercial Operations

Commercial operators represent a large share of the parking market, especially in larger urban centers. There are myriad commercial operators that own, manage, and/or maintain private parking operations. These entities primarily support urban areas, event centers, and destinations, and even smaller downtowns and universities and institutions. Often, municipalities will contract out to these organizations for third-party management, especially of off-street resources, namely surface and structured parking. These companies comprise a large cross-section of the industry.

Suppliers and Consultants

A summary of the industry would not be complete without addressing the multitude of suppliers of products and services that support parking owners and operators. These include technology providers of software, hardware, and consulting; planners, architects, engineers, and construction companies that provide infrastructure; and goods and services providers of physical equipment that run the gamut from tickets to meters of all kinds.

The Role of the Parking Professional

Parking is a career that is rarely discussed; college parking degree programs aren't the norm. Most industry professionals did not plan to pursue a career in parking; their journey took them there by chance.

As referenced, there are more than 1 million estimated employees in the parking industry working in municipalities, airports, colleges and universities, hospitals, corporate campuses, hotels, commercial operations, and major event venues. This number doesn't include transportation and mobility professionals who also address parking in the scope of their employment.

Each industry segment mentioned has its own customer base and audience, with its own specific focus, but there are commonalities across all segments. These include parking resources, revenue (and expenses), and customer service and training.

Here are a few differences for consideration:

- Personnel in airport operations are primarily focused on the traveler; efficient and timely communication and access is key. They are also concerned with the speed and process of payment and both ingress and egress of customers.
- Municipality operations and their staff are focused on driving economic development and getting customers downtown. They shape policies that drive parking decisions to create turnover and maximize space use. They may also manage residential parking needs and regulations to balance potentially competing priorities for residential and downtown commuter and visitor parkers.
- Parking professionals working in hospitals balance the demands of medical and other staff with the needs of the patients and their visitors. Staff in this industry segment must understand the customers' needs and the possible stress and emotion generated by any hospital visit, especially in an emergency.
- Colleges and universities host many varying customers, all with differing needs. Faculty park during classes and office hours; staff park for longer periods of time nearly every day; students and visitors are always coming and going; and events bring large numbers of patrons wanting to enter, park, and exit simultaneously. These professionals balance supply, demand, and customer expectations.

Skills Sets, Resources, and Aspects of the Profession

As discussed, industry professionals cover a multitude of issues and play many different roles. Parking operates at the intersection of real estate, technology, logistics, consumer behavior, and transportation.

Degrees in planning, management, economics, finance, or behavioral sciences can provide a solid foundation that will enable a professional to manage a parking operation in these segments. Understanding strategic planning, developing financial forecasts and benefit analyses, and managing and motivating employees are crucial to leadership in these roles.

Planning, engineering, architecture, and design are the specialized (and licensed) practitioners most often associated with industry consultants. These individuals build parking structures and lots, and engineer the best design for ingress and egress, traffic flow, load, visual aesthetics and location. They perform inspections and recommend preventative maintenance or help restore these investments in infrastructure.

A focus on safety, security, and emergency management can be well-adapted into a career as a parking professional. The health, safety, and welfare of all patrons and employees (as well as their vehicles) is of paramount importance in every segment of the industry. Understanding passive and active security as well as best practices in emergency management translate well in this environment.

Specialists in information technology and data are critical to the success and innovation in the industry. As operations increase integration with the connected car, real-time data, and eventually the autonomous vehicle, these skills sets are and will continue to be in extremely high demand. Planning appropriately for the implementation of new technology, and understanding the value of the data parking systems generate, is critical for operational success. As concepts of mobility as a service are innovated, these skills will be of great importance as traditional parking models change.

Sustainability is an increasing priority as mobility patterns change and shift. Transportation demand management and reducing the use of the single-occupancy vehicle is central to sustainability efforts. Professionals with a sustainability or TDM background work to change customer behavior by providing viable transportation options, including carpools, vanpools, mass transit, and bicycles. Additionally, these professionals assist with the planning and implementation of sustainable features into facilities and operations.

Lastly, communication through marketing and branding, public relations, and social media all enhance customer service. Customers have come to expect immediate communication and information about parking resources. These professionals communicate with patrons, interact with the media, and essentially, tell their organization's story.

Every parking and transportation professional touches upon aspects of each of these skills sets in the scope of their career. While it is not expected that any one person develop a specialty in all of these areas, the successful industry professional will be both literate and seek a basic understanding of this wide range of skills.

Notes

1   Shoup, Donald. *The High Cost of Free Parking*, (U.S., Routledge Publishing, 2011).
2   http://blogs.cornell.edu/armapp/2013/03/27/revenue-management-in-car-parking-industry/.
3   2013 U.S. Department of Labor, Bureau of Labor Statistics.
4   www.nrdc.org/experts/david_b_goldstein/does_every_car_need_8_parking_spaces_ride_ sharing_can_save_emissions.
5   www.parking.org/2016/01/02/2012-05-08-new-report-highlights-importance-of-parking/.

CHAPTER 2

Laws, Regulations, and Related Policy

Michael J. Ash, Esq.

Parking laws exist at the intersection of municipal law and land-use regulations. While there is no uniform code of parking regulation in the U.S., most parking is regulated in the same manner in different jurisdictions. Parking laws and regulations are the result of local legislation by the governing body of a municipality, county, or other public body with delegated legislative authority. Parking regulations fall into two general categories: on-street and off-street.

Individual laws vary in different jurisdictions and from state to state, based on the supply and demand of parking facilities. Further, parking regulations vary from town to town based on the demands and customs of the community. Rather than focus on the various regulations in a municipality, an analysis of the general legal theories that form the basis of on- and off-street parking laws will provide proper context to understanding parking regulations and related policy.

Regulation of Parking: Adoption of Parking Laws

Throughout the U.S., on- and off-street parking is regulated by the governing body of the local government through the legislation of laws, rules, and policies. Actions by local governing boards typically take the form of ordinances, resolutions, motions, or orders. The appropriate legislative action of the governing body may vary depending on the intended parking policy. Legislation intended to make a permanent change to a parking regulation or parking requirement in the land development code requires the adoption of an ordinance. In most jurisdictions, an ordinance requires at least one public hearing and advanced notice by publication prior to adoption. The result of an adopted ordinance is a permanent change to the municipal code such as a change in off-street parking requirements or a change in on-street parking rates. A governing body typically uses a resolution to approve agreements, direct executive functions, or for an expression of governing-body opinion of a factual determination that conditions necessary for the operation of an ordinance have been met. Governing bodies should consult with parking professionals to review best practices for the regulation of on- and off-street parking. By the same token, parking professionals should offer their opinions and insight into parking policies to governing bodies to assist them in drafting legislation. To inform the opinions of the governing body, a parking professional should be aware of the legal basis and public policy considerations that provide the basis for valid on- and off-street parking regulations.

On-Street Parking Permits

While there is little doubt that on-street parking can be regulated throughout a municipality with the establishment of parking meters, signage, and a program of penalty enforcement, expanding these typical police powers sometimes requires review and approval by the courts. The existence of a residential permit parking program in a densely populated residential area seems routine, however some of the first residential permit parking programs were the subject of lawsuits alleging discrimination against non-residents and an improper allocation of the public resource of on-street parking. Residential permit parking programs were established in cities to restrict nonresident motorists in the use of on-street parking spaces.

The U.S. Supreme Court in the case of County Board of Arlington County Virginia, et. al. v. Rudolph A. Richards, et. al. 434 U.S. 5 (1977), upheld the constitutionality of a residential permit parking program and reversed the decision of the Virginia Supreme Court [Cty. Bd. Of Arlington Cty. v. Richards, 231 SE 2d 231], which held that resident permit parking programs violated the Fourteenth Amendment—equal protection clause—by discriminating between residents and non-residents. The U.S. Supreme Court in its opinion stated:

> To reduce air pollution and other environmental effects of automobile commuting, a community reasonably may restrict on-street parking available to commuters, thus encouraging reliance on car pools and mass transit. The same goal is served by assuring convenient parking to residents who leave their cars at home during the day. A community may also decide that restrictions on the flow of outside traffic into particular residential areas would enhance the quality of life there by reducing noise, traffic hazards, and litter. By definition, discrimination against nonresidents would inhere in such restrictions.
>
> The Constitution does not outlaw these social and environmental objectives, nor does it presume distinctions between residents and nonresidents of a local neighborhood to be invidious. The Equal Protection Clause requires only that the distinction drawn by an ordinance like Arlington's rationally promote the regulation's objectives.

The findings of the Supreme Court in upholding the legality of a residential parking permit program can be interpreted to support additional aspects of on- and off-street parking regulations. The rational objectives of a residential permit parking program include:

- Enhancement of the quality of life for residents of a community.
- Properly regulating the utilization and balance between off-street parking facilities and on-street parking resources.
- Promoting the flow of traffic by limiting the circling of non-residents searching for free on-street parking.

When considering the implementation of new parking regulations, the parking professional should be able to identify the rational basis for the policy. In addition to the desired regulatory changes, the legislation, whether by ordinance or resolution, should clearly articulate the objectives of the regulation. If the objectives are clearly articulated in the legislation, the likelihood of a legal challenge will decrease and the likelihood of surviving scrutiny by the courts will increase.

Off-Street Parking Requirements

One of the biggest challenges facing urban communities is the regulation of off-street parking in downtown environments. The ability to accommodate the parking needs of competing land uses is key to the success of a functioning municipality. The varied types of land uses in the municipality will dictate parking needs based on the characteristics of the respective uses.

For example, residential uses may require less available parking than office or retail uses. In addition to the variety of uses, their locations will have an effect on required parking supply. Consideration must be given to the context of the municipality: an urban downtown within walking distance of multiple modes of public transportation will have less parking demand than a suburban location without access to public transportation whose residents are dependent on personal vehicles.

Off-street parking requirements are typically found in municipal zoning codes. Zoning aims to create an orderly framework of development and separate incompatible land uses, such as industrial and residential uses. A form of zoning has existed since individuals began living together in cities, largely including desirable uses within the center of the city and relegating less desirable uses to the outskirts. The modern form of zoning in the U.S. can be traced back 100 years to the development of the first skyscrapers in New York City. When the Equitable Building was completed in downtown Manhattan in 1916, surrounding buildings were suddenly cast in its shadow. For the first time, New York City was forced to promote the efficient development of new skyscrapers with the legislation of policy to protect existing uses from adverse effects to light and air.

The first legal challenge to zoning ordinance survived judicial scrutiny in Village of Euclid, Ohio v. Ambler Realty Co., 272 U.S. 365 (1926), in which the Supreme Court held that the zoning ordinance was not an unreasonable extension of a municipality's police power and was based on a reasonable desire to regulate compatible uses, and thus it was not unconstitutional. This important decision established the modern Euclidian zoning that shapes development in U.S. cities today based on the segregation of land uses into specific zones and dimensional standards that place limitations on development activity within those zones. Some say the most limiting factor of modern zoning is a lack of flexibility in the way policies merely become a list of permitted and proscribed uses.

Parking is a key component of modern zoning and can dictate where certain development occurs. Usually development code includes a required minimum number of off-street parking spaces to be provided for a proposed development. A public parking professional should be consulted to study parking supply and demand to ensure the adequacy of the parking requirements. However, public parking professionals must also recognize the opportunity to use zoning considerations to balance the challenges of requiring sufficient parking supply and flexibility of desired development characteristics through the legislation of zoning ordinances.

The public parking professional has the ability to shape development and desirable parking policy through the implementation of the zoning code. While a formula for providing onsite parking for different uses may work in a suburban setting, successful planning for transit-oriented development and mixed-use development in an urban downtown setting must incorporate additional zoning considerations. Zoning codes should be implemented that seek to create pedestrian-friendly environments while maximizing parking efficiencies. For example, to maximize a pedestrian-friendly environment, public parking professionals should create zoning legislation based on the following policies:

- Proscribe off-street parking between a public street and the required frontage of a building.
- Require off-street parking supply to be located in surface lots at the rear of the building, underground, or in a structured facility.
- Create incentives for developers to provide retail space at grade or decorative façade elements along street walls lining structured parking facilities.
- Eliminate conflicts between vehicular parking access and pedestrian walkways.

Flexible options for the relief of parking requirements as described below should also be created to avoid rigid onsite parking requirements that may prevent development or waste precious real estate with overbuilt parking.

Relief from Off-Street Parking Requirements

Planning boards and municipalities must have a rational basis to waive off-street parking requirements or make sufficient findings to grant a variance of off-street parking requirements. Municipalities can benefit from proactively establishing checks and balances in their land development code that provide developers with flexibility in providing a supply of off-street parking that will not exceed demand based on the needs of the community. By having rational waiver options established in the land-use code, developers can maximize the efficiencies in their projects, municipalities can adequately manage off-street parking inventories, and the grant of a waiver or variance will have a rational basis that will withstand scrutiny by the courts. With flexible parking policies regulated in the land-use code, parking requirements can be applied fairly and uniformly, thereby avoiding a challenge to the municipality acting in an arbitrary or capricious manner.

Payment-In-Lieu of Parking

Another program designed to create flexibility in the development of new off-street parking is a Payment-in-Lieu of Parking (PILOP) Program. PILOP programs offer a developer the option to pay a fee for each parking space deficiency in a proposed development application in lieu of providing the number of parking spaces required by local land-use regulations. The PILOP fees are collected and held by the municipality or parking authority until such time as they can be used to construct a public parking facility that serves the same community. A PILOP program creates a mechanism for the municipal planning board to waive parking requirements without burdening the municipal taxpayers. The developer is given the opportunity to maximize the commercial development uses of the property by making a PILOP rather than dedicating more space or cost to the provision of off-street parking. The urban municipality promotes redevelopment, gains new real estate tax revenue, and receives a dedicated funding source for the construction of a public parking facility in concert with the city's or parking authority's master plan and future public parking needs.

The benefits of adopting a PILOP program are:

- Developer flexibility.
- Public parking facilities can be shared by multiple users.
- Consolidation of multiple small and single-user parking facilities into a larger, strategically located facility.
- Reduction or elimination of parking variances granted by a municipality.
- Ensures a uniform application of waivers for off-street parking compliance by developers.
- Provides a dedicated source of funding for public parking improvements and facilities.

The PILOP program should be created by ordinance as an amendment to the land development code of the municipality. The ordinance establishing a PILOP program should clearly define the guidelines for the implementation of the program, establishing the parking fees and procedures for the dispensation of the collected fees to develop new public parking facilities.

Shared Parking

Most local zoning ordinances continue to require dedicated, off-street parking for each individual project, missing valuable potential for shared parking among complementary uses. In addition, the high costs of building and operating structured off-street parking facilities and the minimum economies of scale related to such facilities can defeat proposed projects in the absence of significant public subsidies in all but the most expensive real estate markets in the U.S.

The concept of shared parking has become an effective way to regulate the parking supply for new development in a transit-oriented or mixed-use development. Simply put, the ability to share an off-street parking space in a mixed-use development project reserves more space in the development footprint for the principal uses and ensures that scarce real estate resources are not dedicated to a parking over-supply.

The concept of shared parking requires that off-street parking spaces serve multiple complementary uses. The shared parking space must be used for overlapping trips. For example, a person who drives to a central business district during the morning commute for work and parks his or her vehicle may also walk to nearby shops at lunch or after work in the evening. The commuter has driven to a central business district for work and patronized other establishments throughout town while using one off-street parking space. Here, the multiple uses—office, retail and restaurant—all share the same parking space. A parking supply saving is achieved when this occurs. It is the challenge of parking professionals to recognize these parking supply savings and structure off-street parking supply policy with opportunities for shared parking in mind.

The benefits of a shared parking policy are also achieved when off-street parking can serve non-competing uses. For example, residential tenants park in an off-street parking facility at night, typically between 7 p.m. and 7 a.m. They take their cars to work elsewhere and the spaces they vacate during the day are available to meet the demands of office, retail, and commercial tenants who typically require parking from 7 a.m. to 7 p.m. The result is that 300 (for example) parking spaces in a downtown context may fulfill the parking demands of both residential and nonresidential users that would otherwise require 400 to 500 parking spaces.

There is a variation on this complementary parking construct in transit-oriented developments. Given the recent trend in transit-oriented developments, a reliance on public transportation has decreased the use of personal vehicles. Instead of multiple complementary uses sharing off-street parking facilities or the possibility of multiple users of the same space in a 24-hour time period, the new horizon for shared parking concepts will rely on a combination of bicycle-share programs, car rental services, and ride-sharing applications. With more options for personal transportation available, the less beholden residents will be to personal automobile ownership. Such diversification in modes of transportation made available by the sharing economy will lead to gains in parking efficiency.

The Law

If it is a challenge for parking professionals to identify shared parking opportunities, it is even more challenging to codify the concept into a valid law. The inherent benefit of flexibility in the application of the shared parking concept can easily be lost in the rigidity of the codification of an ordinance, and the shared parking tool can only be available for deployment if duly adopted into law. Accordingly, best practice should be to highlight the essence of the shared parking concept in an ordinance.

First, the concept of shared parking should be clearly defined in the ordinance together with the stated purpose of the program. Second, the ordinance must outline the specific criteria in which a developer may invoke a shared parking arrangement, the factual circumstances upon which a municipality can grant a waiver for parking compliance based on a shared parking alternative, and the formula to calculate the amount of shared parking permitted in a proposed development. Third, the ordinance should specify the documentation required to justify a shared parking plan, including the options for a parking study, shared parking plan, and shared parking agreement. When all aspects of the shared parking policy are duly considered in a well-defined ordinance, the policy can seamlessly be integrated into law.

Public parking professionals should recommend flexible options for the relief of parking requirements to avoid rigid onsite parking requirements that would otherwise prevent development, or waste precious real estate with overbuilt parking. The success to any legal challenge will be to demonstrate a rational basis for the implementation of the parking policies in a uniform manner to prevent allegations of arbitrary and capricious action by a municipality.

Compliance with Federal Parking Regulations

While parking requirements are typically regulated and enforced on a state and local (municipal) level, federal statutes ensuring access and accommodation for disabled individuals must be accounted for in parking compliance. The Americans with Disabilities Act (ADA) provides requirements for access and accommodation to public and private facilities. The U.S. Justice Department updated regulations on parking requirements through the promulgation of new design standards outlined in the 2010 ADA Standards for Accessible Design.

ADA rules are applicable to all government facilities under Title II and all public and commercial facilities under Title III. The standards in design include new requirements for the quantity of accessible parking spaces and requirements for van-accessible parking spaces.

- Medical facilities require more accessible parking than other types of uses.
- Furthermore, the location of accessible parking spaces must connect to the building entrance by the shortest possible route and must be dispersed throughout a parking facility serving multiple buildings.
- Accessible parking spaces must comply with strict design criteria to accommodate width, access aisles, and loading areas.
- Accessible parking spaces must be clearly marked with signage and striping to identify the availability of the accessible space and discourage others from parking.
- Accessible parking spaces should be maintained with a heightened standard of care to remove snow, debris, or other impediments to access.

Best practice to enforce these mandatory regulations under the ADA is to have local ordinances incorporate the required standards and design criteria in land development ordinances.

Conclusion

While specific parking requirements may vary depending on local customs, governments should strive to adopt regulations that will provide sufficient supply and demand, encourage sound planning principles, and ensure compliance with uniform design guidelines.

CHAPTER 3

Planning Parking: Functions, Analysis, and Strategy

Richard W. Willson, PhD, FAICP, Dennis Burns, CAPP, and Brett Wood, PE, CAPP

Parking is an integral element of land use and transportation systems. Planned well, it supports mobility, economic vitality, and driver convenience. Planned poorly, parking creates automobile-dominated environments that can be detrimental to the environment, undermine community livability, frustrate parkers, and are socially unfair.[1] During the last few decades, parking experts and stakeholders have rethought how parking is supplied and managed. Parking planning has moved from a one-size-fits-all, standard approach common in engineering fields to one in which parking is an integral part of planning and policy, aligned with a community's vision and goals. This approach encompasses both transportation and land use planning.

Innovation and change are the watchwords in parking planning. Uniform best-practice approaches are being replaced by ones that are tailored to local objectives and that place parking in a broader planning context. For example, while minimum parking requirements are the norm in North American cities, Buffalo, N.Y., recently eliminated them for economic development and environmental reasons. While the norm of fixed curb parking prices exists in many cities, San Francisco and others are dynamically varying parking charges by time of day and blockface. And the norm of hunting for a convenient parking space with wits and luck is being replaced by systems that guide parkers to their space of choice.

This chapter provides a framework and perspective for the more detailed chapters that follow. It has three elements: an introduction to functions and types of parking, a review of parking study procedures and techniques, and a presentation of a strategic planning framework for parking planning.

Functions of Parking

Parking is part of the multimodal transportation system that provides access; think of the trip from home to work. That system includes facilities such as roadways, rail transit lines, bike paths, and sidewalks, and services such as transit, goods delivery, and transportation network companies that match riders with drivers. Planners are developing ways to provide access with methods other than driving and parking, including increased land use density that places destinations closer together, mixed land uses that encourage walking, new rail transit and bus rapid transit, and the development of shared mobility.

Parking is both a land use, occupying a large part of land and building area in cities and suburbs, and an aspect of transportation infrastructure. Accordingly, many stakeholders are involved in parking planning, and it relates to a variety of policy issues. On the land use side, city planners, zoning regulators, property owners, parking operators, lenders, and developers make key decisions about the supply of parking. On the transportation side, planners and traffic engineers consider the design of parking facilities, their effects, and how they coordinate with other transportation modes.

In the past, having a plentiful parking supply was widely viewed to be in the broad public interest. When there was a complaint, the default response was to build more. In some ways, parking was the tail that wagged the dog of transportation and land-use planning. Now, many plans consider parking additions as a last resort, only after land-use strategies, other mobility strategies, shared parking, and parking management have been fully explored.

Parking (and transportation systems) are undergoing rapid change due to new transportation options and technology, as discussed in Chapter 5. The current supply of parking far exceeds the number of vehicles, and estimates say there are more than three parking spaces for every vehicle in the U.S.[2] This presents the opportunity to make better use of existing parking resources. Further, the rise of shared mobility services and the prospects of autonomous vehicles suggest that household vehicle ownership may decrease in the coming decades in some areas, and new parking management technologies will reduce traditional problems such as searching for an available parking space.

City planners and engineers know how controversial parking can be. Residents, customers, and employees have territorial feelings about parking arrangements and often complain when parking conditions change or new approaches are proposed. Sometimes, controversies about parking block the implementation of otherwise desirable development projects.[3]

Types of Parking

A community's parking system is comprised of many types of parking. While some parking is planned and provided by public agencies, other parking is provided by private entities as the result of parking requirements in zoning codes, and still other parking is provided as the result of private decisions. Despite this variety, it is important to look at total parking supply as a system and to seek integrated management strategies that treat it as such.

While each parking space occupies roughly the same land or building area, there are important distinctions among the types. Planning for parking addresses on-street (curb) parking and off-street parking in lots, structures, or underground. Taken together, all these forms of parking comprise a community's parking inventory.

Parking spaces vary widely in their usefulness, as measured by how many person-trips they serve per day.[4] Some spaces are seldom if ever used, such as excess parking in an office complex. Others are intensely used for specific time periods but empty the rest of the time, such as parking at a sports stadium or that offered as overflow for busy shopping centers during the holiday season. Still others serve multiple users throughout the day and night. The legacy of parking planning is that each use and type was considered discretely, and not part of a shared system. This meant that a lot of parking is unused a significant portion of the time.

Progressive communities now take a systems view that considers sharing of parking between land uses and advanced parking management tools to utilize the parking they have more efficiently, as noted in Chapter 2.

Curb Parking

On-street (curb) parking is found in cities, in residential neighborhoods, at employment centers, and in commercial districts. In the case of neighborhoods, this parking is the result of minimum street width regulations established by municipalities. In general, these require a wider paved surface than is needed for vehicle movement, creating curb parking opportunities. In built-up areas, curb parking exists where there is sufficient right-of-way and it is compatible with traffic conditions. Sometimes, curb parking is prohibited because street space is prioritized for faster vehicle flow. In those settings, the act of backing into a parking space would disrupt traffic and become a safety issue.

As noted in Chapter 2, cities determine rules for the use of on-street parking, such as how long a vehicle may be parked, prohibitions or limitations on overnight parking, time limits in high-use areas, parking charges, spaces reserved for drop-off or loading, and requirements to remove vehicles for street cleaning or during weather emergencies. These rules may include priorities for certain parkers, such as residents of a neighborhood or short-term parkers in a business district. Of late, other uses of curb space, such as loading, pick-up and drop-off, and bus or bike lanes, have been competing with curb parking.

Curb parking is often the most sought-after form of parking. For shoppers, parking in front of a store is more desirable that navigating an off-street parking facility. In neighborhoods, curb parking is prized sometimes because it allows garages to be used for other purposes, such as storage or home offices. Much of the controversy over parking—and there is plenty—relates to who gets to use curb parking and under what conditions.

Off-street Parking

Off-street parking includes a wide variety of facilities, such as surface parking lots, parking structures, and underground parking facilities. Off-street parking is owned and managed by public, non-profit, or private sector entities. Private parking associated with new construction is provided as the result of zoning rules, which mandate a certain amount of parking be provided with new construction and changes in use. Jurisdictions commonly establish required ratios of parking supply, parking dimensions, aisle way and driveway provisions, landscaping requirements, and other features in their zoning codes.

Off-street parking may also be provided directly by municipalities; this is common in downtowns and at special facilities such as convention centers. As well, the private sector may build or provide parking separate from a development project. This could be a market response to parking demand in a district, but parking prices rarely justify parking construction as a freestanding business enterprise. There is usually another reason for private parking construction, such as surface parking being a temporary use of land being held for subsequent development or parking being used to support another objective, such as the success of a real estate development.

Changing Attitudes in Parking Supply Practices

Parking provision was an assumed part of post-war development patterns and was seen as an efficient way of accommodating travel in an automobile-based transportation system. Cities established minimum parking requirements in zoning codes, as discussed in Chapter 2. This compelled developers to provide off-street parking for new developments and changes in building use. Justifications for this practice included avoiding traffic congestion associated with searching for on-street parking, preventing conflicts between property owners if occupants of one building poached the parking of other uses, and establishing a level playing field between developers.

This system, however, came under criticism for its effects on communities:

- The amount of land devoted to parking, producing sprawl and a self-reinforcing advantage for travel by private vehicle.
- Urban design effects related to sense of place and walkability and affecting the feasibility of transit and active transportation modes (buildings set in the middle of a sea of parking).

- Environmental impacts, including direct impacts such as urban heat island effects and polluted runoff, as discussed in Chapter 6, and indirect effects such as encouraging private vehicle transportation and associated greenhouse gas emissions.
- Social impacts related to an uneven playing field between those who can drive and those who cannot, by virtue of income or ability. This includes access to jobs, education, shopping, and other essential needs.
- Economic impacts, such as driving up the cost of housing and thwarting economic development in built-up areas.

Donald Shoup's landmark book *The High Cost of Free Parking*,[5] offers a three-part prescription—eliminating zoning ordinance parking requirements, charging a market price for curb parking, and returning parking revenue to communities—based on economics rather than engineering standards. In response, many communities are rethinking their approach to parking requirements, as evidenced by parking requirements that are reduced or eliminated. Stakeholders often equate these reforms with cessation of parking construction, which is not the case. These changes simply place decisions about parking supply in developer and property-owner hands.

Parking Demand and Use

The commonly-used term "parking demand" is tricky. Its common meaning is to indicate how much parking is used. Economists point out, however, that in locations where parking is free or subsidized and is generously provided, the level of parking use observed cannot be considered demand in the formal sense. Economic demand is the level of parking purchased at a certain price, where demand is sensitive to higher and lower prices. Because parking is free to the parkers in most locations in North America, there is no information on how much parking drivers are willing to pay for. All we know is how much they consume of a free good, which is likely to be an overstatement of how much they would pay for.

Free parking is the norm in some urban areas and most suburban areas in North America. Residents don't pay extra for parking where they live, employees generally park for free at work, and parking is free or validated at retail and other destinations. What we observe, therefore, is parking use at a price of zero and under plentiful supply. This is more than would be used if the parker had to pay for it and if developers could decide how much parking to provide. Only in dense, urban areas can we say that the observed parking use is demand, and this is only true if:

- There is a market for parking.
- Parking is not subsidized.
- There are no parking requirements.
- There is no supply legacy of past requirements.

Data on parking use levels are found in compilations of use studies such as the Institute of Transportation Engineers' *Parking Generation Handbook*,[6] the Urban Land Institute/International Council of Shopping Centers' *Shared Parking*[7] report and model, and local parking occupancy studies completed by cities, parking operators, and business districts.

Parking Management

In the past, the common approach to parking management was "set it and forget it." Cities required developers to provide parking and then had nothing to do with that parking.

Employers offered parking free because everyone else did. Cities set rules for curb parking, such as a two-hour limit, and left those rules in place for decades. When the parking supply is greater than the level of parking actually used, this practice can be understood. But as a community grows and requires more efficient ways to use parking resources, and as spot parking shortages emerge, active parking management is necessary.

In suburban areas, shared parking is a promising management technique. Parking at a shopping mall may be half-empty most of the year, but during the peak December shopping period, it is full. Developing a program for mall employees to park in a nearby office complex on weekends and evenings is a low-cost way to free up parking for shoppers. Planning can enable these shared parking schemes by not over-requiring parking, and generating site and facility designs amenable to sharing.

In urban areas, sharing is more common since densities are higher, parking supply per unit of development is lower, and prices provide a natural incentive for shared agreements. One way to comprehensively measure how well parking spaces are used is to measure the percentage of time in a year (24 hours/365 days) that a space is occupied. A shared space in a downtown may be used 65 to 75 percent of the available occupancy hours, as compared to a use in a suburban baseball stadium, for example, where parking occupancy-hours may be less than 5 percent.

In downtowns and denser activity centers, parking pricing increases turnover in the most desirable spaces and directs long-term parkers to off-street spaces that would otherwise not be well used. This reduces cruising for parking, since the parker makes a choice between price and convenience and finds spaces generally available at each combination. Without this parking management, those seeking a parking space are like lions hunting antelope on the Serengeti, engaged in a competitive sport that results in distracted drivers and increases vehicle miles travelled, traffic congestion, and crashes.

Metrics and Methods in Parking Studies

Parking systems are complex, comprising several components. Incremental changes to one or more of the components can have large effects on the system, which in turn affects the surrounding community. It is important to evaluate conditions and ensure that the performance of the program meets community needs and goals. The parking study is the typical catalyst for determining parking conditions within a community, district, or campus, as well as evaluating specific strategies and solutions to mitigate potential parking issues.

Why is a Parking Study Necessary?

Parking studies are often a reaction to parking system conditions that are objectively and subjectively deteriorating, whether a demand problem, a supply problem, a perception problem, or a complaint problem. Sometimes, parking managers conduct a study proactively in advance of known growth or significant impacts; this proactive approach often leads to the best results.

The parking study is typically driven by a combination of real and perceived parking problems. Real problems are data driven and can be easily observed by the study team or a casual observer. For example, a real problem could be the constant issuance of parking citations for a specific type of infraction, which can be solved with an adjustment in policy or education. Perceived problems are uncovered through stakeholder interaction. For example, the perception of a parking shortage might be incorrect if parking is available just around the corner. But to a business owner or patron, the parking problem may result from the lack of visibility or wayfinding to that parking supply.

Types of Parking Studies

A number of analytical parking study types are used to define and address community parking issues:

- Supply/demand. Identification of parking demand challenges triggered by various community development proposals or parking management changes. The intent is to define shared parking opportunities, new parking infrastructure needed, or site-specific parking demands.
- Parking efficiency study. Emphasis on data collection to define areas of high occupancy and demand vs. areas of lower occupancy and demand, and strategies to balance the two.
- Parking behavioral analysis. Emphasis on data collection, with the combination of occupancy, turnover, duration, vehicular movement, and origin-destination data used to define user types and policies to support them.
- Curb lane management study. Focus on the on-street environment and the prioritization of users within the system to help define mobility access and parking provision. The study should include evaluations of signage, policy, and user needs.
- Site assessment studies. Evaluation of available lands or sites that could be suitable for new parking infrastructure investment. The study includes parking site configuration, site/civil evaluations, and identification of site challenges and opportunities.
- Financial feasibility analysis. Evaluation of operating budgets, potential revenues, capital expenditures, and the ability to finance new parking improvements for the parking system. Ongoing monitoring of parking revenues and expenses for reporting to stakeholders.
- Best practices review. Evaluation of a parking program against peers and industry best management practices. Helps to define new approaches and trends programs should consider, as well as define key performance indicators (KPIs) for ongoing evaluation.

Who Should Be Involved in the Parking Study?

The goal of involving different stakeholders is to help define real and perceived problems and build consensus for recommendations and strategies. The list below is a common set of parking study participants:

- Parking program management and staff. Essential team members tasked with implementing and managing strategies from the study. This could include public sector, non-profit sector, e.g., business improvement district, or private sector managers.
- Other department managers influenced by (or influencing) parking. They can provide perceived and real challenges and opportunities with the implementation of certain strategies.
- Community or campus stakeholders who would be affected by results of the study—residents, employers, students, visitors, faculty, etc.
- Developers or landowners. They provide information that could influence parking demand and behaviors in the future.
- Elected officials and commissioners who will make final decisions.
- Stakeholders outside of the study's boundaries. Often overlooked, but have some influence over parking.
- Parking consultant. A specialist who understands the implementation of parking management strategies can help create a smoother evaluation and implementation process.

- Planning community. Local and regional land use, economic development, and special district planners whose plans depend on parking management.
- Transportation professionals. Local, county, and regional transportation planners whose projects influence parking demand.

What Should Drive the Study?

Many studies are driven by political context or an intended result, which can lead to shortsighted evaluations and nominal implementation strategies. Four key elements should drive a parking study:

- Data. The collection and analysis of data provides a strong foundation for building consensus and finding strategies. Perceptions may be different from actual data, so they must be understood as well.
- Community engagement. Engaging the community often uncovers unseen issues and provides a strong platform for defining community-specific recommendations.
- Local context. The use of local context to define parking solutions often leads to more successful implementation. One-thousand-space parking garages are not ideal for Main Street USA; free parking will not solve problems in a major urban area.
- Alignment with community vision. Parking is just one piece of a larger community transportation system. With that in mind, the outcomes of the study should align with the goals and strategies of the larger community.

Gathering and Analyzing Data

Good parking management is dependent upon solid parking data, data interpretation, and preliminary decision-making. It is not always necessary to collect data on every detail of the parking system and the type of data collected depends on what one hopes to get out of it. Before defining field data collection efforts, it is important to understand two things:

- What are the goals of the study?
- What specific issues are driving the perceived or real problem?

What Data Should Be Collected?

A variety of data points can be collected for a study:

- Parking inventory. Communities should consider creating a database of parking that can be can used to better understand existing and future parking assets. The database can be as simple as a notebook of information or as complex as a geospatial database that provides both mapping and tabular data. It should include:
  - Number of spaces, including regular and specialized spaces.
  - Parking prices.
  - Time restrictions.
  - Types of control devices.
  - Permit restrictions.
  - Other restrictions worth noting.
  - Parking resource ownership and management (public vs. private).
- Parking occupancy. Parking occupancy studies determine parking patterns on a seasonal, daily, or hourly basis. An occupancy study inventories the number of vehicles parked in an area to determine the percent of occupied spaces at defined times

throughout the day. Occupancy data should be collected for each blockface and off-street facility (public and private, where available). Parking occupancy data is best collected on an hourly basis to identify trends throughout a day and on multiple days to normalize against unusual conditions and define trendlines for normal weekdays and weekends. Ideally, parking programs would collect and maintain at least an annual understanding of parking occupancy.

- Parking turnover and duration. This study documents the length of time vehicles are parked in a particular space or area and defines specific behavioral characteristics within the study area, helping identify policies such as time limits and space allocation. Collection requires a unique identifier, often the vehicle license plate, to compare between data collection periods. Turnover data is best collected on a short interval basis, such as 15 minutes or a half-hour.
- Other community and program characteristics. Sometimes, the basis for the study defines the need to collect additional supporting data:

  - Community demographics. Includes types of area users and their perceptions of the parking system. Often accomplished through face-to-face interaction or surveying.
  - Land use mixture. If the study includes demand projections, the quantification of land use types and intensities must be conducted. This includes the square footage of office, commercial, and restaurant uses; the number of residential and hotel dwelling units; and any other types of uses.
  - Parking regulations. Includes geographic allocation and usefulness of regulations and restrictions.
  - Parking budgets and expenses. Includes operating and expense budgets, large expenditures, and expected budget effects.
  - Parking enforcement practices and outcomes. Includes enforcement beats and citation data such as issued citations, fines, revenue collected, and types of citations, compliance rates, and disabled permit use, preferably by area.
  - Transportation choice. Includes mode-split choice data for transit, cycling, walking, and other mobility options.

Much of this data can be found in existing sources within the parking program, including on-and off-street parking revenue control equipment, citation data, and output reports from license plate recognition equipment. Other data can be found in previous or supporting planning efforts within the program or other departments.

If data cannot be obtained from existing monitoring systems, in-the-field data collection is required. While this is normally accomplished using manual labor, it also can be automated using video, analytic camera, sensors, tube counts, and more recently, drones.

Interpreting Results

Data analysis and interpretation is a critical step in evaluating issues facing the parking system and defining recommendations and strategies. Based on the primary data points in the previous section, the following steps should be considered:

- Parking occupancy. The data is entered into a table that shows the number of total spaces and number of occupied spaces for each blockface and/or facility for each hour the data was collected. The percent of spaces occupied is determined by dividing the total number of spaces occupied by the total number of spaces. Using this data, the study can provide peak conditions and average parking occupancies for the study area or sub areas. Parking occupancies below 50 percent are underutilized; those between

50 and 75 percent are operating with room for additional demand; those between 75 and 90 percent are approaching capacity; and those above 90 percent are considered at capacity.

- Parking duration. Duration is calculated by averaging the observed durations for all vehicles for a blockface, facility, sub area, or the study area as a whole. These values are compared against parking regulations for the observed area to determine if the durations are less than or greater than the prescribed regulations. If the durations are consistently greater than the regulations, the study should recommend that the policies be re-evaluated for the intended and actual use of the facility.
- Parking turnover. Parking turnover rates are calculated by dividing the number of vehicles observed in a blockface or facility during the entire observation period by the total number of spaces available. This metric is useful in defining the activity of the spaces. In a highly commercial area, on-street parking spaces turn over four to six times per day.
- Programmatic data. Citations, transactions, and operational budgets and approaches are evaluated to determine if specific approach or policy changes can be attributed to deficiencies noted in the data.
- Public perception. Public input is compared against actual observed data to determine if problematic patterns can be solved by messaging, marketing, or education. Sometimes, perceptions about parking challenges can indicate unnoticed gaps in the system.

When the data has been analyzed, the evaluation determines the types of problems the community faces:

- Lack of public parking. An appropriate amount of parking, respective to the needs of the community, is a key component to supporting businesses, residents, and visitors by providing access to destinations.
- Parking demand. Areas with insufficient parking can lead to conflicts between residents and businesses and create a negative image of the parking system. Areas with too much parking result in valuable space that is underused.
- Balanced use of parking. If parking use is not managed properly, it can restrict access to businesses and increase public frustration. Shared parking can help balance parking supply.
- Cultural changes. Changes in community character often mean a shift in parking needs or how parking needs are met.
- Outdated policies or technologies. Outdated policies and technologies can limit the capabilities of the parking system (e.g., inefficient enforcement and maintenance practices, lack of parking data, etc.). This can lead to issues with customer service, management of parking, and communication of appropriate policies.

Communicating Results

The results of the data collection and analysis are typically communicated through the study report and community presentations. Each medium has unique communication methods but they are served by four key mantras:

- Keep it simple. Simple mapping and charts that clearly communicate the findings of the data are more likely to support your message than complex charts or graphics.
- Keep it on point. The data should answer key questions about the study and clearly communicate the primary issues.
- Provide context so the audience understands. Mapping and graphics should clearly communicate what and where. When using maps, clearly label street names and

Data communication tools include:

- Heat maps. These maps use color palettes to communicate variations in data. For parking occupancy, the thresholds 0 to 50 percent, 50 to 75 percent, 75 to 90 percent, and more than 90 percent are good starting points to evaluate areas of concern. Durational data can also be shown as a heat map, which can point out the areas where policy and time limits may need to be adapted to meet community needs.
- Supply/demand charts. These charts show the variation in supply and demand and help communicate which portions of the system need further evaluation for parking demand mitigation.
- Public perception graphics. Results from survey questions can be used to support or augment field data collection. Survey responses will help solidify the message from the field collection. They may be contradictory to the data, indicating that the public perception of parking is influenced by external factors (e.g., visibility, wayfinding, restrictions).
- Summary graphics or dashboards. The use of a dashboard or infographics is a meaningful way to communicate the trends observed in field-collected data and identify areas of primary concern or opportunity.

destinations so the public can quickly determine locations. Heat mapping of occupancy can clearly define where the issues are.

- Don't make up data! If the data does not communicate the message you were hoping it would, realign your message, not the data. Data does not lie and the community will pick up on abnormalities.

Of course, an analytical parking study does not indicate what policies, programs and projects should be adopted. That step requires a planning process.

Parking Strategic Plans

A parking strategic plan takes a higher-level view of the parking program. Parking and transportation are essentially support systems for the larger institutions or communities that they serve. Therefore, it is important to define the overarching goals of the program as they relate to helping the larger institution or community achieve its broader strategic or master plan goals. The importance of properly aligning a parking or transportation program's philosophy and programs to better serve the businesses, customers, and residents it serves cannot be overstated.

A range of studies are commonly performed within the parking arena:

- Financial feasibility.
- Facility condition appraisals.
- Revenue control audits.
- Operational assessments.
- Best practice reviews.
- Organizational assessments.
- Marketing and branding studies.
- Technology planning assessments.

Parking strategic plans include the development of program-guiding principles, extensive community outreach and engagement, and an external scan of issues related to the competitive environment, regulatory issues, and relationships with partner agencies, departments, or affiliated institutions.

What's In the Plan?

Parking strategic plans help integrate parking with a variety of other plans; they tend to be focused on implementation and are action-plan oriented. They are broad-based in nature and cover a wide range of operational areas:

- Vision and mission.
- Parking planning.
- Organization structure.
- Staff development and training.
- Safety, security, and risk management.
- Communications, marketing, and branding.
- Program scope and services.
- Financial management.
- Operational efficiency.
- Facilities maintenance programs.
- Effective use of technology.
- Positive customer service programs.
- Special events parking.
- Parking enforcement.
- Transportation demand management.

Why Conduct a Strategic Plan?

There are several reasons for an organization to consider undertaking a parking strategic plan. They might want to reassess organizational objectives, enhance accountability, address market changes, leverage new technologies, enhance customer service, resolve conflicts, or change outdated procedures. Key strategic plan outcomes might include enhanced buy-in from leadership or community members, improved focus and better-defined priorities, consensus-building, and alignment of future goals.

Parking Strategic Plans Defined

The key components of strategic planning include an understanding of the institution's vision, mission, values, and strategies. Good strategic plans also identify critical success factors and specific action items that are in alignment with core values and guiding principles designed to achieve targeted results. In parking, there may be multiple responsible organizations with their own strategic plans, so coordination between these plans is often required.

The vision outlines what the organization wants to be or how it wants the world in which it operates to be (an idealized view of the world). It is a long-term, future oriented view. It can be emotive and a source of inspiration. For example, a charity working with the poor might have "A world without poverty" as its vision statement.

The mission defines the fundamental purpose of an organization or an enterprise—why it exists and what it does to achieve its vision. For example, the charity noted above might have "Providing jobs for the homeless and unemployed" as its mission statement.

Core values are beliefs shared among the stakeholders of an organization. Values drive an organization's culture and priorities and provide a framework in which decisions are made. These might also be called guiding principles.

There are several other sections that might be included in a parking strategic plan. They attempt to better orient the readers to the plan's objectives and use. Good plans explain how they are to be used, why they were done, why parking matters in the community, who might be affected, and some basic explanations of parking management.

The Process

Parking strategic plans typically involve several organizational and process elements:

- Project management team. This usually involves the client team, the consultant team (including sub-consultants if applicable), and potentially other invested parties. A small core team is responsible for managing the project.
- Technical advisory committee. This engages a broader group of related parties or key community stakeholders with technical insights beyond the core project management team. Normally, this group is made up of representatives from other departments, agencies, or community groups that can provide technical expertise or information that could help inform the planning process.
- Public engagement processes. Public engagement processes are critical to strategic planning efforts and typically include public meetings, focus groups, individual stakeholder meetings, city council workshops, etc. Social media and community surveys are also important and growing elements of successful strategic plan projects.
- Project schedules. Providing a well-organized and well-published project schedule improves project management and also ensures more effective project communication and public meeting attendance.
- Background information/context. It is important to review and understand the planning context in which the parking plan is being conducted. This typically involves reviewing and documenting related project plans such as downtown or campus master plans, economic development strategies, larger community or regional transportation plans, bike plans, mobility plans, traffic impact studies, community marketing or branding strategies, etc.
- Review of existing plans and policies. Conducting a review of current program plans, policies, and operating procedures is important. Typically, most plans will include a current program assessment process as a core plan element.
- Limited supply/demand update. While a parking strategic plan is not a parking supply/demand study, as discussed in the previous section, an understanding of parking supply/demand factors is important. The better the data, the more strategy can be tailored to local conditions.
- Issues identification. Following the initial data collection, planning context reviews, and community feedback, a more focused picture of key parking issues will emerge. It is important to capture these key issues (and their community effects) and feed them back to the community so stakeholders know that they have been listened to and heard. Having a clear definition and acceptance of the issues is a critical step. This process should include identifying future issues and trends, which can be done with forecasting and community assessments.
- Primary and secondary recommendations. Parking is more complex and important than most community members appreciate, at least initially. A relatively short list of primary action items keeps the report focused on the key action-oriented recommendations. This is often supplemented by a listing of secondary action items that may be more important for staff. The primary action items become the key elements that the community and elected officials will focus on.

- Implementation strategies. For a parking strategic plan to be truly effective, the primary recommendations must be accompanied by specific implementation strategies. This often takes the form of an action plan with an accompanying communication strategy.
- Implementation timeline. Placing the defined recommendations and implementation strategies into a concise, logically presented, and realistic timeline helps define priorities and assists with plan implementation budgeting, roll-out, and potential approval.
- A concise report. One of the core challenges in developing these plans is to keep the reports concise, understandable, and digestible. As a result, these plans are often condensed into executive summaries or even infographics. Another strategy is to provide a parking management toolbox, often as a set of report appendices.

Conclusion

Parking must be understood in terms of its role in broader transportation and land use systems. Data on parking supply and use characteristics is the foundation for parking planning. The most successful parking and transportation programs have one common denominator: they have all embraced the importance of having a strategic plan to guide their programs.

Notes

1   Willson, R. 2013. *Parking Reform Made Easy*. Washington DC: Island Press.
2   Chester, M. A. Horvath, and S. Madanat. 2010. "Parking Infrastructure: Energy, emissions, and Automobile Life-cycle Environmental Accounting. *Environmental Research Letters*. 5:1–8.
3   Willson R. and A. Allahyar. 2015. "Indirect Uses of Minimum Parking Requirements." Paper 15–3403. Transportation Research Board Conference, Washington, D.C.
4   Willson, R. 2015. *Parking Management for Smart Growth*. Washington DC: Island Press.
5   Shoup, D. 2011. *The High Cost of Free Parking*. Chicago IL: American Planning Association Press.
6   Institute of Transportation Engineers. 2010. *Parking Generation*, 4th ed. Washington, DC: Institute of Transportation Engineers.
7   Smith, M. 2005. *Shared Parking*. 2nd Ed. Washington, DC: ULI-the Urban Land Institute and the International Council of Shopping Centers.

CHAPTER 4

Approaches to Parking Management

Casey Jones, CAPP

Introduction

The management of parking facilities, programs, and services closely followed the advent of the automobile, when spaces were offered to accommodate parked cars. Indeed, the first recorded parking garage in the U.S. was a converted skating rink in New York City owned by the Electric Vehicle Company; it opened in 1897. The first public parking facility for automobiles is thought to have opened two years later in Boston, where a bicycle repair shop was adapted to provide parking accommodations.[1]

In the early days of the automobile, like today, management of most roadways and associated right-of-ways was the responsibility of the public sector, and allowing cars to park on unused portions of streets was common practice. In 1935, the first parking meter was installed in Oklahoma City, Okla., to help address traffic congestion and low traffic turnover, which local merchants felt was hurting their business.[2] These are the earliest examples of parking management in practice in the U.S.

Though the parking industry currently lacks a formal and comprehensive historical record, Shannon Sanders McDonald's *The Parking Garage: Design and Evolution of a Modern Urban Form* provides a starting point for understanding the evolution of parking management. One can also glean historical information about the early days of the industry by the account of the founders of this industry's organizations. Though admittedly far from exhaustive, a glimpse at the available record helps us understand the industry's evolution and management models.

The complexity and sophistication of parking management has evolved, and today is as varied and intricate as the cars and drivers for which parking management is a critical and necessary activity. In many places, parking spaces are a scarce commodity, and even if it isn't scarce, the parking space provides access to important or desired destinations. It is often said that people don't park to park, they park to do other things, and the ability to access any number of destinations is impeded if the parking spaces designed for these destinations is not proactively or thoughtfully managed. For the purposes of this discussion, parking management is broadly intended to mean all manner of decision-making relating to the provision of parking spaces for commercial or civic purposes. Where should parking be located? What hours should parking be available? At what price should parking be offered? What action is appropriate when parkers fail to use parking as intended or fail to pay the designated amount? These questions and many more are left to parking managers to answer based on achieving certain goals and objectives.

This chapter will discuss approaches to parking management. It will define parking management as the daily oversight of a parking program or service; as such, the act of managing parking is operational in nature. Management differs from strategic oversight, which focuses on the accomplishment of broad overarching objectives and is therefore less centered on tactical or operational considerations. It will consider the types of organizations that manage parking, contemporary management models, and common arrangements between the various actors involved in parking management. These arrangements are referred to as "relationship structures" because they define the relationship between an owner of a parking asset and the provider of parking management services.

Abridged Parking Management History

The first entrant into parking management was the private sector, which required storage and maintenance facilities for fleets of electric cabs. Private automobile clubs also provided facilities that provided electric charging stations, upholstery repair, and storage.[3] Cities, which first sought to manage their growing municipal fleets (ambulances, fire trucks, delivery vehicles), soon realized the income potential for also providing public parking accommodations. Cleveland, in 1916, was perhaps the first city to offer a parking facility that stored its own vehicles, while allowing public usage for a fee.[4]

It was not until the mid-1930s that the first account of involvement by the public sector was seen in on-street parking management in a form resembling that practice today. As noted above, this occurred in Oklahoma City with the installation of the nation's first parking meters. Being responsible for the public right of way, the City of Oklahoma City must have installed the meters, collected monies the meters produced, and enforced any associated parking rules. It's also probable that the holder of the meter patent and Oklahoma City's meter vendor provided any needed meter repairs, thus becoming the first U.S. parking meter manufacturer, equipment vendor, and third-party meter service provider. How quickly other cities followed Oklahoma City in on-street parking enforcement has not been fully documented but it wasn't until the late 1940s that the public sector took an interest in off-street parking. This did not sit well with the private sector, which saw the provision of off-street parking as their domain.

The economy was booming following World War II, and urban America was at the epicenter of growth and prosperity. Because suburban shopping centers, sprawl, and expressways were yet to come, the majority of growth experienced post-WWII happened in America's major downtowns. International Parking Institute founder James A. Hunnicutt, CAPP, noted that:

> Complaints were beginning to be heard from motorists with no place to park, merchants whose customers had no place to park, and business people whose customers and clients could not come downtown because of a lack of parking. A chorus of cries for parking began to be raised with most noise coming from a number of major northern cities, including Chicago, Milwaukee, Detroit, and Pittsburgh.[5]

The resulting response was that cities began organizing themselves to manage their own parking resources in a variety of ways including "the establishment of parking authorities, parking commissions, city parking agencies, and revenue authorities."[6] Public officials from major U.S. cities banded together to create the burgeoning industry's terminology, to discuss common challenges and potential solutions, and to develop procedures, policies, and practices that others could replicate to provide the foundation for parking management as we know it today.

Typical Parking Management Duties

Regardless of the size, scale, or nature of a parking operation, similar management functions take place. At a high level, these duties include supervision and staffing, equipment and facility maintenance, financial oversight and revenue control, training of staff, record keeping and reporting, program marketing and communications, parking facility safety, and operating parking facilities to accommodate modes other than automobiles, such as bicycles, walking, and transit. Parking management also includes development of parking policy (defines who can park where and when), pricing policy (defines how much to charge for various types of parking accommodations), and planning, designing, building, equipping, and caring for parking facilities.

Organizations that Manage Parking

There are three general types of organizations that manage parking: public, quasi-public, and private entities. Government entities that perform parking management activities include departments, bureaus, and agencies from all levels of government. Quasi-public organizations are special-purpose entities that are authorized legislatively or statutorily to assume specific parking management duties and responsibilities. Private entities vary as well, and include everything from sole proprietors of a single parking facility to national and multinational corporations responsible for millions of parking spaces.

Public Organizations

Parking management is not just an activity for municipal governmental entities—all levels, including cities, counties, states, public universities, public airports, and the federal government, perform parking management activities. As such, public sector parking management organizations take various forms. Typically, parking management responsibilities are either housed in a single department or across several entities. In a decentralized model, the various facets that comprise parking management are assigned to different governmental entities based on the general role of the department. For example, in a municipal environment, enforcement of on-street rules and regulations may be the responsibility of the police department; care and maintenance of facilities and equipment—such as parking meters—may be the responsibility of public works; and permitting and payment for parking may be assigned to the treasury and parking citation appeals by the city clerk.

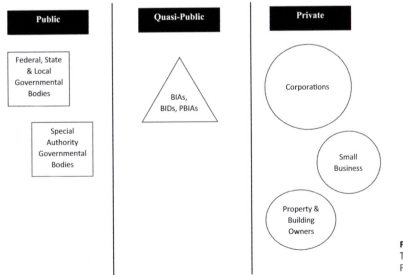

FIGURE 4.1
Typical Organizations Involved in Parking Management

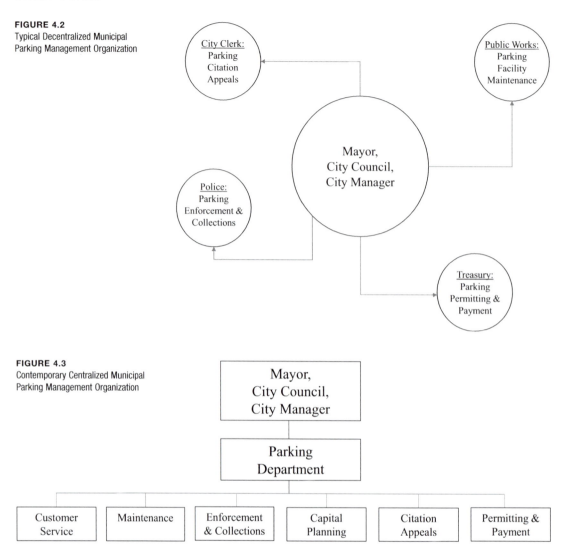

FIGURE 4.2
Typical Decentralized Municipal
Parking Management Organization

FIGURE 4.3
Contemporary Centralized Municipal
Parking Management Organization

The more contemporary model consolidates parking enforcement, maintenance, permitting, customer service, appeals, and most, if not all other parking related duties within a single governmental department. Just as with the decentralized approach, there are variations on the consolidated theme. A parking department may have most responsibilities for daily management and operation of parking programs and services but may not be responsible for the capital needs of the parking system—such as repair of parking infrastructure.

Authorities and Commissions

An authority or commission is a special-purpose governmental entity that may function autonomously from the legislative governmental authority that established it. An authority normally has its own elected or appointed governing body, and may also have decision-making capabilities (taxing, fee setting, for example) that are typically reserved for traditional governmental bodies. The key distinction between an authority and traditional governmental body is that the authority's responsibilities and purpose are narrowly defined: a parking authority is a governmental entity that is only involved with parking. Additionally, parking authorities are typically responsible for all facets of public parking for a specific jurisdiction, including land acquisition for parking development, funding parking facilities, and managing parking programs and services. It is also not uncommon for transit authorities to manage specialized parking such as park-and-ride facilities that further use of mass transit.

Public entities are involved in parking management for a variety of reasons, first and foremost of which is that publicly owned parking assets are a public resource and must be managed by the public sector. Public entities also manage parking because the effective management of parking can and often does help government achieve larger goals, such as community and economic development, access and mobility, and revenue generation to pay for programs and services deemed important to the general public. Governments may also manage parking so they may provide parking for public-sector employees and as may be necessary to support other governmental functions—such as a motor pool for storage of public vehicles.

Quasi-Public Entities

There are a variety of quasi-public entities that may be involved in the management of parking. Commonly referred to as parking benefit districts, business improvement districts or areas (BIDs, BIAs), and parking, business improvement districts or areas (PBIDs, PBIAs), these are publicly sanctioned, privately directed quasi-public organizations that supplement public service to improve shared, geographically defined, outdoor public spaces, and to promote economic and community development goals. These entities typically provide services that enhance the safety, cleanliness, image, and competitiveness of city centers. They are occasionally also given responsibility for the direct management of parking facilities, and are frequently involved with efforts that influence the delivery of parking services (such as marketing parking and managing validation programs).

Private Entities

All shapes and forms of private entities manage parking, from single proprietors to large corporations. Building owners and managers also manage parking for their facilities, and there are third-party businesses that specialize in the management of parking on behalf of building owners and managers. Private interests may be involved in parking management for a variety of reasons, with the most obvious being that charging for parking can be a lucrative commercial enterprise. Another reason may be that a property owner plans to develop the lot on which a surface parking facility exists, and parking provides income until the development can occur. Parking may also not be financially profitable on its own, but it may be essential for another use as might be the case with a property manager who is interested in tenanting their building. The presence of proximate parking may make the building attractive for a tenant, making the management of the parking an important ancillary activity to commercial and residential leasing.

Private interests may also manage public parking facilities as would be the case if a public entity elected to divest itself of its parking assets. This is a form of privatization that will be discussed below.

Management Models

Management models describe how parking management activities are arranged. As is the case with parking management organizations, parking management models vary broadly.

BOX 4.1 **Example: Parking and Business Improvement District Authorization (Spokane, Washington)**

State Authorization: The Revised Code of Washington State under RCW 35.87A allows for the establishment of special assessment districts including parking and business improvement districts (PBIDs).

Purposes: To aid general economic development and neighborhood revitalization, and to facilitate the cooperation of merchants, businesses, and residential property owners which assists trade, economic viability, and livability, the legislature hereby authorizes all counties and all incorporated cities and towns, including unclassified cities and towns operating under special charters:

(1) To establish, after a petition submitted by the operators responsible for sixty percent of the assessments by businesses and multifamily residential or mixed-use projects within the area, parking and business improvement areas, hereafter referred to as area or areas, for the following purposes:

   (a) The acquisition, construction or maintenance of parking facilities for the benefit of the area;
   (b) Decoration of any public place in the area;
   (c) Sponsorship or promotion of public events which are to take place on or in public places in the area;
   (d) Furnishing of music in any public place in the area;
   (e) Providing professional management, planning and promotion for the area, including the management and promotion of retail trade activities in the area;
   (f) Providing maintenance and security for common public areas; or
   (g) Providing transportation services for the benefit of the area.

(2) To levy special assessments on all businesses and multifamily residential or mixed-use projects within the area and specially benefited by a parking and business improvement area to pay in whole or in part the damages or costs incurred therein as provided in this chapter.

For the purpose of this introduction, this section will focus on three general models: fully self-managed, partially self-managed, and fully contractor managed.

Fully Self-Managed

Fully self-managed parking systems are those where the daily decision making resides with the owner of the parking facility, program, or service. This is an internal approach in which no or very few outside management resources are used, and that the major management tasks (as noted above) are completed internally.

Partially Self-Managed

Partially self-managed systems are typically those in which a private entity outside the system's owner provides some of management functions. An example of this would be if a city outsourced parking meter enforcement to an outside company while maintaining all other facets of parking management.

Fully Contractor-Managed

Some parking system owners prefer to outsource all facets of their operations to an outside contractor. This model is known as fully contractor-managed. The owner may maintain strategic decision-making for the system—such as rate setting, capital improvement planning, and overall program goals and objectives—but daily management is outsourced.

Making a choice between an internal arrangement and outsourced parking management is complex and there are many variables to consider when deciding the best course for an owner. Here are a few common considerations an owner must weigh:

- Will managing our parking assets take away from another priority, goal or objective?
- Do we have the expertise, human resources, and time to effectively manage our parking?
- What are the financial implications of outsourcing vs. self-managing?
- Are there labor savings to be realized or additional costs related to outsourcing?
- Are there risk avoidance advantages/disadvantages to outsourcing?
- What are the political advantages/disadvantages to outsourcing?
- Can we improve performance by outsourcing?
- Are there facets of parking management that would be more advantageous to outsource than others?

These and more considerations drive the decision about how much, if any, an owner should devote to managing parking assets. If they do decide to outsource, the arrangement under which the outsourcing takes place will influence whether an owner can realize his or her goals.

Parking Management Relationship Structures

Relationship structure refers to the specific contractual arrangement between an owner of a parking asset and the provider of outsourced parking management services (contractor). In large part, the structure establishes how risk is managed between two parties. It will define the business terms of the relationship and establish high-level decision-making authority. The relationship structure provides the roadmap for parking management activities and our focus here will be on the common types: management fee; reverse management; performance-based fee; lease; and concession.

BOX 4.2 Management Approach and Risk

Shifting Risk: Management Fee vs. Reverse Management Fee

Let's suppose that a municipality contracts for parking management services and that snow removal is included in the responsibilities of a private contractor. Under a basic management fee relationship structure, the city agrees to pay the contractor a management fee of $50,000 per year and it assumes responsibility for all other expenses that are required. For illustration purposes, let's pretend that the only parking management expense beyond the management fee is for snow removal. In a given year there is significant snowfall and the contractor spends $10,000 on snow removal. The city pays the $10,000 and also owes the parking contractor its management fee of $50,000 for a total outlay of $60,000.

With a reverse management fee structure the parking contractor agrees to provide parking management services for an all inclusive $55,000 including an estimate for $5,000 in snow removal. If in that year snow removal cost $10,000, the contractor must make up the difference between what they anticipated it would cost and what it actually cost. The city owes no more to the contractor than the $55,000 and the contractor now only has $45,000 left after absorbing the higher than expected snow removal expense.

Management Fee

The management fee approach is the most basic and common structure. The owner agrees to pay a set fee to the parking management entity to perform a specific set of duties. Any revenue from the parking system or asset goes to the owner. The owner is also responsible for paying all necessary expenses that are incurred. The owner assumes the majority of risk in the management fee arrangement and has strategic decision-making authority.

Reverse Management Fee

A reverse management fee structure is similar to the basic management fee structure but the parking contractor agrees to provide its services for a fee that includes both profit and expenses. Overages in expenses are the responsibility of the contractor. Again, any revenue from the parking system or asset goes to the owner and strategic decision-making rests with the owner. Management and reverse management structures are common in both the commercial and public sectors.

Performance-based Fee

Performance incentives can be used in both the management fee and reserve management fee structures, and mean that parking contractors receive additional fees when agreed-upon outcomes are achieved. Outcomes may be financial (such as increasing the revenue received in the parking operation or reducing operational costs), customer-service-based (the extra fee is earned when a certain customer service score is achieved), based on achieving certain milestones (such as training a certain portion of the parking staff on a particular topic), or a composite of several factors. Strategic decision-making and risk do not change under this structure from the structures described above, but the incentives can create a dynamic between the owner and the contractor that can be viewed as more collaborative, in which the contractor can be rewarded for achieving objectives the owner deems important. Performance-based structures are also common in commercial and public sectors.

Lease

A lease structure is essentially the opposite of the management fee structure. Here, a parking contractor agrees to manage an owner's parking asset and assume risk and decision-making authority in exchange for a negotiated payment to the property owner. At base, the contractor agrees to pay a set amount to the owner regardless of how much the parking operation makes or costs to operate. The contractor makes all decisions including what rates to charge, what hours to operate, what services to provide and how to staff the operation, and is responsible for all associated costs. Leases are typical in the commercial sector.

Concession

The final basic model covered here is the concession structure. Compared to the other structures, this is not common but at least one university and several municipal governments have chosen to privatize their parking assets in the recent past. A concession is essentially a long-term lease where public parking assets are converted to a private enterprise and turned over to a private owner and a concessionaire in exchange for a single lump sum of money (compared to periodic and frequent payments under a lease structure). Typically, a concessionaire is a private equity investor or similar type of organization that hires a parking contractor to manage the parking asset once the concession is in place.

The time frame varies but can be anywhere between 20 and 99 years. In this model, most decision-making shifts from the previous public owner to the private owner, as does

TABLE 4.1 Parking Relationship Management Characteristics

Relationship Structure	Decision-Making Authority	Expense Responsible	Receives Revenues	Operating Environment
Management Fee	Owner	Owner	Owner	Public/Commercial
Reverse Management Fee	Owner	Contractor	Owner	Public/Commercial
Performance-Based Fee	Owner	Owner/Contractor	Owner	Public/Commercial
Lease	Contractor	Contractor	Contractor	Commercial
Concession	Concessionaire	Concessionaire	Concessionaire	Public

all risk and future reward (parking revenues). This approach has not been without controversy, as there is some question as to whether it is appropriate to transfer what is considered a public asset to the private sector while divesting public decision-making and responsibility for the asset.

Case Studies

Capital City Development Corporation (Boise)—Municipal Quasi-governmental, Outsourced Operations

Capital City Development Corporation (CCDC) is the redevelopment and urban renewal agency for Boise, Idaho, founded by the City of Boise in 1965 as the Boise Redevelopment Agency (B.R.A.)., CCDC is a public redevelopment agency serving as a catalyst for quality private development through urban design, economic development, and infrastructure investment with a goal of "igniting diverse economic growth, building vibrant urban centers, and promoting healthy community design." CCDC's nine-member board of commissioners directs the activities of the agency. The commissioners are appointed by the mayor and confirmed by the Boise City Council. They serve five-year terms and are not compensated for their service. The agency employs a staff of 15 people.

CCDC, in partnership with the City of Boise, continually assesses and studies downtown parking to drive innovative and cost-effective parking solutions. CCDC owns and operates six parking garages throughout the downtown area, but also supports and works to expand alternative parking opportunities such as bike share and convenient bike parking throughout the city.

In addition, CCDC prioritizes work with local developers to make parking solutions affordable. CCDC understands that communities who look for innovative ways to manage off-street parking—a key link between land use and transportation—will be best prepared to tackle ongoing parking challenges. This is important to keep in mind as downtown Boise continues to enjoy significant growth and development.[7]

City of Alameda, Calif., Decentralized, Outsourced Municipality

The City of Alameda, Calif., owns four parking facilities that accommodate public parking. In addition to on-street parking spaces, these include one parking structure and three off-street parking lots. The parking structure is managed by a third-party operator. Permits to park in the surface lots are issued by two different downtown business associations. Parking enforcement and citation appeal processing duties are performed by the Alameda Police Department. Other parking management duties outside of those listed above, such as capital planning, meter collections, and maintenance, are performed by the city's public works department. This approach is considered decentralized because multiple city departments manage different aspects of parking management.

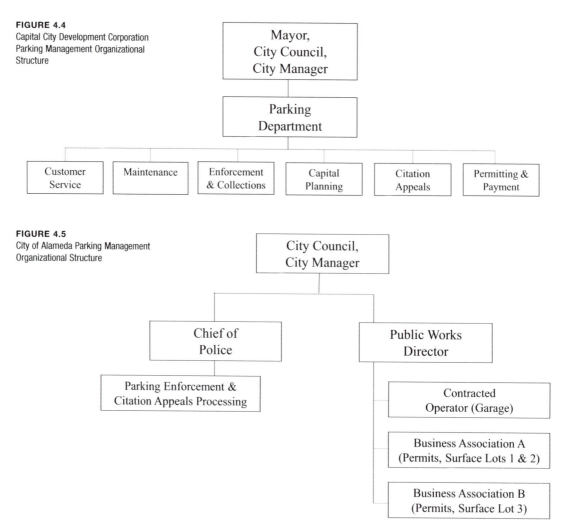

FIGURE 4.4
Capital City Development Corporation
Parking Management Organizational
Structure

FIGURE 4.5
City of Alameda Parking Management
Organizational Structure

Ohio State University—Higher Education Concession (to concessionaire QIC Global Infrastructure)

In 2012, The Ohio State University entered into a long-term lease with Australian investment firm QIC Global Infrastructure. In exchange for a cash payment, QIC operates the university's parking system and earns parking revenue. QIC created a limited partnership entity known as CampusParc to provide parking management services under the agreement, and CampusParc, in turn, hired a third-party parking operator to provide daily parking operational duties.

CampusParc is responsible for the operation of The Ohio State University's parking system, including management of the permit system, parking enforcement, customer service, motorist assistance, event parking management, and parking facility maintenance, including major renovations. The parking system, one of the largest of its kind, is comprised of 5 million square feet and 13,000 spaces within 16 garages, and 7 million square feet and 23,591 spaces within 196 surface lots, for a total of 36,591 system spaces.

CampusParc operates the parking system through a 50-year parking concession (lease), which began in September 2012. As a result of the concession, the university received a one-time, up-front payment of $483 million that is expected to provide $3.1 billion in investment earnings for academic initiatives. In the first 24 months of the concession, the initial $483 million created $112 million in interest, funding teaching, learning, research, transportation, and sustainability.[8]

University of Central Oklahoma—Higher Education, Self-Managed

The University of Central Oklahoma's transportation and parking services (TPS) department exists to provide its university community a safe environment and ready access to campus facilities by efficiently using all available transportation and parking resources. TPS establishes parking rules and regulations, distributes parking permits, and manages on-campus parking facilities. The department also manages alternative transportation programs consisting of the university's shuttle service, carpool program, and bicycle program. TPS does not rely on any outside contractor to provide parking related programs and services. TPS is comprised of 10 full-time staff and several part-time student positions. This includes the director, assistant director, administrative supervisor, field supervisor, customer service representative and two lead parking enforcement officers and two parking enforcement officers.[9]

Summary

Governmental entities, sole proprietors, property owners and managers, corporations, and many more organizations and individuals manage parking for a variety of reasons and motivations. What's certain is that providing parking, whether at a charge or for free, is an increasingly important activity for an increasing number of organizations. What's also clear is that the complexities surrounding the parking industry have increased, and this has led to equally complex and varied ways in which parking is managed and the relationships between all parties involved in offering parking services. Each approach and relationship structure offers tradeoffs in the sharing of risk and reward.

Notes

1   Shannon Sanders McDonald: The *Parking Garage: Design and Evolution of a Modern Urban Form*, (Washington: Urban Land Institute, 2007), 14.
2   "Carl Magee," Wikipedia,org, last modified, November 12, 2017, https://en.wikipedia.org/wiki/Carl_Magee.
3   McDonald, 16.
4   McDonald, 21.
5   James A. Hunnicutt, "The Founding of IPI," *The Parking Professional*, January 2012.
6   Hunnicutt.
7   "Capital City Development Corp" www.ccdcboise.com.
8   "CampusParc at The Ohio University" http://osu.campusparc.com/home/about-us/about-us/our-values.
9   "UCO Transportation & Parking Services (TPS)," last modified January 3, 2018. http://sites.uco.edu/administration/safety-transportation/transportation-parking-services/index.asp

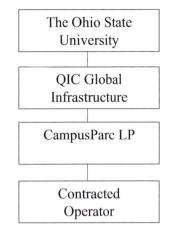

FIGURE 4.6
The Ohio State University Parking Management Organizational Structure

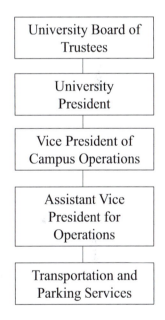

FIGURE 4.7
University of Central Oklahoma Parking Management Organizational Structure

CHAPTER 5

Technology

*Michael Drow, CAPP, PMP and
Blake Laufer, CAPP*

Every day, technology becomes more integrated into our lives. Similarly, technology is becoming an important part of managing parking and transportation operations. Effectively integrating technology into a parking and transportation operation allows a parking professional to:

- Enhance customer service and communication to customers.
- Offer new services and customer conveniences.
- Reduce operating costs and improve efficiency.

Technology by itself is not a solution but a tool to help accomplish an operation's objectives. Many new and innovative technology solutions are developed every year; however, to effectively select and use a technology solution, the operation should understand its service goals, its customer needs, and its operating procedures and constraints. A technology should not be selected simply because it looks innovative. Unless a manager understands how it will support the customer or adjusts the operations to leverage the technology, it may not deliver the desired effect.

Technology evolves over time, and the reader is encouraged to stay abreast of these changes. This is not an exhaustive review of relevant technologies and their uses, rather, it is a primer to enable research and evaluation of technology in detail.

While there are many ways to describe technology, this chapter approaches technology in four categories:

- Field technology: the hardware (meters, gates, etc.) and software found on site and used to collect information about the environment (video, space sensors, loops) and interact with customers and onsite personnel (handhelds, ticket dispensers, signs, intercoms, apps).
- Infrastructure technology: the hardware, software and data/voice bandwidth to connect the facility with the world. This technology includes communication services (T1 lines, Cable, WiFi) plus the necessary hardware devices to manage network security and system integrations.

FIGURE 5.1

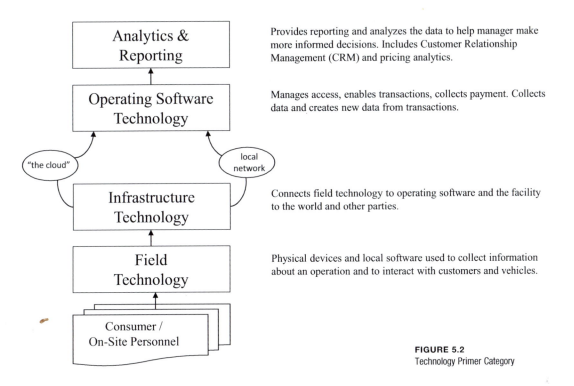

Provides reporting and analyzes the data to help manager make more informed decisions. Includes Customer Relationship Management (CRM) and pricing analytics.

Manages access, enables transactions, collects payment. Collects data and creates new data from transactions.

Connects field technology to operating software and the facility to the world and other parties.

Physical devices and local software used to collect information about an operation and to interact with customers and vehicles.

FIGURE 5.2
Technology Primer Category

- Operating software technology: solutions that interact with the field technology to control access to a facility, process parking and enforcement transactions, process financial transactions, enable customer-service support, or interact with third-party systems to enable customer conveniences such as mobile payment, prepaid parking, reservations, and transportation.
- Analytics and reporting technology: solutions that collect the data from operating software and field technologies, and analyze the data to help managers make informed decisions or identify new trends. This includes graphical reporting, demand prediction engines, budgeting & forecasting, pricing analytics, etc.

Field Technology

This is the largest and most diverse of the technology groups and covers the many physical devices in a parking and transportation facility. Field devices are sometimes referred to as "edge devices" because they are on the front edge of data collection and at the furthest point from the centralized data management systems. The popular technology term "Internet of Things" (IoT) refers to edge devices that collect and transmit data.

This technology group can be further segmented:

- Access and revenue control systems (ARCS): the technology that manages access verification of a parking area, either in an on-street, ungated or gated environment, as well as managing the calculation of fees based on specific parking activities. This technology group includes gates, ticket spitters, payment kiosks, and cashier stations used to control access into a parking facility. These systems issue access credentials or read electronic credentials from phones or vehicles to grant access. Common examples

FIGURE 5.3
Advances in Parking Technology Have Transformed the Industry and the Customer Experience

of these technologies include multi-space meters, single space meters, and cashier and automated systems used in parking structures. The first ARCS solutions were designed as standalone systems, possibly on a local network; today's ARCS systems offer a self-hosted/onsite or cloud hosted configuration.

- Parking guidance systems (PGS): technology designed to convey parking space availability to a driver prior to arriving at the parking space. Guidance systems observe vehicle (and pedestrian) entrances and exits at various points in a parking facility, compute occupancy or use counts, and distribute the information to customers via mobile apps or signage. A key capability of PGS systems is to share data with other parties in real time.

Vehicle movements are collected several ways:

- Space sensors that detect when a vehicle is physically in a single parking space or when the vehicle passes a specific point in the facility. There are a variety of technologies used, including ultrasonic to detect an object, inductive loops to measure metal mass in an area, Bluetooth to detect the presence of a Bluetooth radio in a vehicle or phone, and infrared/optical to sense a physical object in the target area of the sensor. A sensor typically includes multiple detection methods to improve its accuracy and a means to communicate with a central collection station to aggregate the data for distribution. Space-sensing technology is accurate but also more expensive to implement due to communication and wiring needs to support the space sensors.
- Video (image) analytics that monitor for change in a video stream (image) to detect the movement or presence of vehicles in specified areas or parking in specific spaces. This technology also enables an operation to identify vehicles by license plate and help customers find their car location when they forget. While cameras and software tend to cost more than a single-space sensor, a camera can usually monitor a larger area

FIGURE 5.4

FIGURE 5.5
Technology has Improved Wayfinding, which has a Positive Effect on the Overall Customer Experience

with many spaces resulting in lower costs on a per space basis. In addition, the video stream can be used to support the many other needs of a facility, including the security department, enforcement, and customer service. The use of video analytics to support parking guidance activities is but one of many operational capabilities the technology can support. Additional uses are described in the Video Analytics section below.

- Real-time payment information to estimate current occupancy in a facility. By collecting current payment data and/or crowdsourced data and understanding enforcement history of a facility, a solution can predict the current occupancy through statistical methods. This approach has the least accuracy but is also the least expensive to implement. Parking guidance can be accomplished by monitoring individual spaces or a zone. In many situations, a combination of approaches is appropriate to monitor occupancy in a complex facility. As an example, video can be used to manage large parking areas and space sensors used to manage special use, premium parking areas, or areas not visible by the camera.

Access Credentials

Related to access and revenue control systems (ARCS), this technology group includes the media that enables a parker to use a parking facility. A unique identification is required to verify access rights or collect payment via operating software technology, typically in a real-time approach.

Access credentials vary from simple paper permits issued by a garage office to an AVI tag that allows a vehicle to identify itself via shortwave radio to a mobile app that communicates with the access control technology and possibly provides payment information; credentials may be assigned to an individual or a vehicle. A parking operation's policies determine transferability of credentials between cars, parkers, or facilities.

Types of access credential media include:

- License plate technology: uses video analytics to read a vehicle's license plate and verify access rights. Technology typically requires good lighting to improve the readability accuracy rate of license plates; license plate recognition can be tuned (manually or using machine learning) to provide improved results against specific plates.
- Bluetooth Low Energy (BLE): relies on a Bluetooth radio in phone or vehicle to connect to a listening (receiving) device in the facility. Once detected, a user can be identified from the unique Bluetooth signature. The Bluetooth signal can be "sniffed" by a reader if the Bluetooth device's signal is activated, even if the Bluetooth device is not paired to the reader.
- Automated vehicle identification (AVI): a grouping of technologies that use shortwave radio to identify a vehicle associated to a credential and includes RFID, transponder, etc. Readers require specific placement and tuning to work effectively, especially in complex entry/exit lanes.
- Custom credentials: an employee or student ID badge or unique identifier provided by the user. This is typically an extension of AVI technologies that allow a custom ID card or badge to be used in a parking facility. Some ARCS systems will allow a parker to use multiple credential media, for example an AVI tag and a custom credential, and still can prevent misuse of the system.
- Barcode ticket: a 2D scanner/imager can read paper barcodes as well as barcodes presented on a digital display. Barcode tickets are easy to print and track, and the readers can also support e-commerce activities and mobile payments. 1D scanners cannot read digital screens as the laser does not reflect the barcode back to the scanner,

while 2D imagers can read from printed materials as well as a digital screen such as a smart phone. Many technologies are migrating to QR codes and other 2D style barcodes.

- Mag stripe ticket: an older technology that relies on a paper ticket with a magnetic stripe on one side to store the relevant parking event information. The magnetic stripe contains encoded information about the parking transaction. This type of media is being replaced by barcode-based tickets.
- Video analytics: a rapidly advancing area that relies on software to analyze a video stream and/or image to identify objects or specific types of movements. Images can be collected using a camera in a fixed location, or can be mounted on a vehicle. The software analyzes the image for changes, often in real-time. Video analytics are used to manage license plate recognition (LPR) in on-street parking and facilities, count cars, categorize cars (i.e. big car vs small cars), examine tire valve-stem locations (to see if a car moved), provide new services (find a car), identify operational issues such as a car parked in wrong space or stopped in an exit lane for a long duration. Machine learning is a developing aspect of video analytics in which a computer learns from the activity it sees in a video and learns to identify exception cases and process them correctly.
- Handheld and mobile devices: as our lives become more mobile, so do parking operations. Handhelds can be found in event and valet operations, supporting parking enforcement activities, and for validating towing/immobilization needs in real-time. The industry is experiencing rapid growth in the use of handhelds in urban garage operations with the ability to collect payment and verify access credentials, the ability to look up information on a customer or vehicle in real time, and the ability to manage facilities from a different location by monitoring operations. Handhelds and many mobile phones and tablets are enabling operating personnel to access critical information necessary to manage multiple facilities with a single internet-connected device while on the move. In addition, mobile software is providing field cashiers with the full capabilities of a cashier station in a mobile device.
- Payment: a data-sensitive technology group that covers the collection of payments as well as the management of payment data security. Of course, this includes common payment methods such as cash and credit card, however we are seeing an explosion of new, alternative payment methods as well.
- Automated cash collection requires sophisticated mechanical devices that analyze a paper note or coin to determine the value and authenticity. Some devices can recycle the notes and coins to reduce operating members having to visit the device to replenish currency.

When it comes to credit cards, the Payment Card Industry (PCI) has established several standards (PCI-DSS) to improve card payment transaction security and reduce fraud. PCI-DSS requirements define hardware, software, network, and work practices to improve the security of card payment data storage and transmission. Another type of electronic payment technology leverages a driver's mobile phone or payment account; Apple Pay, Android Pay and other electronic wallets offer a tap-and-go model that uses near-field communications plus biometric security (a thumbprint, for example). Other mobile-based payment options such as Paypal, Venmo, and even Bitcoin are being explored.

Additional technologies to explore related to payments include end-to-end encryption (E2EE) and point-to-point encryption (P2PE), which define methods to securely transmit credit card data from the reader to the bank, improving compliance with PCI requirements. EMV is a separate technology not related to PCI, that defines a standard for accepting chip cards in physical locations. EMV reduces fraud associated with duplicated and stolen credit cards at physical pay terminals.

The Connected Car

This technology group is in its infancy, and will increase in importance as autonomous vehicle and connected car usage is adopted. Connected cars and specifically autonomous vehicles will need to communicate with the parking facility to identify space availability, access the garage, navigate to a specific space, and process payment. It may also need to activate equipment and services, such as an electric vehicle charger. In addition, when a vehicle is in the facility, it may need to access the facility's network as a communication bridge to access the outside world. This will be accomplished with technologies being developed to support vehicle-to-vehicle (V2V) and vehicle-to-infrastructure (V2I) methods. These methods rely on the use of DSRC technologies (dedicated short-range communications) which operate on a specific radio frequency.

FIGURE 5.6
Autonomous Vehicles and Vehicles
that Can Find and Reserve Their Own
Parking Spaces are Forecast to be
on the Horizon

FIGURE 5.7
EMV vs PCI, Flow
of Credit Data

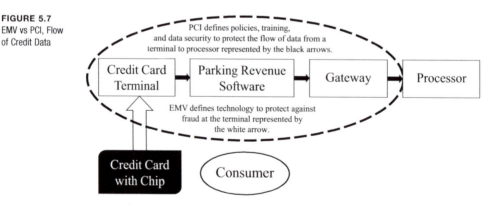

Customer Support

Customer support technologies are more important to operations as customer self-service and remote operating capabilities are deployed. This technology group enables customer support operations to be more efficient and incorporates desktop software to access cameras that monitor traffic and customer areas, and to see a customer interacting with a device. Intercom systems enable customers to talk with customer service agents.

Using digital intercom and voice-over-internet-protocol (VoIP) technologies, agents can talk to any location via software-based customer support software from any location with an internet connection; in some cases, video intercom (two-way, real-time) is implemented. Finally, there are the tools and software that an operating organization uses to support customers. This includes customer relationship management (CRM) systems, customer service ticket management, and maintenance management systems to manager repairs.

Ancillary Technologies

As facilities evolve to support additional use scenarios there is an increasing number of technologies that a parking manager needs to be aware of:

- Smart lighting: LED and fluorescent lamps controlled by a software system to adjust light and energy usage based on activity in the garage. Fewer lights are activated on a sunny day than on a cloudy one. This technology monitors the facility for pedestrian and vehicular movement and increases lighting in areas where activity exists.
- EV charging stations: as electric vehicles become more common, parking facilities and street parking are natural places to recharge. While there are a variety of charging options and capabilities, there are two popular types of charging units today that a manager should understand—a Level 2 charger and a DC quick charger. Level 2 chargers can charge an electric vehicle in four to six hours and require 240v electric circuit. These chargers can be installed on a wall or a kiosk and do not require much space for installation. DC quick chargers can charge an electric vehicle in about 30 minutes. These chargers require 480v electric service, which typically requires enhancements and upgrades to a facility's electrical system.

  In addition to charger hardware, a facility will need to decide if it wants to associate with one of several charging networks. Charging networks manage the chargers on behalf of a facility and manage payment collection from chargers. There are a few national networks and several additional regional networks, each of which provides a mobile app that allows users to find, use, and pay for charging.
- Transit ticket kiosks/information kiosks: depending on the location of a parking facility there are several kiosk type devices that might be installed. Kiosks are used to allow customers to purchase transit passes and entertainment tickets, provide information for local business and attractions, and many other information services. These devices typically require access to a reliable internet service.

  While there are many different groups of field technologies, there are several desirable characteristics to confirm when selecting a specific solution. As new technologies are introduced, they should include the following capabilities to ensure they will support an operation into the foreseeable future.
- Internet-based: devices in the solution should be IP addressable and connect via network technology versus serial wiring. This enables easier installation and makes remote support possible. It also improves the ability of network security tools to better manage the devices and remote updates without having to physically visit the equipment.

FIGURE 5.8
A Variety of Electric-Vehicle Charging Options Offer Choices for Both Drivers and Parking Facility Operators

- Interoperability: Devices and on-site software should allow remote access with appropriate security and have an application programming interface (API) library that easily enables integration with other systems. The use of an open and robust API library is very important in today's operations. A valued solution is one that can easily integrate with other solutions in a secure manner.
- Reduce or eliminate moving parts in devices: Moving parts wear out and require maintenance, leading to higher cost-of-ownership in the long run. This includes limiting the use of ticket transports and bill acceptors. Encourage the use of credit card swipe or dip style readers versus card machines which ingest a card to process a payment.
- Data ownership: Edge devices and the operating systems create large quantities of data. Ensure that the parking operation owns or has a license to the data (data may be stored elsewhere, such as a cloud provider) and has the ability to authorize the dissemination of data as desired. Data is a critical asset in managing and processing transactions and as such, data formats should be standard and non-proprietary.

Infrastructure Technologies

The technology infrastructure is the foundation on which parking technology is built. Monitoring and securing the infrastructure is critical to parking and transportation operations, but unfortunately, these key technologies are forgotten in solution implementation. Poor deployment of infrastructure technology can create significant service and reliability issues and, in the worst case, can bring the operations to a halt. Infrastructure technology includes the data and voice circuits used by an operation to connect to the outside world, the network switches and firewalls that route data traffic in and out of a facility, and the wireless network and internal cabling used to connect devices in the facility.

A facility should regularly monitor its data use and compare it to available bandwidth. An overused data circuit (network connection) results in lost or slow data, which will cause operating and payment issues as the devices cannot consistently communicate with third-party systems.

Often the components of infrastructure technology can be described as supporting "data in transit" and "data at rest". The first term refers to the ability to move data securely across a network, while the second term refers to how data is stored, locally or online.

Firewalls and other network devices should also be monitored and maintained on a regular basis. As a high-level summary of critical infrastructure needs:

- Install a firewall.
- Train staff on internet use, passwords, and access policies.
- Physically protect local systems and devices.
- Maintain software and operating system with necessary patches and updates.
- Maintain antivirus software.
- Monitor the network activity for unusual activity and performance.

As more solutions become cloud-based or hosted off-site in professional data centers, a facility will need a more robust data circuit and network to manage the flow of data and ensure connectivity to the data center(s). In addition, critical operations should consider implementing dual data circuits or high-speed cellular wireless back up (automatic failover) connections to ensure a location can always access its data center to continue to operate.

In addition to ensuring that data moves quickly and correctly in a facility, infrastructure technology plays an important role in ensuring a secure data environment is maintained, from network appliances that manage access to various devices in the network, to software that analyzes data traffic to identify suspect activity and notify and shut down access of the offending source. Some PCI-DSS (credit card) compliance can be solved by moving financial transactions to a separate physical network or even a virtual private network.

Data storage is a key part of the infrastructure, regardless of where the data is stored (locally or cloud). Consideration must be given for sensitive data. This includes PCI data as already mentioned but should also include personally identifying information (PII) such as names, addresses, email address, phone number), and adhere to any other applicable data standards. A parking operation should implement a data management policy and should choose to err on the side of caution.

As smart city and smart parking initiatives expand, the ability for a parking location to interact with other parties will become more important and more robust. The infrastructure technologies will be critical to the success of a facility to integrate with other systems and share data in an appropriate way.

Operating Software Technology

This can be considered the brains of a solution; it is the technology that coordinates and manages all the activity and transactions for a parking and transportation operation. This technology group connects to the field technology, stores the rates to charge customers, manages access credentials for users, processes parking transactions and payment transactions, identifies enforcement actions for scofflaws, and manages many other operational parameters. This technology maintains the key functions to drive operational efficiencies and customer conveniences.

The common functions of operating software include:

- Rate management: managing rates and performing calculations on the proper amount to charge for a parking activity.
- Inventory management: tracking usage of spaces and sharing the information with reservation platforms and other systems.
- Access control: managing both transient tickets issued and contract parking credential rights for access to parking. Managing the various rules associated with a specific rate and user (e.g. contract parker allowed to park only on certain days and at certain times, or event parking on a specific date and time).
- Payment processing: sending proper amounts to the appropriate clearing service to collect payment from a customer.
- Billing and customer account management: generating appropriate invoices for recurring and one-time charges related to credentials, managing vehicle registration and associating to credentials, managing receivables and communicating to the access system valid credential accounts
- Daily accounting and auditing: generates reports on daily activity and provides audit trails to reconcile with cashflows related to the operation.
- Enforcement and violation: similar to rate management but includes functionality to report violations for adjudication and to monitor escalation of violations for repeat offenders.

While operating software comes in a wide variety of solutions, most solutions fall into one or a combination of the following categories:

- Access and Revenue Control (ARCS): manages the entry and exit to a gated parking facility or collects payment in ungated facilities. Tracks open transient tickets, verifies electronic validations, calculates parking fees, and manages contract parker access.

- Billing and customer account management credential/accounts receivable/asset/billing: manages the invoicing of customers for credentials, often using integration to payroll or student systems, assignment of credentials to customers, and tracks the inventory and status of active and inactive credentials suitable for an access control system. This includes support for gated operations as well as non-gated operations where permission-based credentials such as hangtags or residential permits are deployed. This also typically handles payment for such credentials, as well as supports vehicle registrations and assignment to credentials.
- Event system: manages the entry and exit to events that are typically operated in ungated parking operations. The solution issues event parking passes, tracks cash, credit, and prepaid transactions, can maintain a VIP list, and is typically run on hand-held devices.
- Valet system: manages the acceptance and retrieval of vehicles in a valet operation. Like an ARCS, it also manages vehicle location in addition to recording damage to a vehicle and monitoring valet attendant performance and efficiency in moving vehicles.
- Meter system: revenue control system that manages rates, calculates parking fees for parking events, and distributes active parking sessions to the appropriate enforcement solutions. Can apply to both single-space or multi-space meters, most typically used for on-street parking, but frequently appearing in non-gated garages and surface lots.
- Enforcement: solution that identifies vehicles that have not paid for parking, are parking on an expired credential, parking in an illegal error, or have past parking violations. The solution manages the issuance of a violation, tracks payment of the violation, and processes through an adjudication (appeal) process.
- Transport: a solution that sells rights to use a transportation service. The solution manages rates, calculates fees, and distributes appropriate credentials to use transportation. Solutions can also assign specific seats and scheduled routes/trips.

As online marketing of parking becomes a more important source of generating demand (see Chapter 16), operating software will need to manage the distribution of inventory and rates across the various marketing channels. Channels will include local business website, parking marketing websites, event ticketing platforms and many other sources of demand. Social media is also a marketing opportunity, as well as a direct feedback mechanism from parkers.

Analytics and Reporting

In a connected world, the amount of data generated is unfathomable.

While data itself can be interesting, it's the actionable data that is most valuable. Actionable data enables a parking operator to meet or exceed performance management metrics. This is a result of analyzing the data to identify trends and improve operations and then implementing changes to the operation and measuring the results of those changes.

Analyzing millions of transaction data generated by a typical parking facility is impractical to perform manually. As Big Data initiatives and IoT concepts continue to be applied in parking and transportation scenarios, even more interesting data will be generated. This is where the analytics and reporting technologies come to the rescue.

With billions of bytes of data generated in an operation, a management team needs effective tools to collect, segment, and compare data. As shown in Figure 5.13, the merging of math and statistics with computer skills to access systems, and domain knowledge inherent in the management team creates the field of data science—the processes and systems to extract knowledge or insights from data.

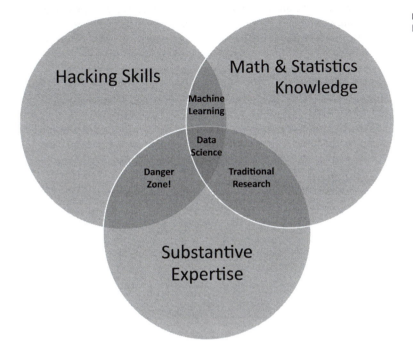

FIGURE 5.9
Drew Conway Venn diagram

A picture is worth 1,000 words. The most effective way to represent data is through a graphical interface, particularly one that highlights the relationship being illustrated. Key capabilities of reporting software include the ability to plot data visually versus reading tables of data. Most commonly this is a chart or heat map to show variances, or placing data on a map to provide geospatial references. Viewing the data enables trends and outliers to be more readily identified. Additional key capability of reporting tools is to allow a user to quickly explore information by probing into details accepting new data sources and merging it into the reporting framework.

Key performance indicators (KPIs) are a type of reporting tool that enable a management team to identify the critical measurements to effectively manage the operation. By implementing the appropriate reporting tools, managers will be able to reduce the effort necessary to collect data and report KPIs, and therefore focus on understanding the story being told by the KPIs and implementing actions to drive improvements in the KPIs.

KPIs help a management team with what is important; these are the building blocks of reporting. Benchmarking enables a parking operation to measure its performance against other parking operations, to ask the question, "Why is my number different than someone else's?" A parking operation can also benchmark against itself, to ask the question, "Why is my number different than it was last month?" The latter is useful when considering that parking operations are different and what is important to one operation may be different from what is important to another.

Once a manager understands their KPIs, they can act and monitor the results of that action in the KPIs.

In addition to reporting capabilities, the ability to analyze data and generate new information is readily available in our computer-based world. Data analytics and processing tools have evolved to the point where even a novice can generate insightful results based on trends or historical data. For example, analytic tools can assist in analyzing budgeting variances and projecting cost and revenue forecasts, allowing a manager to focus on making improvements based on the reporting. With the lower cost of processing power, a manager can develop pricing algorithms that can suggest pricing for various events and situations. Other tools can predict occupancy levels based on historic activity and predicted events (local events, weather conditions, etc.).

As operations expand their usage of analytic tools, an understanding of data analysis processes and statistics is a valuable knowledge base. Managers must understand the data being used in an analysis to ensure that the output of any analytics has a high level of confidence, especially as systems begin to manage activities automatically, such as pricing and inventory allocation.

Analytics will require a plan to store and retrieve data. It will be difficult for a location to store 100 percent of its collected data in one place. In addition, it is likely that the analytics an operation wants to perform will require access to other data sets, such as weather, construction, hotel activity, etc., which are not collected by the operation directly. As such, a manager should consider where and how they will store and access data to support its analytic activities.

Big Data is the term used to describe sets of data that are so large and unwieldy that they cannot be comprehended by the human mind. Big Data merges large data sets with analytic tools to uncover relevant trends and insights. As an example, one might ask which are the characteristics that impact a parker's decision where to park. The answer could include the time and day, the price charged, the anticipated duration of stay, the availability of alternative transportation, the number of people in the car, proximity to the parker's true destination, the weather forecast, amenities near the parking lot (such as a gas station or car wash), and dozens of other factors that are difficult to measure or model. The promise of Big Data is that through the analysis of large amounts of data, a predictive model of parking can be developed so that the manager can offer the right parking to the right parker at the right price.

Key Steps to Selecting Technology

This section offers a brief review of the key steps used to evaluate and choose technology. A parking operation will never be at a loss to find technologies to implement in a facility. However, as outlined in the beginning of this chapter, not every technology is appropriate for every location, regardless of how innovative the technology might appear.

The following steps will assist an operating team to understand theirs and their customer's needs and to identify the technologies that fill the needs:

1) Understand operations today and in the future.

    Define customers today and in the future. What are their transportation and parking needs? Remember parking is just one step on a person's journey; parking is not the destination but rather a transition point from driving to some other modality. Does the facility support office workers in the building or in buildings in the area? This drives whether custom ID credentials should be supported or not. Does the facility support local attractions and events on the weekend? This might indicate the desire to support online marketing firms that will generate electronic barcode permits or LPR based credentials.

    a) What types of businesses might need access to the facility? Does the organization support downtown-based universities or a convention center that requires dedicated access to specific spaces? Is there a business in the building that has a large number of daily guests who may desire the ability to park near an elevator (i.e. a nested area)? Does the operation serve a medical facility with a greater-than-mandated requirement for disabled spaces?

b) What type of parking and transportation services will the operation offer? Will the facilities allow rideshare vehicles to drop off and pick up customers? Are car-share services parking in the facility? Do companies rotate a fleet of vehicles across several facilities? Will amenities like EV chargers be provided?

c) How will customers interact with facilities? Will the organization have a mobile website that allows customers to search and pay for parking online? Will the operation work with third party marketing and ticketing firms? How will customers access the facility—will they use barcode, license plate, toll tag credentials?

d) What data is required to manage the operation? To share with others? Data examples include occupancy, pricing, enforcement, and access credential details with building security or hotels.

e) Are there operational or financial constraints? Everyone wants to implement the best solution, but most live with budgets and need to prioritize their wants. Will the management team have the resources to support a new technology? Are the necessary IT resources and maintenance resources available to support the technology?

f) Develop a roadmap or timeline highlighting when key parking and transportation services will be started or launched. When will the valet service start? When does the operation intend to work with the local restaurant for validations? When will the new building security system be installed that provides one access credential to the parking and building? Understanding when these operational services will launch is a key step in defining priorities for technology. It is likely that the services will be introduced over time. Documenting the rough timing will help to prioritize and sequence a facility's technology needs.

g) Identify the technology needed to support the rollout of the services. Evaluate the technology needs for each service. Identify the technology that needs to be implemented first to support future services and understand the relationships and dependencies of the various technologies being considered.

2) Coordinate your plan so that the launch of a new service offering includes the correct amount of technology needed, while staying within financial and operational constraints (i.e., the budget). This brings the desired plan in line with the realistic plan that considers financial and operations constraints. The ability to be objective will ensure a successful plan can be defined. With a successful plan, the probability of delivering innovative solutions on time and on budget increase significantly.

a) Taking the time to develop a technology roadmap will prove to be invaluable. Understanding the services an operation wants to deliver for its internal use or to support customers more effectively will make it much easier to identify the technology needs. Once an organization understands the technology needs to support its operation's goals, a manager will be able to prioritize the selection and implementation of technology solutions in an orderly fashion. More important, the plan will ensure that the sequence of technology implementation is correct and that the technology solutions are effective and support the organization's goals.

CHAPTER 6

Sustainability

Paul Wessel and
Rachel Yoka, CAPP, LEED AP BD+C

Context

There are more than 1.2 billion motorized vehicles in the world as this book is published and that number is expected to double by 2030.[1] By 2050, perhaps the only element of personal mobility common to the turn of this century will be the act of moving around in self-contained vehicles on wheels. Many of today's businesses will be gone, but new ones will emerge, and current players will evolve to stay relevant–and profitable–in this new transportation environment.[2]

Transport accounts for about 60 percent of global oil consumption, 27 percent of all energy use, and 23 percent of world CO2 emissions.[3]

As an integral element of the transportation network and a specific land-use type, parking resources and operations have significant effects on environmental sustainability.

There are a few ways to consider the relationship and links between parking and sustainability—as a land use, building type, form of transportation. Before addressing these three relationships, it is important to address the effects of parking generally, and then define sustainability. This chapter will primarily address the infrastructure of parking, namely garages and the built environment as well as the impacts they have on customer behavior and parking operations.

FIGURE 6.1
Parking has a Significant Effect on Sustainability

Environmental Effects of Parking

The parking industry, like all industries, has both generalized and specific environmental effects that stem from the specific land use, building type, and operations. The specific impacts are difficult to quantify, given a shortage of available data on the industry as a whole. The effects can be discussed by category, however, and relate to the specific industry as detailed in the examples provided below. This summary is neither comprehensive nor all-inclusive, but highlights major effects at a high level.

- Pollution. Perhaps one of the most direct environmental effects of parking comes from the carbon emissions and fuel waste generated by vehicles traveling to, in, and around parking facilities.

  - The layout, equipment setup, and payment configurations of the garage or lot can reduce idling and travel time, reducing emissions and fuel wasted during vehicle trips.
  - Significant gains can be made using transportation demand management (TDM) strategies aimed at reducing both the number and duration of single-occupant vehicle (SOV) trips. These strategies include access to transit as well as multi-modal options including biking, walking, and ridesharing.
  - Technology improvements that increase the availability of real-time occupancy data and directional guidance (wayfinding) can decrease these effects as well, allowing for reductions in the amount of time and emissions drivers spend searching for parking spaces.

- Land Use. Significant land resources are dedicated to parking in lots and garages, as well as on-street spaces. It's important to note that parking is often not the highest and best use of land, especially within urban areas.

  - The concept of right-sizing parking is a common best practice. Building only what is necessary based on accurate supply/demand studies, applying shared-use principles, and seeking appropriate variances for new facilities can reduce the number of spaces to be constructed, as well as maximize turnover in parking operations, as discussed in Chapter 3.
  - Zoning laws and ordinances, addressed in Chapter 2, can often require parking owners and developers to build more parking than is truly necessary. This is a challenge that remains for the industry and policy makers, yet it can be successfully tackled by political leadership, urban and transportation planners, and parking professionals on a case-by-case basis depending on location.

- Energy Use. Parking structures (and lots) are not significant energy users as compared with other building types (commercial, residential, hospitals, laboratories, etc.). The single greatest cost after labor in parking operations is generally considered to be lighting, followed by mechanical ventilation in structures, if required.

FIGURE 6.2
It's Important to Note That Parking is Not Always the Highest and Best Use of Land

FIGURE 6.3
Significant Advances in Lighting Technology Have Increased Sustainability in Parking Garages

- Significant strides have been made in the industry as evidenced by more efficient lighting technologies and sensors, more efficient ventilation systems and sensors, and renewable energy sources, namely rooftop solar arrays.
- Significant gains stand to be made by the greater application of commissioning,[4] re-commissioning, and retro-commissioning, but these practices are not yet widespread, with the exception of LEED-certified facilities, which commonly mandate commissioning.[5] These are also encouraged by Parksmart,[6] the standard for sustainable parking that will be covered later in this chapter.
- Embodied energy and life-cycle assessment is not yet common in the industry, and will develop in time as sustainability strategies become more sophisticated.

- Water. Again, parking structures (and lots) are not significant water users as compared with different building types. There are some operational procedures (i.e., washdowns) that are done as part of regular maintenance and cleaning of parking structures, and use significant amounts of water on a periodic basis.
- Waste. Waste impacts from the parking industry are limited when compared with other real-estate.

    - Limiting construction and demolition waste, and considering the deconstruction of facilities and possible reuse of materials when a property's useful life is over will result in the reduction of major waste streams in the parking industry.
    - Recycling is common in operations and maintenance and gain can be made in effectively managing these programs.

Applicable Definitions of Sustainability

The International Parking Institute's Sustainability Framework[7] references two common definitions or models for sustainability in parking: the Triple Bottom Line and the Brundtland Commission definition.

The Triple Bottom Line provides a framework for sustainability in any industry. This approach, first coined by John Elkington in, *Cannibals with Forks: The Triple Bottom Line of 21st Century Business*, is often referred to as "People, Planet, Profit," "TBL," or the "three pillars." This definition focuses on balance—that without the three pillars, long-term sustainability cannot be achieved or maintained.

Another good reference comes from the Brundtland Commission of the United Nations. First proposed in March 1987, this definition has stood the test of time: "Sustainable development meets the needs of the present without compromising the ability of future generations to meet their own needs."

Together these provide a foundation for our decision making, aiming to achieve balance among these three often-competing priorities.

A Sustainability Framework for the Parking Industry

In early 2011, the International Parking Institute conducted a landmark survey to solicit the feedback of parking professionals to define the sustainability movement and the role of parking professionals to shape it.

Respondents identified critical elements for sustainability in the parking industry but felt the

FIGURE 6.4
The Triple Bottom Line of People, Planet, and Profit Offers a Framework for Sustainability in Any Industry

two most important elements were "green building and high-performance building standards for parking structures" and "parking facility operations supporting alternative transportation modes."

Based on this information, as well as industry research and collaboration, the International Parking Institute released the *Framework on Sustainability for Parking Design, Management, and Operations*. Updated regularly, the resulting framework takes a generalized approach to sustainability and applies it specifically not only to the parking industry, but also to the industry's strengths and capacity to engender positive change.

The Framework identifies strategic sustainability goals, as well as accompanying action items to advance and strengthen the parking profession and the greater application of sustainability within it. These key priorities are grouped into the following areas:

- Knowledge and Research:

  - Gather data, conduct research, and document case studies to create a body of knowledge about best practices in parking and transportation.
  - Identify innovative technologies that support sustainability goals.
  - Increase education, awareness, and information-sharing to disseminate gained knowledge widely throughout the profession.

- Programs and Operations:

  - Prioritize transportation demand management (TDM), access, and mobility management programs that decrease single-occupancy vehicle trips and vehicle miles traveled.
  - Decrease reliance on fossil fuels by increasing energy efficiency, using alternative fuels, or generating renewable energy as part of daily operations.
  - Protect water quality by reducing potable water use, using biodegradable cleaning products, and implementing stormwater control practices.

- Planning, Design, and Construction:

  - Promote practices in the planning, design, and construction of parking facilities that reduce the long-term environmental effects of land-use decisions.
  - Encourage alternative energy sources and energy-saving technology, reduce reliance on fossil fuels, and accommodate alternative-fuel vehicles.
  - Make informed decisions based on long-term environmental effects related to material and technology selection, including effective natural resource management and waste reduction.

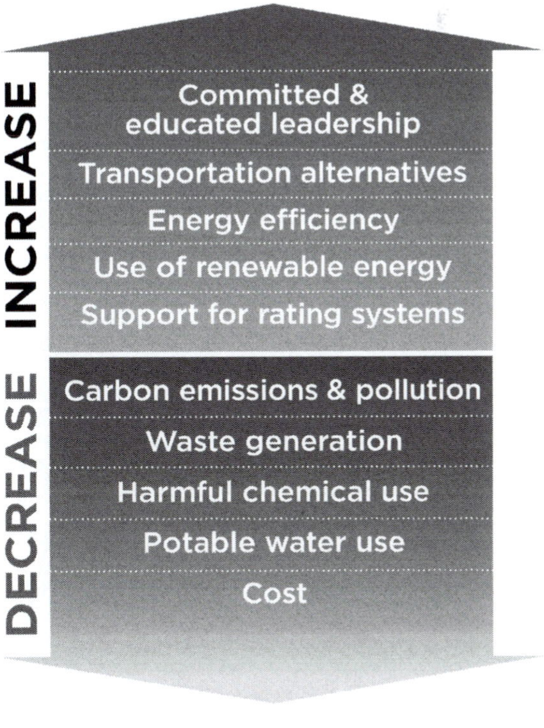

INCREASE
- Committed & educated leadership
- Transportation alternatives
- Energy efficiency
- Use of renewable energy
- Support for rating systems

DECREASE
- Carbon emissions & pollution
- Waste generation
- Harmful chemical use
- Potable water use
- Cost

FIGURE 6.5
Sustainability Objectives

This approach is specific to the parking industry and relevant to its business practices and opportunities. It is detailed further in *Sustainable Parking Design & Management: A Practitioner's Handbook* (IPI & NPA, 2014). This reference book addressed the complex interplay of parking, transportation, and sustainability, and is recommended reading for readers interested in a deeper dive into the subject.

Parking's relationship to sustainability is complex; a good starting point is to approach parking as a land use, as a building type, and as a form of transportation and mobility.

Parking as a Land-Use

There's a key consideration that links land-use and transportation: Parking is often the connection between where we are and where we want to go. And decisions about travel and transportation have significant environmental impacts.

Parking is a significant land use that appears in urban environments to suburban and rural ones. This chapter addresses parking as a land use, excluding only private, residential parking (namely, the driveway). Parking as a land use has specific attributes and specific environmental considerations.

Parking as a land use includes structured parking, surface parking (lots), and on-street operations (parking at the curb). General considerations that reference these three uses:

- The "greenest" space is one that is never constructed because patrons used other modes of transit.
- An empty space is a wasted resource; and "free" parking isn't a reality.
- Parking resources should be used to the greatest extent possible (maximum turnover and usage), often through shared parking.
- Structured parking can support greater density.
- Surface parking can serve as a land bank for future uses.
- On-street parking can support a vibrant, walkable street system.
- Consideration should be given to the re-use of facilities (lots and garages) as mobility choices transform how we travel, given the rise of transportation network companies (TNCs) and autonomous vehicles.

Parking as a Building Type

Parking as a building type addresses structured parking, including planning, design, engineering, and construction choices. Considerations for surface lots are also included in this category, as there are physical attributes that influence sustainability outcomes.

Sustainable building design is now mainstream. The United States Green Building Council (USGBC) and the LEED Ratings System have moved the market, proving that a rising tide lifts all boats. Consumers factor environmental effects into their buying decisions—a trend that looks to continue and intensify with the millennial generation. Renters and homeowners are willing to pay more for high-performing and better-quality housing based on environmental standards. Companies recognize that indoor air quality and daylighting improve employee performance and boost retention rates. And even bottom-line businesses are investing in benchmarking and efficiency projects that have the right return on investment rates. The emergence of sustainability rating systems serves as a prime example of the ways garage owners and operators implement benchmarking, energy efficiency, and high-performance standards, just as in other sectors: office, retail, industrial, multifamily, and hotel.

Energy efficiency gains and higher-quality buildings in each of these sectors will be essential to reducing emissions and energy use. The parking industry has implemented its own standards and benchmarking tools to achieve greater levels of sustainability in parking facilities as a building type.

When examining parking as a building type, consideration should be given to:

- Location of facilities in relation to destinations and other modes of travel.
- Choice of building materials and structural systems for long-term durability and maintenance. Proactive operational maintenance contributes substantially to the life-cycle of the asset.
- Mechanical and electrical systems and their life-cycle return on investment (ROI) and sustainability effects, versus a simple, first-cost approach.
- Efficiency of travel and level of service in the functional design to limit unwanted idling, travel, and queuing.
- Safety and security of patrons—the human factor. People are the first in the list of the Triple Bottom Line approach, and the health, safety, and welfare of patrons and employees are paramount.

Parking as a Form of Transportation and Mobility

Parking is an essential element of transportation and mobility networks. The rise of the connected car and the journey toward automated vehicles and transportation allows for even greater linkages to existing and evolving transportation networks that include all forms of mass transit, as well as alternative modes of transportation.

The goal of sustainability initiatives in this approach focus on reducing the need and frequency of the SOV. As technology improves the software and applications that provide information on transportation options, efficiencies can be increased by maximizing parking resources (using spaces to the greatest extent possible) and reducing waste and pollution.

Approaching parking as a transportation and mobility enabler (or access management) is a means to expand and accelerate the choices that consumers want. Parking as a hub for mobility facilitates access to mass transit, car-sharing, ride-sharing, bicycles, alternative fuel vehicles, etc.

Sustainability Rating Systems for Parking Structures

Although multiple ratings systems can be applied to parking garages nationally and internationally, one system exists that was developed considering the unique impacts and attributes of the building type.

The USGBC acquired the Parksmart program in 2016. GBCI, as the certification arm of the USGBC, administers Parksmart, which defines and recognizes sustainable practices in parking structure management, programming, design, and technology.

Parksmart is a voluntary certification program enabling high-performance parking facilities to increase mobility while using fewer resources. The program guides parking structures toward solutions-oriented strategies that accelerate the growth and adoption of business models integrating connected cars, consumer choice, multimodal mobility options, smart parking and intelligent transportation innovations, and rapidly advancing technologies.

Serving existing and new parking structures in all markets—including commercial, university, municipal, hospital, retail, and hospitality—the program aims to:

- Reduce operational costs.
- Reduce environmental impacts.
- Increase energy efficiency and performance.
- Offer better lighting and ventilation.
- Develop efficient parking structure management.
- Promote alternative modes of transportation.

- Integrate sustainable mobility services and technologies.
- Diversify mobility options.
- Create stronger community relationships.

Parksmart recognizes 48 measures across four categories that offer a variety of options to maximize the sustainability of a parking structure, allowing asset owners to select approaches best suited for their operation:

- Management recognizes how garage operations maximize the use of a parking asset while minimizing waste.
- Programming promotes effective vehicle ingress/egress, access to alternative mobility solutions, and leverages the garage's potential as a public space, producing new revenue sources, greater customer satisfaction, and stronger community relations.
- Technology and Structure Design includes the physical attributes that increase energy efficiency, reduce waste, and support customer mobility choice in a parking facility.
- Innovation credits new and creative sustainable parking and transportation initiatives.

Points are assigned to each measure based on environmental impact, achievability for new and existing structures, and relevance to the economics of the asset. A total of 248 points are available; Parksmart certification is achieved by meeting minimum thresholds.

The certification system is applicable to both new construction and renovation and rehabilitation of existing facilities. In new construction, Parksmart promotes integrated design, pulling in operators, managers, and the sustainability team into the architecture, engineering, and design process. For existing structures, Parksmart provides tools to assess, benchmark, and improve parking assets.

Best Practices in Sustainability and Parking

Although each of the measures included in the Parksmart standard is relevant to the building type, summaries of a few selected strategies illustrate how the standard approaches the certification process. These best practices apply to parking structures and operations regardless of certification.

Parking Pricing

This measure is listed as the first in the entire standard. The objective states: "Parking structure charges for the use of parking spaces, allowing for economic and market conditions to impact patrons' decisions on mode of travel." Parking pricing has significant transportation effects; even marginal parking fees affect patron travel choices and patterns. This measure is supported by data from multiple sources, including Donald Shoup's *The High Cost of Free Parking* and the Victoria Transport Policy Institute. "Shifting from free to cost-recovery parking (prices that reflect the full cost of providing parking facilities), typically reduces automobile commuting by 10–30 percent, particularly if implemented with improved transportation choices and other complementary TDM strategies."[8] Options for compliance in this category are relatively straightforward—the facility charges for parking and provides the relevant documentation as listed in the requirements.

Third-Party Sustainability Certification

This measure allows for both high-impact and high-point values in the system. To recognize their comprehensive commitment to environmental sustainability, garages that have achieved a third-party sustainability certification (that complements and aligns with the goals of the program) will receive points in this measure, including LEED.[9] This measure recognizes and reinforces third-party rating systems, aligning with the shared sustainability goals as depicted previously. Structures that achieve a platinum LEED rating are awarded the highest point values on a weighted scale through to Certified LEED rating. The measure also allows for credit under other performance systems, including Energy Star Portfolio Manager.

Placemaking

This measure acknowledges that parking structures exist within the context of a community. As businesses, these facilities can contribute to the social well-being of a community and serve as positive neighborhood features, as discussed in Chapter 10. Placemaking examples include a suggested range of corresponding point values. Initiatives with higher community value (i.e., greater event frequency, more extensive physical features) are awarded higher values. Listed options include engaging arts and civic associations through events; providing public access to facilities for sporting events, exercise, or youth activities (as appropriate); creating parks and green space for the public good; and more. Documentation for both physical and event-based placemaking includes narratives and images, and additional listed resources include the Project for Public Spaces.[10]

Car-share Programs

This measure recognizes that "car-share programs reduce the number of miles driven by single occupancy automobiles. On average, a shared car removes between 9 and 13 vehicles from the road.[11] Additionally, the average carsharing participant decreases his or her driving by 27 to 56 percent,[12] reducing traffic congestion and automobile emissions." Options under this measure include partnering with an established car-share provider to create a car-share hub, or creating a standalone program. Populating the car-share hub with only hybrid or alternative-fuel vehicles is encouraged. The standard also provides a list of Related Measures, when applicable to the measure at hand. For car-share, these related measures include transportation management association (TMA)/organization (TMO) affiliation, low-emitting and fuel-efficient vehicles, alternative fuel vehicles, and marketing/educational programs.

Idle Reduction Payment Systems

This measure's objective is the implementation of payment systems that reduce idling at entry, payment, and exit. Properly configured, these systems allow efficient exit, reducing the amount of time vehicles wait in line and conserving energy, time, and natural resources while limiting greenhouse gas emissions. Specifically identified technologies include pay-on-foot, pay-by-cell, automated vehicle identification (AVI), license plate recognition (LPR), and toll transponders. Like parking pricing, this measure also specifically addresses the nature of the parking industry and parking facilities, using emerging technology to limit environmental effects.

Electric Vehicle (EV) Charging Stations

Plug-in electric vehicles (PEV) use EV charging stations and the intent of this measure is to facilitate EV infrastructure to foster further adoption of this emerging technology. According to Navigant Research, annual sales in the U.S. alone are estimated to surpass 467,000 vehicles by 2020 and will represent a significant percentage of the total vehicles on the road. Replacement of traditional fuel-combustion engines with EVs by consumers will

A century after the emergence of the Model T, parking facility owners, developers, planners, architects, operators, policy makers, and others are moving from a narrow "Where do we put the cars?" approach to an integrated vision of "How do we move more people, more efficiently?" And evolving technology, new business opportunities and a growing awareness are also expanding the role of parking as a transformative force for sustainable mobility in our cities, campuses, entertainment venues, and elsewhere.

reduce greenhouse gas emissions, but this trend requires widespread deployment of charging technology, especially in U.S. cities and metropolitan areas. This measure allows multiple compliance methods to accommodate Level I, Level II, and DC Fast Charging systems. Point values range and increase as charging durations improve, and facilities that provide EV charging to customers for free are encouraged. This measure includes the best practice of integrating charging stations with on-site renewable energy generation or renewable energy purchase programs to enable vehicles to be charged with clean energy.

Roofing Systems

The objective of this measure is to employ roofing technology that provides environmental benefits, and the measure allows for a wide range of options. These multiple options accommodate the reality that all buildings and operations have unique considerations. This range includes green roof systems,[13] blue roof systems,[14] and cool roofing applications, photovoltaic arrays, and high Solar Reflectance Index (SRI) value materials. The U.S. Environmental Protection Agency encourages the adoption of cool roofs to reduce energy use, air pollution, and greenhouse gas emissions, and improved human health and comfort.[15] For most parking operations, the roof of the structure is used for parking cars, making high SRI values the simplest and most cost-effective compliance path.

Conclusion

In sum, parking and transportation are not necessarily at odds; indeed, a vibrant and healthy society must enable the transport of both people and goods effectively and efficiently. The best sustainability approach takes advantage of the unique attributes of parking and transportation to create opportunities to limit the incidence of the SOV while increasing the efficiency of trips as well as the infrastructure that supports them. Advances in technology, especially software and analytics tools, have the ability to support sustainability initiatives. Parking resources can be carefully planned, designed, constructed and managed properly to increase their positive impacts on the environment while mitigating negative outcomes.

Notes

1   Unlocking the Power of Urban Transport Systems, The New Climate Economy—2016. http://newclimateeconomy.report/2015/wp-content/uploads/2016/04/Unlocking-the-power-of-urban-transport-systems_web.pdf.
2   Navigant Research White Paper, 2Q 2016—Transportation Outlook: 2025 to 2050: How Connectivity, Autonomous Technology, On-Demand Mobility, and Vehicle Electrification Will Transform Global Passenger Transportation. https://www.navigantresearch.com/research/transportation-outlook-2025-to-2050.
3   Paris Process on Mobility and Climate (PPMC), 2015. www.ppmc-transport.org/common-messages-2015/Sustainability.
4   Building commissioning may be defined as providing documented confirmation that systems are functioning as designed and meet operational needs.
5   For additional information, reference the Building Commissioning Association at https://www.bcxa.org/.
6   Parksmart includes commissioning in its criteria in the Parksmart Certification Standard, Measure 9.
7   International Parking Institute's Framework on Sustainability for Parking Design, Management, and Operations www.parking.org/2017/05/08/sustainability-framework-2017/.

8   Victoria Transport Policy Institute, www.vtpi.org/tdm/tdm72.htm.
9   It should be noted that most garages are ineligible for LEED certification. Structures with mixed-use or ancillary occupied spaces may qualify. For additional information, reference usgbc.org.
10 Project for Public Spaces, www.pps.org.
11 www.uctc.net/access/38/access38_carsharing_ownership.shtml.
12 www.uspirg.org/sites/pirg/files/reports/Apercent20Newpercent20Waypercent20topercent20Go percent20vUS1.pdf.
13 Green roofs also known as 'vegetated roofs' or 'living roofs'—are ballasted roofs consisting of a waterproofing membrane, growing medium (soil) and vegetation (plants) overlying a traditional roof. www.gsa.gov/about-us/organization/office-of-governmentwide-policy/office-of-federal-highperformance-buildings/projects-and-research/green-roofs.
14 A blue roof is a roof design that is explicitly intended to store water, typically rainfall. https://en.wikipedia.org/wiki/Blue_roof.
15 www.epa.gov/hiri/mitigation/coolroofs.htm.

CHAPTER 7

Managing Staff and Professional Development

Colleen M. Niese and Vicki Pero

This chapter will discuss the various processes associated with the employee life-cycle, starting with a section on how to determine the organizational structure and required staff to manage a parking location and carrying through to talent acquisition, on-boarding, training, and development. It ends with guidance toward developing and pursuing a parking career, including how professional certification can play a vital role in education and career development.

Organizational Structure and Staffing Levels

When designing the organizational structure for a parking location (on- or off- street), there are two roles typically required to manage operations, service customers, and report revenue:

- The Location Manager. While this job title can vary, the primary responsibilities for this position are centered around the ability to manage the daily activities of a parking facility, including managing staff, ensuring operational policies and procedures are followed, and guaranteeing a safe and seamless experience for parkers.
- Front Line Associates. Depending on the type of facility, these roles can be titled as attendant, cashier, enforcement officer, or valet. All front-line associates have two main responsibilities: ensure that patrons are able to park safely and efficiently through customer service, and accurately collect and report revenue from their respective shifts.

Given the broad spectrum of parking facilities, additional job roles may be involved including bookkeeper, accountant, field auditor, etc., but generally speaking, each facility will require at least one supervisor/manager with a team of front line associates.

Regardless of whether the parking facility is public or private, a combination of factors is used to establish staffing plans:

- Internally vs. Externally Managed. Facilities are either managed internally by an entity such as a university or municipality, or outsourced to a third-party management group (externally).

  - Internally Managed: Given that all employees are employed by the entity itself, managers set staffing plans according to both short-term needs and long-term objectives.

- Externally Managed: A parking professional should closely examine the contract requirements, whether the agreement in question is a lease or management agreement. If management, the terms will largely dictate the organizational design and staffing levels. If a lease, the parking professional will be more dependent on two criteria to evaluate staffing needs:

  1) Data: Parking professionals lean heavily on occupancy, ticket volume, parker mix (transient vs. monthly) and seasonality to determine staffing levels.
  2) Facility Type: The facility type, along with customer profiles, will drive material consideration toward staffing. For example, a self-park lot with 200 spaces, largely serving special events and collecting revenue manually, will likely require a staff of five to six frontline associates and one supervisor. In contrast, a large 365/24/7 hospital complex that has multiple parking lots and garages, some of which self-park while others offer valet service, will require a much more comprehensive staffing schedule.

Employee Job Descriptions

Employee job descriptions serve two purposes: they attract applicants who possess the skills and experience to perform a job, and they ensure hiring practices align with external compliance requirements. This table lists each section of a typical job description along with its definition and purpose.

TABLE 7.1 Job Descriptions

Job Description Section	Definition/Purpose
Job Summary (Job Title, Direct Supervisor, Department, FLSA Status, Position Summary Statement)	• Defines role and place in organization. • Helps establish salary band. • Distinguishes between specialist and generalist. • Represents the overall role. • Indicates if the position has supervisory responsibility.
Essential Duties and Responsibilities	• Lists the core responsibilities, typically in order of priority and/or frequency. • Further supports FLSA duties test. • Only those responsibilities that are requirements of the position are listed.
Non-Essential Duties & Responsibilities	• Additional duties that applicants will be asked to complete, not requirements to the position.
Minimum Requirements	• Lists the minimum number of years of experience, minimum education and baseline certifications, as applicable.
Other Requirements	• Includes other desired qualifications, however not required to be considered for the position.
Physical Demands & Working Conditions	• Lists the environment where the position works and any physical demands. • This section helps determine ADA accommodations, as applicable.

When drafting job descriptions, it's important to be as accurate as possible, especially when identifying minimum essential duties and minimum requirements These two aspects play key roles when interviewing and hiring.

Job descriptions should be reviewed on an annual basis to ensure that they are current and consistent with actual job duties. Lastly, it's highly recommended that employees sign the job description when they are hired, transferred, or promoted, or if the job description itself changes, to ensure that they understand and acknowledge their duties.

Recruiting Staff

Successful recruiting is largely based on the ability to cast the widest net to gain a robust applicant pool and respond to each applicant. Listed below is each step to the recruitment process, along with associated definitions and best practices.

TABLE 7.2 Recruitment Steps

Recruitment Step	Definition and Best Practices
Draft Job Ad	• Job ads contain a high level description of the position along with benefits and aspects of the ideal candidate. • Use the content of the job description to draft the job ad.
Place Job Ad	• Post job ad on the employer's website, career websites and through social media (e.g., LinkedIn, Facebook, Twitter). • Recent studies show that more job seekers visit the company's website over career websites.
Applications/Resume Review	• A process to ensure the applications/resumes received align with the job description. • First review and sort those that meet minimum qualifications vs. those that don't.
Phone Screen	• Typically, a 15-20 minute phone conversation to validate the application as compared to the job description. • During the phone screen the following is verified: education, years of experience, availability, and base compensation desired.
Face to Face Interview	• An opportunity for the hiring manager to better understand the applicant's knowledge, skills and ability while the applicant learns more about the organization and the opportunity. • The hiring manager should prepare the list of questions before the interview and verify legal vs. illegal questions with Human Resources and/or Legal.
Evaluation	• This is the point in the process where the hiring manager evaluates each candidate based on the responses during the interviews. • Commonly, Human Resources will provide an evaluation sheet so that the hiring manager can objectively determine the best candidate.
Job Offer	• Once the finalist is selected, the hiring manager either offers the position verbally first or in writing. • Job offers typically include base salary, benefits, bonus (if applicable) start date and any pertinent company policies. • They can be contingent, if the company practices background and/or drug tests.

Onboarding Staff

Hiring managers and new hires themselves typically want to be productive as soon as possible. Listed below are the most common, leading practices to support new hires learning their job efficiently and successfully.

a. *Reach out to the new hire before start date.* It creates a great first impression, will likely alleviate any anxiety the new employee may experience, and demonstrates the hiring manager's leadership profile. Reaffirm to the new hire when and where they should arrive, along with any items (e.g., I-9 credentials) they should bring on the first day.

b. *Be prepared for the new hire's first day.* If the new employee is to meet with other coworkers, be sure to schedule calendar appointments and review the agenda each should cover. Also, all logistics should be addressed: security access, laptop, business card, office space, etc. before the start date.

c. *Training.* Schedule the order of training activities based on job priorities, commonly during a 60- to 90-day period, to ensure the employee has time to practice what's been learned and balance it with daily job duties. Check in often throughout the entire process to discuss what the employee has learned, questions they may have, and if applicable, ask the employee to demonstrate skills to ensure that performance aligns with expectations.

d. *Set the same expectations early and often throughout.* A common pitfall that should be avoided is to provide a lengthy list of all the outstanding items, issues, and projects that have been on hold to the new employee. Many hiring managers have good intentions in thinking the employee will perceive how much they are wanted and needed, but often the new hire ends up overwhelmed. The next section will address this in more detail.

Establishing Performance Goals

The best way to set expectations during the new employee's first week and connect his or her job to the company's bigger picture is to establish performance goals. Managers should meet with a new hire on their second or third day on the job and plan two to three goals he or she can complete in the next 90 days. These can be as simple as completing the new hiring training plan, as involved as managing a project, and everything in between.

These goals should be tied directly to the employee's essential job duties, and the employee should be provided with all of the support and resources needed to develop and complete each. Agree upon the deadline for each, and the hiring manager should also share how he or she will check in on progress and, as importantly, provide feedback. Lastly, the employee should clearly understand the expected outcomes, who is going to use it for what reason, and have a direct line of sight regarding how it fits into the organization's overall scope of services/products.

As referenced above, be sure the employee understands and completes the first set of goals agreed upon before moving onto the next set. It is important for the employee to gain a sense of accomplishment by completing the initial goals before moving onto other projects. Too often, with volume, some goals are started, but not completed, which may lead the employee to question the validity of the goals overall.

FIGURE 7.1

New employees are eager to contribute and setting initial performance goals helps them feel part of the team and experience contributing to the organization's success from the start.

Scheduling

Scheduling employees is central to effective management of a parking operation for two reasons. First, payroll is typically the most significant expense within an operation, ranging between 20–35 percent of total operating expense. Second, adequate staffing levels are needed to deliver expected levels of customer service.

Typically, managers set a schedule in one-week increments, and best practices dictate that the schedule is set and made available to employees a week ahead of time. Many organizations use online scheduling tools, such as whentowork.com, that allow employees to view their schedule, trade shifts with coworkers, and request time off through an online portal.

Managers take several things into consideration when establishing the weekly schedule:

- The previous week's schedule and any roles/employees shifts that are part of a standard schedule.
- Events that will occur and related anticipated traffic volumes.
- Staff availability and vacation requests.
- Special projects that may require additional employee support.
- Staffing requirements for the same period during the previous year.

When the schedule is set, managers use a few common practices to plan for unforeseen events such as employee call offs and higher than expected traffic volumes. The most common of these is to have a few team members who act in floater/on-call positions. These individuals can perform multiple roles within the operation and are called in on short notice.

Performing Staff Internal and External Training

Leading organizations provide employees with ongoing training opportunities to continue to develop skills that result in higher quality performance and a reduction in undesirable events such as workplace accidents. Training delivery ranges from in-house to external opportunities and from formal classroom delivery to informal on the job learning.

Successful training programs provide in-depth education regarding the logic behind the job responsibility to guarantee better learning retention and engagement from the employee. Specifically, these programs address a need of adult learners to know *why* specific tasks are done certain ways, not just the related steps to completing a task to obtain buy in and impact job performance.

The following are guidelines managers use when planning, developing, and sourcing training programs for employees.

The best way to identify learning needs is to conduct a needs analysis by reviewing team member job descriptions. The skill areas identified in the job descriptions are the core competencies for each role, which can be used to identify the training requirements.

Training program learning objectives should be measurable, so it is clear if the employee learned these objectives when the training is complete. Managers should always be able to answer the question "How will I know if this learning objective was completed?" following the training. Quality learning objectives use action words such as create, complete, describe, and perform to accomplish this.

The learning objectives should provide a good indicator for the best way to deliver the material. Some things are easiest to convey in a classroom, while others make more sense through hands-on learning, job shadowing, or computer simulation. Making this determination for each module will dictate the rest of the process in terms of materials to gather, resources involved, and who has the skill sets to develop and deliver the program content.

FIGURE 7.2

Team Leadership Practices

Successful parking team leaders deliver results through goal setting and execution, balancing emotions and data when making decisions, and receiving and providing feedback.

Goal Setting and Execution

Psychologists have theorized for years about human motivation. Psychologists Edwin Locke and Gary Latham pioneered goal setting research in the workplace and found that employees are motivated by clear goals and appropriate feedback. Through their research, they also demonstrated that working toward a goal provided a major source of motivation to reaching the goal—which, in turn, improved performance.

Team leaders are expected to stay informed regarding the organization's priorities and ensure these are shared with team members in ways that relate to their roles through communications and goal setting. Leaders commonly use the S.M.A.R.T. model to set goals, which is based on Locke and Latham's Goal Setting Theory.

> ### The S.M.A.R.T. Model
>
> Much has been written about the S.M.A.R.T. model for goal-setting, but what does it mean? It's a checklist to ensure goals are realistic and achievable and says they should be:
>
> - Specific.
> - Measurable.
> - Agreed upon, achievable, action-oriented.
> - Realistic, results-oriented.
> - Time-based, trackable.

Emotion and Data Balance

Team leaders are constantly pulled into different directions on any given day, with each situation triggering a requirement of balancing a spectrum of emotions with data. Emotion and data balance revolves around *what* individuals know and *how* they feel about it. Successful leaders give equal weight to both to ensure they communicate with the appropriate degree of emotion and don't risk expressing with too much or too little.

Emotions are powerful when motivating others, creating a sense of urgency and leading the team through good times and bad. When balanced with data, the direction, guidance, and expectations given are heard and retained.

Receiving Feedback

There are two truisms for leaders: they influence more than they think they do, and moments they receive authentic feedback from team members and peers are few and far between. At the same time, understanding in the moment how team members and peers value a leader's decisions and overall leadership are crucial components to ensure continued high performance. Effective leaders regularly seek feedback on what is working, what isn't, and apply what they learn to future situations.

The next section provides more detail regarding delivering feedback to employees.

Monitoring Performance and Conducting Evaluations

While it remains a common practice for organizations to deliver annual performance evaluations, it has also become commonplace to provide ongoing performance feedback throughout the year.

Studies have validated that the more feedback (both positive and constructive) an employee receives, the better his or her productivity and engagement will be. When an employee understands how their role and performance affects the bigger picture—the company's financial and strategic goals—he or she is motivated to deliver the results associated with his or her responsibilities.

Identify the Core Competencies and Expectations

One of the challenges of providing effective performance feedback and evaluations is the mutual understanding between the hiring manager and the employee in defining the position's core competencies. For example, the employee may think that timeliness of reports is crucial, whereas the hiring manager thinks this a secondary responsibility.

Core competencies should be identified for each position type and shared with employees. Use the position's job description as the source document for this documentation and discussion, highlighting those sections that are paramount in terms of being successful on the job.

If appropriate, include in this discussion key goals that leadership and and/or the employee have set. The goal itself doesn't necessarily have to be big; its only criterion is that it's aligns with the company's overall objectives.

Ongoing Feedback and Core Competencies

When employees understand priorities in terms of job responsibilities and the supporting performance expectations, the hiring manager can reinforce through both monitoring and coaching. This is done by identifying reports, projects, etc. associated with the core competencies that an employee is responsible for producing and using those deliverables as the basis for providing feedback on an ongoing basis.

Annual Performance Evaluations

The annual performance evaluation should be a summary representation of the employee's performance during the course of the past year. Because of the ongoing feedback discussions taking place throughout the year, there shouldn't be any surprises for the employee in terms of how he or she has been performing or even the examples discussed as part of the review.

Organizations typically use a standardized performance review form that is customized to include position core competencies where the hiring manager is able provide a rating for each competency, as well as a feedback example that supports the rating.

FIGURE 7.3

Parking as a Career

It's an exciting time to be part of the parking industry. As technology expands capabilities, new roles and opportunities for different types of careers are also becoming available.

Certification programs such as IPI's CAPP can complement and round out institutional knowledge gained through formal education programs and industry work experience. Making this investment in staff is a way to accelerate development for a promising career path within the parking industry.

CHAPTER 8

Parking Enforcement

Shawn McCormick

arking enforcement is necessary to ensure that chaos does not occur related to the use of motor vehicles when they start and end their journey. Every vehicle trip has a start and end point that requires a parking space, whether at a private residence, public or private parking lot, or on the street. In most metropolitan areas, enforcement of parking regulations is an essential service.

The need for parking enforcement began around the time that the first parking meters were installed in 1935. Their primary goal was to provide access to parking spaces to support local businesses by limiting how long a car remained parked in a space on the street. Over time, the goals of parking enforcement have expanded to include not only space turnover and access, but also service and safety. In addition, agencies have found that the additional revenue generated from parking enforcement can supplement budgets for many essential programs unrelated to parking enforcement.

The effectiveness of parking regulations is only realized when vehicle operators expect that the regulations will be applied regularly. Things can disintegrate quickly when enforcement does not exist, limiting access to businesses, impeding traffic flow, and creating an unsafe environment for the public.

Parking enforcement is a benefit for the area where enforcement takes place, either by creating a better quality of life for residences (which will be addressed in great detail in this chapter), or improved business access, which results in increased sales and business tax revenue for the community. When turnover at parking meters occurs at regular intervals, the revenue that results can be used in many ways to benefit programs specific to the local business area, as well as other wider-spread programs.

Effective parking enforcement requires more than assigning an officer to write parking tickets. Without any thought as to where or what problem is being addressed, the results will be random at best, and the effectiveness over time will be limited. Before assigning an officer to enforcement, there needs to be an enforcement program plan.

FIGURE 8.1
Parking Enforcement Prevents Chaos on City Streets

Data is the key to creating an effective plan. Historical data is the basis for setting up the plan. Real-time data can be used to better react to changes and improve effectiveness and efficiency.

Chapter 3 discussed parking surveys and data collection. It is now time to take that data and analyze it to create an effective enforcement strategy. Areas to consider include:

1. Where are the heavily parked areas?
2. Where are areas that are receiving parking related complaints?
3. Where and what parking behavior needs to be changed?

Taking a deeper look at data starts with parking occupancy rates and violation rates to determine the need for enforcement in a given area. Other chapters will discuss in more detail how to analyze the data to make policy decisions. The key to enforcement is that data will help determine how to deploy resources.

Occupancy rates indicate the percentage of spaces on a given blockface where vehicles are parked. Violation rates tell how many of those parked vehicles are in violation of the posted regulations. Being able to understand where problem areas exist enables the directing of limited enforcement resources in an effective and efficient way. A high occupancy rate may indicate that the cost to park is too low, while a low occupancy rate may indicate the price is too high or there is nothing drawing people to the area. A high violation rate could indicate the regulations are not aligned with the use of the area.

The capture rate is the number of vehicles in violation that actually receive parking citations. Too high of a capture rate can lead to negative program feedback related to excessive enforcement, while too low a capture rate can lead to complaints related to lack of enforcement and frustration with finding parking. Finding the balance between the two is critical to meeting the expectations of revenue generation and the sense of effective and not overzealous enforcement. The effective capture rate that balances both is usually between 25 and 40 percent.[1]

The absence of parking enforcement basically nullifies parking policy, which is critical to the community.

Tools

There are several tools that are necessary for enforcement. These tools can vary based on budget, agency size, and geography. In this area we will talk about the physical tools, not the most important human aspect of enforcement. Parking enforcement officers need to move from place to place to enforce. On the simplest and most ecological level, walking can be effective in small geographic areas and where traffic is heavily congested. Bicycles can be another effective enforcement transportation option. The ability to patrol larger areas than can be covered on foot, while still being able to move in heavily congested areas is key. Both of these options also lead to more officer interaction with the public, which can have a positive effect on the perception of the enforcement program.

Larger geographic areas require motorized transportation to effectively enforce. Motorcycles, three-wheeled scooters, and cars are all options. It is important to know the laws in your area regarding scooters and motorcycles to know if special licenses may be required for the operators, as some jurisdictions exempt the requirement of a motorcycle license when specifically assigned to enforcement and others do not (and some states don't require licenses to operate some or all scooters). Other specialized vehicles used for details such as boot and tow, abandoned, or nuisance vehicle enforcement might include vans and pick-up trucks.

Some automated tools for enforcement include license plate recognition (LPR) cameras mounted on enforcement vehicles. These devices read license plates as vehicles move down

FIGURE 8.2
Technology has Made Parking Enforcement More Efficient and Effective

the road and can identify residential permit zone violations, time limit violations, scofflaw or stolen vehicles, and alert the operator to the specific vehicle. This automation can increase efficiency and expand the coverage area of an officer who does not have to manually validate each vehicle.

Enforcement Strategies

Enforcement strategies vary by jurisdiction and can even vary markedly within a jurisdiction. One of the key factors to consider is staffing. Staffing is usually the most costly aspect of an enforcement program over time, even for very small jurisdictions. It's important to consider who will do the enforcement. Local police, a unit of employees specifically authorized to enforce parking regulations, or volunteers are common options. The benefits and challenges of each should be considered.

Having local police officers enforce saves the cost of hiring additional employees, and they are already authorized in most cases to enforce parking regulations, in addition to their typical law enforcement duties. The challenge with using police officers to enforce parking regulations is that other law enforcement duties reduce their available time for enforcing parking regulations. Parking enforcement is also not always as great a priority as other police duties. This can create inconsistent and ineffective enforcement of parking regulations.

Identifying a unit to specifically enforce parking regulations as its primary duty can result in a more dedicated, consistent enforcement program as the employees specialize only in parking enforcement. Some drawbacks include additional overhead to manage the unit, and staff turnover can be an issue due to the stress of negative feedback and mis-perceptions during field interactions.

Volunteers are clearly the most cost-effective option, and because they are donating their time, they are likely to be dedicated workers. That said, as dedicated as they may be to the idea of enforcing parking regulations, they may be less committed over time to report to work. If field interactions become increasingly negative, the perception that the position is not worth it leads to turnover. Finally, it is essential to verify if volunteer parking enforcement is allowed in your jurisdiction at the state or local level.

Uniform Standards

No matter what the consideration is for staffing, it is important to ensure that a parking enforcement officer in the field looks like an officer. Uniform standards are important to consider for officer' safety so they are not mistaken for vandals or car thieves. Standards can be a full uniform that is similar to but not to identical to the local police uniform, such as a vest or shirt identifying the individual as parking enforcement staff. Unless a parking enforcement program includes police officers, it is in the parking enforcement officer's best interest to have a uniform that differentiates them from the police department or other related law enforcement agency, sheriffs, state, etc.

Employee Assignments

Once decisions are in place regarding how to staff an enforcement program, consideration must be made based on the survey data and other enforcement requirements as to how employees will be assigned. Assignment areas are usually identified as *beats*. An enforcement beat might be generalized enforcement covering any violations observed in an assigned beat area, or it could be specialized by having officers assigned to enforce specific violations.

Generalized enforcement means the assigned beat officer enforces known beat regulations, meters, time limits, and residential parking permits (RPP) to be enforced as expected, as well as safety violations, red zone, no parking, and no stopping—all of these are among the most common violations. The officer can address abandoned vehicles left parked in the beat and any service calls such as complaints about blocked driveways. This type of enforcement allows the officer to take ownership for the beat area and makes it easier to direct service calls to the assigned beat officer.

Specialized enforcement can be looked at in a couple of ways. One way is an overlay on top of the generalized enforcement beat, or by breaking down the officer's beat assignment by specific regulation or violation type for enforcement. The overlay approach allows the beat officer to focus on more common violations, and specialized enforcement activities that may take more time to complete are handled by a specially-assigned officer. Some types of assignments would be booting, vehicle impounds, and disabled placard enforcement. Each of these tasks requires specialized equipment such as a van or truck, often outfitted with LPR cameras with an inventory of boots for scofflaw vehicles. These units may also be responsible for the release of the boot after outstanding violations have been paid or the vehicle impounded if the payment due date has passed. Impounding vehicles can take additional time away from productive routine enforcement, waiting for the tow truck to respond, and completing the necessary paperwork. Disabled placard abuse teams often need to wait for long periods of time to make contact with a placard user to verify if the placard is valid for that individual to use.

Specialized enforcement as a beat assignment strategy means that different officers enforce specific regulations. For example, a street cleaning unit may only enforce street cleaning violations, while in the same area another officer is enforcing meter violations, and a third is enforcing time-limit restrictions. All of these specialized units could be working in the same geographic area.

The decision to use generalized, specialized, or a hybrid enforcement strategy is a decision that is made based on staffing levels, geographic area to be covered, and transportation choices for the specific agency. No one system is the best fit for all types of environments.

Other Duties

Duties other than parking enforcement often fall to the parking enforcement program. The most common of these is traffic control and the other is attendance at hearings or court for contested violations. Traffic control is the most visible activity parking enforcement programs engage in. Traffic control can support police and fire activities, relieving police officers to resume routine policing activities. Other traffic control activities can support traffic management around event venues, street fairs, parades, and demonstrations or protests. Management of these non-enforcement activities should be monitored, and where possible, cost-recovery efforts should be implemented to reduce the financial effect on the parking enforcement program.

Hiring the Right People

The human side of parking enforcement requires the right people for the job. There is a perception that anyone can do parking enforcement. The truth is, not everyone can be a parking enforcement officer. Many enforcement programs find that large numbers of applicants apply for a limited number of available positions. The minimum qualifications generally require a high school diploma or GED. Many people choose parking enforcement officer positions as a starting point for a public service career without the expectation of a full career in the industry.

The desire to provide public service is a key trait for parking enforcement officers. Successful enforcement officers have a commanding presence without being overly authoritarian, the ability to remain calm under stressful and trying situations, and a cooperative attitude. Programs that include traffic control duties require the ability to work in the street in traffic—most of us were brought up to be fearful of traffic and not to play in the street. Parking enforcement officers are most effective when they have the ability to apply some discretion when enforcing. This discretion should not be abused as an excuse not to do one's job, but is a hallmark of an effective parking enforcement officer and a compassionate and effective parking enforcement program.

Parking enforcement officers interact with a larger percentage of the population than most other public servants and they deal with one of the public's most cherished possessions: their automobiles.

Looking at the case of a car blocking someone's driveway, when a resident is trying to get in or out of their home, the parking enforcement officer has to deal with both the positive and negative perception of the job. The person trying to get in their driveway is glad to see the officer respond to help. The officer issues a parking citation for the violation and may even call for a tow truck to respond to clear the vehicle from the driveway. The resident is usually happy to have parking enforcement available, yet on occasion they are upset if the response time is longer than expected.

The owner of the vehicle who parked in front of the driveway is not as happy when they return to find either a citation on their vehicle, or worse to find that their car has been towed away. This person may have the opposite view of parking enforcement. They may ask, "Why was it necessary to take such drastic action and have the vehicle towed? Why not just issue a parking violation?" This incident shows how the perception of parking enforcement varies.

Parking enforcement officers may face these situation numerous times each day. Officers have been physically attacked, spat on, had beverages or other objects thrown at them, had their vehicles vandalized or their ticket books or handheld computers grabbed from them, been struck by cars driven by angry motorists, and rarely but on occasion killed while doing their jobs. The demeanor of the officer is critical to his or her safety and the effectiveness of the parking enforcement program. An officer must be aware of their surroundings at all times.

Other challenges to parking enforcement programs can be internal or political. There is always a desire to have an effective, efficient parking enforcement program that generates no complaints from the public and generates the revenue that was expected from the program. This is the goal, but usually not the reality. As noted, not everyone is always happy about the citation side of parking enforcement.

Overzealous officers, lack of enforcement, and selectively enforcing only certain violations are common complaints made about parking enforcement programs. Cases of officers being overzealous in their enforcement activities can be handled through internal management and the disciplinary process. Lack of enforcement and selectively enforcing certain violation complaints can come with a couple of different angles to consider. There may be an issue with an officer assigned to a beat who is not performing. Again, management and discipline are available. Other times, the issue can be due to a lack of resources and the inability to have a presence everywhere at all times.

We have already determined that the public perception that officers should issue citations for every violation is a sign of an effective parking enforcement program. However, we also know that if the capture rate is too low, these complaints may require investigation and realignment of resources. Staffing levels can also affect what violation types can be focused on, while also meeting the other goals, including budgetary, both in terms of revenue generation and control of expenditures.

Political pressures can weigh heavily on a parking enforcement program. While most people hope that political leaders honestly do not want to get into situations where they are asked to "fix" or help make a parking ticket go away, they may be asked. Some jurisdictions have codified regulations that prohibit political leaders and their staff from entertaining any requests to intervene regarding a parking violation. This helps to keep the process clear and above board. There are systems in place to allow parking violations to be challenged, either through an administrative process or through the court system.

Political pressure can be also applied to parking programs in response to increased services to a particular district. Parking enforcement is personal and local no matter the level of jurisdictional authority of the political leaders being requested. Challenges can arise when many political districts make requests of the single parking enforcement program. Parking enforcement programs need to be responsive and provide timely feedback to these requests. Program managers should evaluate the requests to determine if they are for information or action. A well-run parking enforcement program can use the data referenced previously to respond to information requests or determine what actions and resources are needed to deal with requests for action.

Data is more readily available than ever before to help drive the strategies and direction of a parking enforcement program. The availability of data is only as good as the analysis. Programs using data must also consider the personnel aspect of parking enforcement. Newly-hired officers must be properly trained to effectively enforce, while applying the occasional discretion not to issue a citation at the right moment; that shows enforcement is also compassionate.

Note

1   www.chancemanagement.com/downloads/presentations/CMA_MEPS2009_OnStreet.pdf.

CHAPTER 9

Economics and Finance

Leonard T. Bier, JD, CAPP and
Mark A. Vergenes

The highest and best use for land within an urban city's core, central business district (CBD), retail shopping district, or adjacent to a transportation node is generally not parking lots. However, this is often where government-owned real estate is and how these valuable assets are used. This situation poses an opportunity for government to actively support urban redevelopment and revitalization by putting its real estate assets into play as development sites.

Public and private land in high-rise cities, such as New York, Boston, and Chicago, is too valuable to be used for parking lots. It is true that small infill parking lots, which often use mechanical car stackers to maximize parking yield, can be found in high-rise cities and that some still have traditional surface lots. However, a parking lot footprint in these environments is often either too small and cannot be economically repurposed for real estate redevelopment, or is part of an owner's long-term land-banking strategy. Because parking resources are often scarce and user demand and market rates in these communities for off-street transient and monthly parking spaces is high, infill parking lots in densely urban cities generate significant parking revenue.

Structured parking is a necessary and expensive resource to build for both the public and private sector as part of a development project. In most small- to medium-size urban environments, structured parking does not generate a profit for private developers and must be subsidized by rents from other components of the developer's project: retail, office, entertainment venues, and residential units. This chapter will discuss the ways governments can finance structured parking resources that may be more favorable than commercial lending sources available to a private developer. The government's decision to repurpose a parking lot as a structured parking facility or include its real estate in a larger redevelopment project and participate in project financing is a critical element of successful government-led urban redevelopment planning.

Unlocking the redevelopment potential and value of well-placed government parking lots can be done in a number of ways:

- A standalone garage can be developed to act as a centralized public parking resource financed by the government. A standalone garage can act as a redevelopment catalyst and encourage new private-sector development and rehabilitation of existing commercial and residential real estate within the garage's area of influence.
- Mixed-use garages can be financed by a government entity as the developer, with commercial retail or service leaseholds available on the ground floor and additional

office space located on liner floors above grade, and office, restaurants, or residential on the garage roof available for occupancy by government, and/or private tenants.

- Public-private partnerships (P3s) are projects in which the government entity sells the parking lot development rights to a private developer in support of a development project that is favored by the government. In a full P3, the government will participate in the financing and operation of the project's parking component.

Identifying an Area of Influence

When repurposing an urban parking lot for structured parking, either standalone or as a component of a redevelopment project, user walkability is important. Research related to parking walkability has identified 1,200 feet as the outer boundary for acceptable walking distance for parking associated with retail, restaurant, office, employee parking, and entertainment venue parking generators. Municipal urban planning departments have generally adopted planning and/or zoning ordinances ranging from 500 to 1,200 feet as the maximum distance from a parking generator to an off-site parking facility, to satisfy a municipality's land use regulations for a redevelopment project's required parking.[1]

The appropriate distance from a parking generator to a parking resource is an important factor both as a matter of parker acceptance and use as well as from a legal planning and zoning perspective because the walking distance will establish the area of influence for the construction of a standalone, mixed-use, or P3 shared parking garage as part of an urban redevelopment project.

When planning a development project that will include a parking component, either private or available to the public, it is advisable to draw concentric circles around the parking resource at distances of 600, 800, and 1,000 feet. The purpose of this exercise is to identify competing parking facilities that may affect economic feasibility by virtue of existing parking market rates. Identify other parking resources to determine if there is excess parking supply and inventory in the immediate area that could compete with the project, which will influence the project's parking demand and the appropriate size of the project's parking component. In addition, this practice can locate other parking generators within the garage's area of influence that may not have sufficient parking and could become users of the project's parking component, which increases the project's parking revenue and economic feasibility. At this juncture, municipal zoning requirements related to the development project are not a consideration.

Defining the area of influence for a structured parking facility in small-to-medium cities or in low-to-medium-rise neighborhoods of large cities, using concentric circles is a useful planning technique that can unlock the redevelopment potential of other public or private parking lots in the main CBD or secondary business districts and neighborhoods.

Development Case Study: Rahway

Every development will have unique and defining characteristics, and there is no single approach that will work for economic development and redevelopment. This chapter offers a case study to demonstrate the variety of factors that influence development and may be required for a successful outcome. This case study focused on transit-oriented development, which often includes structured parking as critical infrastructure.

A comprehensive case study example of a standalone garage constructed for a redevelopment purpose is the city of Rahway, New Jersey (population 26,000). In 2005, the city conducted a strategic planning retreat to create a working plan for the redevelopment of the CBD and to repurpose parking lot assets owned by both the city and the parking authority. The participants included all senior government officials—mayor, council president, city manager, city attorney, city planner, and the parking authority.

FIGURE 9.1

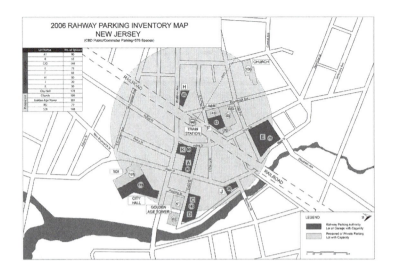

The city and parking authority owned eight parking lots, not including the city hall lot, containing a total of 576 public parking spaces within a 1,000-foot radius of the city's train station operated by New Jersey Transit. Rahway's train station is located on the Amtrak Northeast Corridor Line, running from Washington, D.C. to Boston. The Rahway station is the transfer station where the Northeast Line meets the New Jersey Shore line that services New Jersey's beach communities, such as Asbury Park. Seventy percent of commuters using the city's parking facilities were nonresidents.

The city understood that the highest and best use of its real estate assets and train station was not to have a CBD comprised of commuter parking. The city's plan was to unlock the transit-oriented development (TOD) potential of its CBD commuter parking lot and its vision was to attract private developers to construct 2,000 residential units within walkable distance of the train station.

Prior to 2006, the parking authority was tasked with simply managing on- and off-street parking assets. To further TOD efforts and redevelopment, the city put its strategic planning into action. The city, in addition to the parking authority, created an independent development agency to act as the single point of contact for developers to present redevelopment projects to the city for screening and preliminary approval; make recommendations to the mayor, city council, and planning board for final approval; and intercede and act as a redevelopment project facilitator with various city departments after project approval and during construction.

The creation of the redevelopment agency was important, as the city council, under New Jersey law and absent an independent redevelopment agency, is the designated entity for review and approval of redevelopment projects. Requiring redevelopment projects to go before a city council as a redevelopment entity is a time-consuming arrangement that puts redevelopment efforts squarely in the political arena. The city retains final oversight after creating an independent redevelopment agency as the project must go before the planning board for final site plan approval. The council must then approve the final agreement with the developer, tax concessions, and municipal bonds or notes for public improvements associated with the project.

Rahway also enacted a number of toolbox ordinances or regulations to encourage developer interest. The city's original CBD residential parking requirements were based on a portion of New Jersey's statewide administrative code for new residential development, known as residential site improvement standards (RSIS). A residential development project's parking ratio in RSIS is tied to each dwelling unit's bedroom count. TOD and smart growth parking standards recognize the effects of a mass transit facility in close proximity to residential units in a transit-oriented CBD, and allows for lower parking ratios. The city, as part of its CBD redevelopment plan, adopted the state's smart growth TOD planning principles and reduced the required residential parking to 1.25 parking spaces per dwelling unit for a city redevelopment-agency-approved redevelopment project.

The city also adopted a shared parking ordinance that allows complementary parking uses, such as office/commuter and residential parkers, to share a parking facility and reduce costly redundant parking spaces. Finally, as part of the CBD redevelopment plan, the city authorized a payment in lieu of parking (PILOP) program regulated and administrated by the parking authority. This program enables developers to make a contribution to a dedicated parking replacement fund in lieu of providing required parking onsite, where it may not be feasible. Overflow parking from the development project is directed to an authority-owned or operated parking facility, where the users pay the going monthly market parking rate.

As a result of the city's vision and strategic planning exercises, Rahway decided to construct a standalone parking garage with 524 parking spaces and 2,500 square feet of government offices directly across the street from the train station on one of its eight public parking lots. The Rahway Transportation Center Garage (RTCG) which was completed in 2008 at a cost of $9.5 million, replaced almost all 576 existing surface parking spaces located within the 1,000-foot radius of the train station.

The city determined that four of the remaining eight public parking lots could be repurposed for redevelopment. It selected a private developer to build a 14-story midrise building on the remaining portion of the municipal parking lot that the train station garage was constructed on.

The redevelopment project now known as Skyview faces the train station plaza and wraps the RTCG. The project, completed in 2009, contains 13,500 square feet of retail and hotel lobby on grade, with 102 hotel guest rooms on the next three floors, and 222 condominium and market-rate rental apartments on the remaining 10 floors. Skyview was built without a parking facility. RTCG serves as the parking resource for Skyview's retail, hotel, and residential components necessary to satisfy the parking requirements of Rahway's land use ordinances and regulations. The parking authority negotiated a $500,000 PILOP contribution from the developer, in exchange for providing the project's required parking for the retail residential and hotel components.

The RTCG has functioned exceptionally well as a shared parking facility. During the day, approximately 350–400 commuters park in the garage as Skyview residents leave the facility. Weekday evenings and all-day on weekends, 190 Skyview residents, hotel guests, and Main Street restaurant patrons are the primary users of the RTCG.

While the RTCG and Skyview projects were being planned, the parking authority and city selected developers for two other municipal parking lots, which resulted in the planning, development, and construction of additional residential projects: River Place, with 136 market-rate apartment units completed in 2007, and Landmark Park Square, with 159 apartment units and 6,390 square feet of retail completed in 2010.

The fourth municipal parking lot approved for redevelopment was split between two developers. These redevelopment projects were delayed due to the 2008 recession, and the need for acquisition of adjacent properties by the developers. The Gramercy East Cherry Street project containing 40 residential units and 1,000 square feet of retail is under construction as this book is published. The second project. Slokker Main and Monroe Streets, will contain 200 residential units in two phases. The main building with 110 units, a clubhouse with an outdoor pool, and 4,000 square feet of retail is presently under construction.

FIGURE 9.2

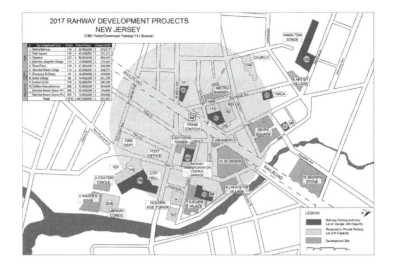

Funding Parking Projects: Bonds or Banks

Big public works projects may require big financing. For many city, state, and national government organizations and authorities, bonds offer an attractive alternative to bank loans. As demonstrated by the case study in this chapter, parking structures also require significant investment. This chapter offers a brief examination of vehicles to finance the design and construction of such large projects.

Whether trying to balance operating budgets or considering a major new investment, financing sits at the heart of any decision. Authorities may finance capital projects or refinance existing debt by accessing the public bond market or by securing a bank loan. Which financing option is the best fit for each authority, owner, developer, etc.?

As these questions present themselves during development, it is important to become familiar with bonds, including the format and issues involved, to make a more informed decision.

Banks and bonds each offer a variety of positives and negatives for large-scale financing. Each organization must weigh its history, financial needs, time constraints, and human resources to decide which format works best in each situation.

What Is a Bond?

The U.S. Bond market plays a vast and important role in American government. On the city, state, and national level, government bonds fund transportation, schools, libraries, commercial development and, of course, parking infrastructure. The next time you drive on a smooth, new highway, attend an event at the local school, or see a city parking garage under construction, remember the role of the U.S. bond market.

While most professionals involved in development understand how bank loans work, the mechanics of bonds are a little less familiar. A bond is similar to a commercial bank loan in many ways, but instead of a bank lending money, the investors who are buying the bonds are behind the loan. Think of it as a big, community-driven IOU.

Bond issuers make a legal promise to investors to repay the amount borrowed back. When dealing with bonds, you may come across some unfamiliar terms:

- The borrowed amount is also known as the principal or the bond's par or face value.
- The bond also must be repaid by a specific future date, referred to as the redemption or maturity date.
- The bond issuer must also pay periodic interest, also called the coupon rate or coupon.

Unlike a loan, which is issued by one institution—usually a commercial bank—municipal bonds are sold in the public capital markets to many investors.

Most bond issues are divided into different yearly maturities and interest rates, such as one- to 30-year maturities, with a different fixed interest rate each year, to appeal to various investor types.

Interest is paid semi-annually, and principal is paid annually until the final maturity of the bonds.

Bonds

TABLE 9.1 Types of Bonds

Revenue Bonds	• Revenue bonds are generally payable from a specific source of revenue and to which the full faith and credit of an issuer with taxing power is NOT pledged.
	• Revenue bonds are payable from identified sources of revenue and do not permit the bond holders to compel taxation or legislative appropriation of funds not pledged for a payment of debt service.
	• A bond issued by a municipal water and sewer authority, for example, involve revenues obtained through local water and sewer assessments. The pledge of revenue would identify specific assessments that can be used to pay principal and interest on the bonds, the authority's responsibility and ability (in any) to raise water and sewer assessments.
Guaranteed Revenue Bonds	• Guaranteed revenue bonds are most commonly referred to as double-barreled bonds.
	• Double-barreled bonds are secured by a defined revenue source as well as the full faith and credit of an issuer that has taxing power.
	• When bonds are sold as guaranteed revenue bonds, a municipality is guaranteeing repayment of the bonds.
	• In addition to the revenue pledge of the authority, the full faith, credit and taxing power of the local government entity are backing the bonds.
General Obligation Bonds	• General obligation bonds generally are backed by the credit and taxing power of the issuing jurisdiction rather than the revenue from a given project.
	• Most general obligation pledges at the local government level include a pledge to levy a property tax to meet debt service requirements.
	• Credit rating agencies consider a general obligation pledge to have a very strong credit quality and generally assign them higher credit ratings.

Financing Overview: The Role and Responsibilities of the Issuer

When the authority is the issuer of revenue bonds (based on revenues of the project):

- Interest rates are based on the credit strength of the authority.
- Debt is issued pursuant to a trust indenture between the authority and the bond trustee.
- Bonds are secured by an assignment and pledge of the authority's revenues.
- Additional security may be provided by funding a debt service reserve fund (DSRF), bond insurance, or a surety policy.
- The indenture will also include many other terms and conditions (such as a rate covenant).

When the authority is the issuer of guaranteed revenue Bonds (taxing power backing up the payment):

- Interest rates are based on the credit strength of the local government unit (assuming a full guaranty).
- Debt of the authority is fully or partially guaranteed by the local government unit through a guaranty agreement.
- The guaranty agreement is among the authority, the local government unit, and the trustee (indenture still applies).
- The local government unit must get approval from the appropriate state authority to guaranty the indebtedness.
- For self-liquidating debt, the bonds will be excluded, or partially excluded from the outstanding debt calculations of the local government.
- The amount to be considered self-liquidating will be determined by an engineer's certificate that projects revenues and expenses of the authority.

The local government must still include in its annual budget the amounts that may become payable under the guaranty agreement.

Bond Financing Team Members

Once the decision is made to issue a bond, several stakeholders should be included in the process. The following worksheet is provided to assist in forming teams and assigning responsibilities.

The Solicitors

The (Parking) Authority Solicitor (attorney):

- Provides a legal opinion regarding litigation, the validity of the bonds, and other matters.
- Coordinates with the engineer and authority personnel regarding upcoming capital projects and funding needs.
- Updates the board during the financing process.
- Works with authority personnel and the financing team to gather necessary documents and information.

TABLE 9.2 Characteristics of Finance Options

Bond Issuance Upsides	Downside of Bond Issuances
Unchanging. Bonds are locked in with fixed interest rates that will be set at time of financing. You won't have to worry about fluctuating rates.	**Higher Total Transaction Cost.** Transaction costs are typically higher, although they are usually amortized over the life of bonds.
Easy to Budget. Locking in the costs provides more certainty for budgeting or planning.	**Limited Use.** There will be imitations placed on the disbursement of the bond. For example, if the money is intended to the construction of a parking lot, this is where it must go. The bond cannot be reallocated to another project.
Tax-exempt Interest. The payment of interest is subject to tax deductions and considered an expense to the organization, and therefore reduces the taxes that need to be paid.	
	More Paperwork. Certain disclosures must be made on a continuing basis through the MSRB's EMMA website.
Longer Window for Fixed Rates. The issuing organization can decide the period of maturity of the bond from three years or thirty years, depending on their preference. This gives you a greater control over your debts.	**Timing.** Transactions tend to take longer to close than bank financing.

The Township Solicitor:

- Provides a legal opinion regarding legal compliance, litigation, binding nature of obligations, and other matters.
- Has discussions with the local government entity board regarding the project/financing.
- Coordinates with the authority solicitor and other finance team members.

Professional Counselors

The Bond or Note Counsel:

- Provides a legal opinion regarding the tax status of the bonds (i.e., tax-exempt), the validity and enforceability of the bonds, and other matters.
- Drafts legal documents for financing.
- Works with the authority board, authority solicitor, and other finance team members to close the financing.

The Underwriter or Placement Agent

- In a bond financing, the underwriter is the investment bank that purchases a new issue of bonds from the issuer for resale to investors.
- In a bank financing, the placement agent is the investment bank that locates a purchaser (i.e., a bank) of a debt instrument.
- Provides advice and recommendations as to terms, structure, timing and other related matters.
- Works with the issuer to design the finance plan.
- Assists in the development of financing documents.
- For a bond issue, the underwriter prepares rating agency strategy and presentation material.

- "Runs the numbers"—provides analyses and models to present alternative financing structures during the course of the process.
- Recommends optimal time for bond pricing (as underwriter), or optimal time for locking in the commitment of the bank as to interest rates and other terms.
- Coordinates activities of financing team.
- In situations where the issuer wants to evaluate both the bond and bank markets, a common practice is to appoint an investment bank to serve as the underwriter/placement agent (known as dual-track financing).
- The placement agent may work with a bank of the issuer's choosing or may conduct a request for proposals to explore bank financing so that the issuer may potentially select a bank based on the interest rate structure proposed and the terms/conditions specified by the bank.

The Engineer

- Performs engineering duties in planning, designing, and overseeing construction and maintenance of building structures and facilities (i.e., water and sewage systems).
- For self-liquidating debt, provides a certificate that projects revenues and expenses to determine the amount of debt that will be considered to be self-liquidating.

The Financiers

The Bank (loan):

- Provides the loan.

The Trustee (bond issue)

- A financial institution with trust powers, designated by the issuer or borrower, that acts, pursuant to a bond contract, in a fiduciary capacity for the benefit of the bondholders in enforcing the terms of the bond contract.
- In many cases, the trustee also acts as paying agent, custodian, registrar and/or transfer agent.
- The paying agent is responsible for transmitting payments of interest and principal from an issuer to the bondholders.

The Rating Agency (bond issue)

- Assign a credit rating to the issue
- Provides periodic updates to the rating while the debt is outstanding

Bonds offer an alternative to bank loans that may be attractive to those looking to finance large parking development projects. As with any financial decision, it's important to understand the nuances of the bond process, particularly as it relates to local or state regulations. This chapter provides an overview, but it's important that industry professionals consult with experts before entering into any finance agreement.

Note

1 "Shared Parking Facilities Among Multiple Users," Table 2, Acceptable Walking Distances. TDM Encyclopedia, Victoria Transportation Policy Institute, Updated December 21, 2015.

CHAPTER 10

Architecture and Aesthetics

Stephen J. Rebora, RA

Throughout the last century, parking garages have often been architectural after-thoughts. They were frequently stereotyped as storage buildings, and therefore often took on the architectural form of monolithic utilitarian buildings. But in recent years, as owners and clients have come to rely more on transportation for a successful campus or development, the role and function of the parking garage has been redefined. In urban, suburban, and even rural development patterns, the storage of cars has evolved into a dominant land use. The role of the designer is to focus parking garage solutions as both an infrastructural and aesthetic contributor to the overall experience of live-work-play communities. Experienced designers will view the design of a parking garage as a needed balance in the built environment.

A successfully designed parking facility uses an architectural design process that combines aesthetics with the building's functional requirements and structural necessities. The structural frame of a garage makes up the largest physical cost and mass of this building type, and it cannot be ignored. The focus of architectural design should be to develop an

FIGURE 10.1

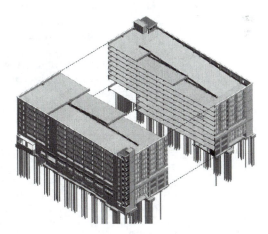

FIGURE 10.2
A Successfully Designed Parking Facility Uses an Architectural Design Process That Combines Aesthetics with the Building's Functional Requirements and Structural Necessities

FIGURE 10.3
The Design Team Works Together to Maximize Attractiveness and
Functionality in a Parking Structure

appropriate appearance for the building—one that achieves tasteful architectural expression while maintaining maximum parking efficiency, constructability, and budget control.

Many diverse factors and decisions that go into the practice of architecture and aesthetics are always subjective. This subject can be amazingly complex. This chapter will not address this subjective topic; it will focus specifically on parking facilities. Good design, as with most things, starts with an organized approach and an understanding of informed design principles.

The Importance of Informed Design

This step can also be referred to as programming. In the project discovery stage, the design team uncovers and documents the client's goals and objectives for the project. A thoroughly documented program serves as the road map and instructions to the design process itself. The objective of this stage is to define the scope and challenges involved. Prior to initiating any schematic design, the designer is encouraged to perform a series of programming sessions with project stakeholders to explore performance and functional objectives that could have an effect: building orientation, massing, space adjacencies, and even material selections. A project's functional and performance needs are integral to achieving a successful design solution for a parking garage. In nearly all applications, a parking garage solution starts with a functioning parking layout and ramping system and then works its way outward from there. Rarely is a project started with an exterior expression, then forcing a solution into the parking layout. The quote "Form follows function" (Louis Sullivan) is particularly apt to parking garage design. The components of a garage's form are essential to the term informed design.

The Importance of Information Gathering and the Evaluation of Existing Context

External research is also essential. Many factors shape a building's design. It is imperative that designers know the restrictions and rules that shape the built environment (see Chapter 2). Building and zoning codes will affect allowable setbacks, buildable footprint, size, height, and type of buildings. In addition, most cities, universities, and corporate campuses have their own design guidelines—architects must seek these out. The guidelines define important features of the established context that should be respected when new buildings are planned. It is important to note that these guidelines typically dictate the client's taste and ensure uniform design, thereby providing valuable information beyond basic restrictions. Design guidelines also provide a basis for making decisions about the appropriate treatment of existing buildings, including historic resources, and the design of compatible new buildings.

Building Site, Views and Axis

Experienced designers always visit a site prior to design. Online aerial photos will not offer enough insight into the hierarchy of important views, allies, axis, context, site topography, and site orientation. All of these elements can inform solutions and should be understood before beginning design.

Of particular note for a parking garage are street patterns, possible vehicular arrival/departure patterns, view corridors, users' likely primary destinations, and a clear understanding of the parking demand generators the garage will serve. Look beyond the immediate surroundings because design cues can also be taken from significant buildings, monuments, or land formations in the areas that are important contributors to the community but may not be immediately adjacent to the site.

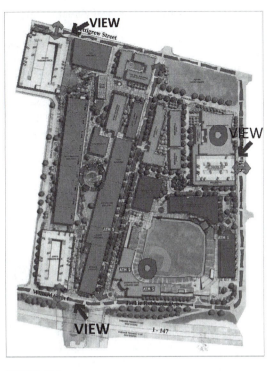

FIGURE 10.4
Considering All Elements of a Building Site Will Inform Solutions and Should be Understood Before Beginning Design

Foreground vs. Background Buildings

The question of foreground versus background design approaches is always an internal battle for architects. It does not refer to the literal placement of the garage. Rather, it is more about whether or not the garage should make an architectural statement. After all,

FIGURES 10.5 and 10.6
Foreground vs. Background Design Concerns Whether or Not the Garage Should Make an Architectural Statement.

a garage is typically a large building and it can be a prominent canvas to showcase design attributes or characteristics. First and foremost, the building should be a tasteful contributor to the surrounding area that meets required functional requirements.

Understanding the client's goals is paramount. A parking garage is frequently an accessory building that serves another use or destination. People rarely drive to a garage for the sole purpose of going to the garage. In this sense, hierarchy of space suggests that the parking garage design should not overshadow the primary building or use that it serves. That does not mean the garage itself should not be attractive and well-designed; it should be a positive contributor to the architectural context. It should provide a welcoming arrival and a positive experience for the user while serving the role of parking infrastructure within the complex. In other words, just because the garage has a supportive role does not mean it should be purely utilitarian or monolithic in design—it should still be an expression of architectural innovation and taste.

Building Scale and Mass

FIGURE 10.7
Considering All Elements of a Building Site Will Inform Solutions and Should be Understood Before Beginning Design

Design Influences

Qualities of scale, material, and articulation predominant in the garage's setting should be influential to the design. In particular, designers need to review heights of adjacent buildings, predominant material palettes, and opening patterns as part of the design process. Massing and density can relate to adjoining buildings and neighboring context to allow the facility to blend into the location and be complimentary or dominant as conditions warrant.

As stated earlier, a parking facility can be quite large, so providing features that are visually interesting and that convey a sense of human scale are recommended. Using a basic approach, these may include storefront windows, ground-level office or retail space, or simply landscaping used to soften the perimeter. A more aggressive solution may include terracing the upper parking tiers or stepping in the lowest tier to form a pedestrian arcade.

Breaking down the mass of building height is important and can be done by using a façade solution that includes a defined base, middle, and top. This is commonly referred to as tripartite design. By the same token, it is no less important to pay attention to the building's length. Parking garages tend to be long and horizontal per their geometric and structural needs. The designer should consider the use of vertical elements and building articulation to provide a sense of rhythm and a visual break. Consider dividing a larger building into modules that are similar in scale to buildings seen in the surrounding area. The designer should consider alignment of horizontal elements along the block with the adjacent properties. Window sills, moldings, and midline and roofline cornices are among those elements that may align. Reflect the established building heights contextual with surrounding buildings. Develop a primary façade that is in scale and alignment with nearby buildings. When considering a taller garage structure, the alignment of building elements is particularly important. Although a new building may be taller than older buildings, the first several stories should visually relate in scale to the surrounding context

Where site conditions allow, articulating away from a strictly rectangular plan can greatly dissipate the imposing mass of a garage by adding visual interest through offsetting façade planes. It should be noted that aggressive shifts can often have a negative effect on parking efficiency, however subtle shifts can often have a negligible effect and can be a better value than adding additional layers to the garage façade.

Aesthetic Drivers and Architectural Cues

The design team can gather many aesthetic drivers from the client during the initial programming phase. Designers should ask the client about formal (and informal) design preferences and guidelines. The team should document surrounding site context and adjacent buildings and use it for architectural cues. Similarly, it is typically useful to research the community's founding, historical events, and past business origins. These items can provide important imagery for the visual story the building may tell. Once the research is complete and the team has documented the steps above, the design can commence. From this stage on, subjectivity increases; this section is intended to provide a brief overview of selected architectural directions.

Self-Expression

While it is important that new buildings and alterations be compatible with the surrounding context, it is not necessary to replicate older building styles. In fact, stylistically distinguishing new buildings from their older neighbors while seeking integration with historical context may be preferred. This approach allows greater opportunities for creativity and self-expression, and presents an opportunity to create a new context in that built environment.

FIGURE 10.8

Environmental

FIGURE 10.9

In the context of design, the term "environmental" does not refer solely to sustainability or energy efficiency. The designer should carefully consider the site context and surrounding environmental cues. Successful environmental design will incorporate these contextual elements into the design of the building:

- Continue the use of similar building materials.
- Emulate the traditional widths of buildings in the area.
- Respect existing paths and axis.
- Respect surrounding architectural style, visual rhythm, composition, and balance.

Catalytic

Catalytic design intends to create or add to the activity in an area. This means that the completed building design will serve as a catalyst within its context. This is often used in garages designed to serve event centers and restaurant districts, or anywhere the client is trying to build social interaction. In such contexts, the parking building can certainly be a signature or forefront building. Introducing a pedestrian use such as a restaurant or retail within the garage often helps spur a client or locale's desired activity.

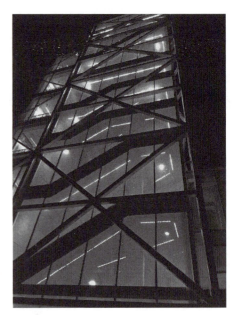

Historic Preservation

Thousands of communities promote historic preservation as part of their positive images. Doing so contributes to a style of livability and quality of life, minimizes negative effects on the environment, and often leads to economic rewards. Many property and business owners are also drawn to historic districts because of the positive image and character they convey.

FIGURE 10.10

FIGURE 10.11

If a proposed garage is in an historic district, there is a need to respect the architectural character dictated by the district itself. Preservation of surrounding heritage is important to the sense of community and its economic development. It is important to consider the significance of their character-defining features, including basic forms, materials, and details, when planning improvements. A new design that draws upon the fundamental similarities among older buildings in the area without overtly copying them is a good practice. This will allow the structure to be seen as a product of its own expression and yet be complementary of its historic neighbors. This balance is often a challenge in designing parking garages, especially those that do not contain retail or residential space. Copying or producing a literal imitation of older historic styles should be discouraged. Instead, a new garage should present a balance of new and historic design.

Interior Environment Enhancements

Parking garages are designed to house cars, and the design must respect the geometry vehicles require. However, it is still a building with human patrons. It is also one of the first things a person will experience upon their arrival to their destination. There are a number of architectural amenities that should be considered within the garage itself. The interior should be open, safe, and welcoming. Introducing natural light and increasing ceiling heights and applying light-colored paint or stain to the interior surface can enhance the space and enhance the patron experience. Proper lighting levels and photometrics are key to promoting safety as well. Lighting and graphics can be used for wayfinding (visual guidance) to pedestrian destinations such as stairs and elevator lobbies. The layout should be intuitive to users and include long, unobstructed lines of sight within the facility. Best practices include eliminating hiding spaces within the garage and making stairways and elevator lobbies and landings open and inviting.

Thoroughfare, Node and Destination—How Aesthetics Can Enhance a Journey

As mentioned, a parking garage is typically not a destination—generally it is an integral part of transportation to the actual destination. The key factor that is most often overlooked is that a parking garage is a momentary stopping point or node on a journey and, most often, is a point to which people will return. It is imperative that the parking experience be easily recalled, to facilitate an uncomplicated return journey.

The parking experience consists of a four-phased sequence: arrival, search, park, and transition. The return journey should be easily directed by the reverse recollection of these experience phases.

In the arrival phase, a parker is most heavily influenced by wayfinding and ready identification of garage entrances. These can become memorable by means of attractive and logical architecture (distractions should be avoided), and the importance of comprehensive wayfinding signage should not be underrated.

Once a parker is within the garage, the next three phases constitute a transitional realm. Interior environment enhancements should be used in concert to shape the experience of the driver as a parking space is sought and the vehicle is stationed for future use. The following pedestrian transition out of the garage should be considered by the designer with great care, as this will be the first step in the exiting sequence. Again, signage is key, however the use of color, texture, imagery, and even sound can all improve the recollections of parkers upon their return—the key is to instill some level of positive familiarity to the place. Maximum utility (satisfaction, in an economic sense) of a node is achieved when familiarity allows for an undistracted return and transition back to the thoroughfare of a journey—such is the stuff of well-designed parking. It is the experience within the garage that will influence the degree to which a parker will choose to select a garage on future journeys.

Conclusion

Through a proper design approach and proper respect for site aesthetics and context, the practice of architectural design when applied to a parking facility can lead to unlimited design options and exciting opportunities for garage owners.

CHAPTER 11

Designing and Engineering Parking Garages

William F. Kavanagh, AIA

Parking garages are a very specialized type of building. They are structures that are designed for the storage of passenger vehicles. Parking garages have many design requirements like other buildings, such as structural, exit design, and fire protection provisions. However, unlike most other building types, parking garages typically have sloped floors for drainage and ramps between floors, and are typically exposed to the outdoor environment.

Building Codes, Standards, and Design Guides

Parking garage design is governed by a variety of codes, standards, and ordinances at the federal, state, and local levels. At the federal level, accessibility codes such as the 2010 ADA Standards for Accessible Design will have effects on a garage design (see more on this in Chapter 2). State building codes also include numerous requirements. Finally, local zoning ordinances typically have off-street parking requirements that may define parking stall and drive aisle dimensional requirements. Where the various codes, standards, and ordinance requirements are in conflict, comply with the most stringent.

In addition to codes and ordinances, there are numerous references, manuals, and design standards developed by technical organizations and industry groups that provide recommendations regarding the design and construction of parking garages. Although not always referenced by building codes, these offer valuable insights into industry best practices in the design of parking structures. The following is a partial list of some of these codes, standards, guides, manuals, and recommendations:

- *International Building Code* (IBC), International Code Council (ICC)
- *NFPA 101 Life Safety Code*, National Fire Protection Association (NFPA)
- *NFPA 88A Standard for Parking Structures*
- *ACI 201.2R -92 Guide to Durable Concrete*, American Concrete Institute (ACI)
- *ACI 362.1R-12 Guide for the Design & Construction of Durable Concrete Parking Structures*, American Concrete Institute (ACI)
- *PCI MNL -129–98 Precast Prestressed Concrete Parking Structures: Recommended Practice for Design and Construction*, Precast/Prestressed Concrete Institute (PCI)
- *Steel Design Guide No. 18, Steel-Framed, Open-Deck Parking Decks*, American Institute of Steel Construction, Inc. (AISC)
- *Use of Composite Steel Floor Deck in Parking Garages*, Position Statement by Steel Deck Institute (SDI)

- *2010 ADA Standards for Accessible Design*
- Fair Housing Act
- ICC/ANSI A117.1 Accessible and Usable Buildings and Facilities, Standard

Open and Enclosed Parking Garages

Building codes have two types of parking garage classifications. Open parking garages are parking structures that provide a code-defined minimum amount of openness. Garages that do not meet this openness criteria are classified as enclosed. Underground parking garages, by default, are enclosed parking facilities. Building codes have several special provisions and exceptions for open parking garages. An open parking garage is usually not required to have sprinklers, fire alarms, or mechanical ventilation. In addition, exit stairs do not have to be enclosed. All of these special code exceptions for open parking garages can result in significant construction cost savings.

Per most building codes, open garages are required to have uniformly distributed openings on two or more sides. Another requirement pertains to the length of openings around the perimeter of each parking tier. Forty percent of the perimeter of each tier needs to have length of opening. In addition, a certain minimum amount of free area must be provided. Twenty percent of the total wall area of each tier must be free area in provided openings. The total potential wall area of each tier is the perimeter of the floor times the height of the tier. Interior walls are also required to be a minimum of 20 percent free area. Finally, openings are not required to be distributed over 40 percent of the perimeter of each tier if the required area of openings is uniformly distributed over two opposing sides.

It is not uncommon for these openings to be infilled or partially obstructed by architectural elements on the garage facades. Cladding systems such as perforated metal panels, expanded metals, woven stainless-steel mesh scrims, grilles, and louver systems can reduce the percentage of openness. Free-area calculations are more involved with such architectural elements on garages.

It is not uncommon for local ordinances or project specifics to negate some of these benefits. Some cities require sprinkler systems and/or fire alarms in all buildings including parking garages. Open parking garages that are part of a mixed-use building project may not be able to utilize all of the special code exceptions. When an open parking garage is located beneath another occupancy such as an office or residential tower, the parking garage is required to be sprinklered.

FIGURE 11.1
Open Stairs

FIGURE 11.2
Louvered Garage

Appropriate Use of Parking Garages

Unless structures are specifically designed to accommodate them, people events should not occur in parking garages. Open parking garages are for the storage of passenger vehicles, not the gathering of people. There are specific reasons why people events such as dances, parties, tailgating, fireworks, and parade watching should not occur in garages that were not designed with those events in mind.

Garages are considered low-hazard occupancies per the building code. Assembly occupancies, in which large gatherings of people occur, represent higher hazards and the building code has higher life safety requirements for them. It is important to understand the building code differences between parking garages and assembly uses as they pertain to structural loading, fire protection, and exit design requirements.

FIGURE 11.3
Tailgating in Garage

Structural Loading

Which is heavier, a person or an automobile?

Obviously, a car weighs more than a person. This may contribute to a common misperception that garages are designed for heavy loads. Now consider which is heavier; a person or an automobile on a weight per square-foot basis? An adult could weigh 250 pounds standing on one square foot of area. A 2010 Cadillac DTS, a large passenger vehicle, weighs approximately 5,347 pounds. It occupies an area of 162 square feet in a standard 9- x 18-foot parking stall. The Cadillac weighs only 33 pounds-per-square-foot (psf). Therefore, people weigh much more than passenger vehicles on a square-foot basis.

The International Building Code (IBC) recognizes this reality—garage live-load design requirements are only 40 pounds per square foot. This is lower than most other buildings. By comparison, office buildings have a 50 pounds-per-square-foot live load design requirement. For assembly occupancies such as theaters and restaurants where large numbers of people can congregate, the live load design requirements are 100 pounds per square foot of area. This is 2 1/2 times greater than the loading requirements for a parking garage.

Dances have been held in garages where the floors of the structure were bouncing significantly as scores of people danced in unison. Most garages are not designed to accommodate the live-load requirements needed for large gatherings of people. Obviously, from a structural perspective, assembly type events should not be held in traditionally designed parking garages.

Fire Protection Systems

According to the IBC, open parking structures are not required to be sprinklered or mechanically ventilated. In addition, open parking garages are exempt from high-rise building requirements such as automatic fire detection, emergency voice/alarm communication systems, and fire department communication systems. These are special provisions afforded open parking garages due to their unique characteristics and low-hazard classification.

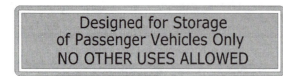

FIGURE 11.4
Sign, Passenger Vehicles Only

When an open parking garage is used for something other than parking cars, the special provisions afforded open parking garages are no longer applicable and the higher life safety provisions of the new occupancy are applied. Most open parking garages are not designed with the additional fire protection provisions necessary to host assembly-use gatherings.

Exit Design Capacity

The building code assigns an occupant load per square foot of space according to the occupancy type. The occupant load is then used to size the exit width capacity of the stairs. An assembly use requires significantly more exit capacity than a garage of similar size area. If an assembly use such as a dance, fashion show, tailgate, fireworks display, or parade viewing are held in a parking garage, the existing exit stairways will likely be significantly undersized for the number of occupants present.

Other Parking Garage Structural Considerations

As noted above, parking garages only have a 40 pound-per-square-foot live load. This is one of the lightest live loads required by the building code. Earlier versions of the building codes used to require a 50 pounds-per-square-foot live load. The building code also requires that garage floors be designed to support a 3,000-pound wheel load acting on a 4.5 × 4.5-inch, or 20.25 square inches. This is a sufficient wheel load for passenger vehicles. Care must be taken that snow removal equipment used on the top level does not exceed these loads.

Vehicular barrier requirements are also specified in the building code. The IBC requires vehicular barriers in passenger garages to resist a concentrated load of 6,000 pounds acting on a one square-foot area at 18 inches or 27 inches above the floor, whichever is greater. This results in a minimum vehicle barrier height of 2 feet 9 inches above the floor.

Another important consideration in parking garage design pertains to the expansion and contraction that occurs in a garage as it experiences temperature changes. The length of the garage will vary depending upon the temperature. Some parts of the U.S. experience a wide range of temperatures throughout the year. It could be more than 100 degrees (Fahrenheit) in the summer and below 0 degrees at times during the winter. The parking garage must be designed to accommodate this thermal movement through expansion and contraction.

Stair and elevator towers are often isolated with expansion joints to keep them independent of the rest of the garage for this reason. The maximum length of a parking garage before expansion joints are provided is a function of many parameters. The anticipated temperature range, the type of structural system, garage configuration, and restraints at the corners are just some of the considerations. Generally speaking, 300 feet of length for a parking garage is not an unusual maximum length before expansion joints would be considered.

Potential Garage Structural Systems

Long Span vs. Short Span

There are several structural systems that can be used for the superstructure of a parking garage. These structural systems generally fall into two categories: long span and short span systems.

Long span systems span the full length of a parking garage structural bay from the front of one parking stall, across the drive aisle, to the front of the other parking stall. This long span between two columns or walls provides a clear span that is uninterrupted by additional intermediate columns. It allows for a more open floor plan than a shorter span system, which would have more columns between parking stalls. These long spans work efficiently for the relative light loads needed to support passenger vehicles. These long spans do deflect, vibrate, or bounce like a bridge does when subject to the movement of vehicles. These vibrations are generally not a problem for parking garage structures since they are not designed for human occupation. Long spans are typical in single-use, free

FIGURE 11.5
Long Span Garage

standing, above grade parking garages, to maximize parking efficiency (square feet per parking space).

Where the long span system spans between two columns over the stall, drive aisle, and stall of a garage bay, the short span system utilizes four columns with shorter spans for the same distance. The additional columns in a short span system leave less floor area available for parking spaces. Obviously, parking garages that use short span systems are typically less efficient than long span systems. Short span systems are often utilized in mixed-use projects when there are other occupancies located above the parking garage. The tighter column bay spaces may work better with the structural requirements for the uses above. Short spans also work better regarding deflection and vibrations, which could be disruptive to the occupied spaces above.

The two most common long span structural systems for parking garages are prestressed precast concrete and cast-in-place post-tensioned (CIP-PT) concrete. Another potential long span structural system includes steel frames with an assortment of floor options.

Prestressed Precast Concrete

Precast concrete parking garages are comprised of a series of individual precast elements that are manufactured off-site and then transported to and erected on the jobsite via a large crane. The individual pieces are interconnected via a variety of bolted, grouted, and welded connections to create a single structure.

The precast elements can include columns, double tees (floors), spandrels (load bearing & non-loading bearing), inverted tee girders, wall panels and stairs. These individual pieces are cast in forms at the precaster manufacturing plant. Precast double tee elements have stems that contain prestressed strands that impart added structural capacity and camber into the double tees.

The cost effectiveness of precast is a function of economy of scale and repetition. Large garages comprised of multiple bays and floors of the same size are ideal for precast construction. Smaller garages comprised of fewer unique pieces are less ideal. It is important to work with the standard piece size or module that precasters manufacture. When they have to alter their standard offering, it become less efficient to manufacture and hence more expensive.

The predominant double tee width in the precast industry is 12 foot wide. Some manufacturers offer 15 foot and 16 foot wide double tees. Bay spacings are usually a

FIGURE 11.6
Precast Manufacturing

multiple of the double tee width such as 30, 36, 45, and 48 feet. A wider tee often can be used to reduce the total piece count required to provide a certain floor area. Five bays of 36 feet each equals 180 feet of length with the use of 15, 12-foot-wide double tees. Four bays of 45 feet equals the same 180 feet of length with the use of 12 15-foot-wide double tees. This is a 20 percent reduction in double tee piece count. A significant cost associated with a precast structural system is the labor and equipment involved in the manufacturing, finishing, handling, shipping, and erection of a piece of precast. If the total piece count can be reduced with the use of larger precast pieces, the cost can be lower and translate into a competitive advantage to that precaster and lower construction costs to the project.

Transportation is a significant cost in a precast concrete system. A parking garage can consist of hundreds if not thousands of precast elements. Some of the weights of these pieces can be substantial. A precast double tee that is approximately 60 feet long can weigh 55,000 to 60,000 pounds. The closer a precaster's manufacturing plan is to the project site, the better. Sometimes a precaster is not located close enough to a project to allow a competitive precast solution, and another structural system makes more sense.

Erection of precast parking garages does not use tower cranes because of the weight of the precast elements. Typically, a large, 100- to 400-ton capacity crawler crane is required. The precast garage is usually erected in one or two structural bays at a time for the full height of the garage, with the crane located within the garage footprint. The crane is then usually repositioned and the next few bays are erected similarly for the full height. The reason this is done is to keep the crane close to where the precast piece is to be set. The closer the crane can be situated, the smaller the crane that can be used. The rental costs on a 100-ton capacity crane are significantly less than that for a 300-ton crane. There are times when larger cranes are required for project-specific reasons. Sometimes a precast pick may require a higher capacity crane for longer reaches than normal or sometime when in close proximity to railroad tracks, the local transit authority may require upsizing the crane capacity for a greater safety factor, to protect against fouling their rails. Sometimes wheeled-over-the-road cranes can be used instead of a crawler crane, when project circumstances warrant the cost.

Future vertical expansion of existing precast garages with precast, even when designed for it, can be challenging. Crane access around the perimeter of the garage is a key consideration. The height and width of the existing garage will determine if a large enough crane exists for lifting the weight and the required reach. Sometimes precast parking garages are expanded vertically with alternate structural systems for this reason.

Another significant characteristic of precast parking garages is the number of joints between the numerous individual pieces of precast. Sealant is installed between the precast double tees to control water infiltration through the garage. Sealant repair and replacement are maintenance items that need to be performed and budgeted for. Sealants at the top level of the garage can be damaged by snow plow activities.

The precast spandrel in a precast parking garage is a very economical building component. It performs multiple roles cost effectively. The precast spandrel supports the precast double tee floors. It also acts as the building code-required vehicle barrier to restrain cars as well as the pedestrian guard. Finally, it also provides for the architectural expression of the garage. Exterior precast spandrels are often cast in pigmented, architectural concrete with reveals and finished with texture provided by sandblasting, acid etching, and/or formliners.

Because of the large precast bay spacings (ex. 36 × 60 feet or 45 × 60 feet), there are fewer, but larger, foundations. It is usually more economical to build fewer larger foundations than more, smaller ones. Lateral resistance systems in precast parking garages are typically provided by shearwalls in both directions.

The labor cost for a precast parking garage can be lower than that of other structural systems. Offsite factory labor costs tend to be lower than onsite labor. Repetitive forms for efficiency and less labor to erect

FIGURE 11.7
Precast Erection

the garage are also benefits. Construction costs for precast parking garages are usually competitive due to lower labor costs and shorter construction schedules. Construction schedules can be compressed since the foundations and superstructure efforts overlap. When the foundations for the garage are being constructed, the precast elements can be manufactured offsite. Once the foundations are complete or sufficiently ahead, the precast erection can commence. Speed of erection is a clear benefit for a precast parking garage.

Lead times for delivery of precast on a job site vary based upon the state of the marketplace. During boom periods, precast lead times have sometimes reached 12 to 14 months. At a minimum, five months' lead time should be expected. This much time is needed for engineering, shop drawing preparation, review, mockups, and manufacturing of a sufficient number of pieces needed to commence erection. Since precast may be on the critical path, it is common for early precast bid packages to be issued so that a production slot can be secured with a precast manufacturer. The rest of the garage design documents can be completed after this initial bid package.

The quality and workmanship of precast elements is usually good. Factory finished, cured, and quality control are usually in controlled offsite manufacturing facilities. PCI-certified plants are regularly audited and have mandatory quality control procedures.

Precast concrete as a structural system is not overly sensitive to weather. The precast elements are manufactured in a factory-controlled environment. Precast erection can occur during hot and cold weather. Some precautions are necessary for temperature extremes. Erection during winter months will require preheating of welds to prevent cracking of the precast and mixing and curing of grout should follow manufacturer instructions for cold weather concreting. Erection during hot weather will require special measures for the mixing and curing of grout.

Precast concrete offers good durability characteristics. The low water-to-cement ratio concrete mixes result in high-strength, low-permeable concrete. Mix designs often include corrosion inhibitor admixtures for protection of reinforcement. Long-term maintenance requirements are good but do need to be maintained. Cracks should be grouted and sealed and joint sealants repaired and replaced as required.

The ceiling heights in precast parking garages often feel compressed. The double tee stems occur every 6 feet for 12-foot double tees or every 7 feet, 6 inches for 15-foot double tees. Such a tight tee stem spacing results in the perception of the ceiling plane at the bottom of the double tee stems. This presents challenges for lighting, exit signs, and signage installations.

Cast-in-Place, Post-Tensioned (CIP-PT) Concrete

This long span, structural system consists of concrete poured into field forms with post-tension strands or tendons. After the concrete has reached a certain strength, the strands are stressed with the use of a hydraulic jack and anchored. The tendons are kept in a permanently stressed elongated state by the anchors, causing a compressive force to act on the concrete. This compression imparts greater load bearing capacity into the concrete. Post-tensioned structures can be designed to have minimal deflection and cracking.

With this structural system, columns, beams, girders, and floors are cast integrally with each other. These rigid frames that are created provide lateral stability to the structure. Parking garage bay spacing for this system is typically in the 24 to 28-foot ranges. Columns spaced at these intervals support beams that span 50 to 62 feet with one-way slabs spanning between the beams. The column bay spacing is tighter and more frequent than those of a precast parking garage. This results in smaller foundations than a precast garage. The labor cost for construction of this structural system can be high, especially in high labor cost markets. Field assembled forms, field labor for rebar and tendon placement, concrete placement, and finishing can be labor intensive. Post-tensioning tendons afterward is another step in the process that takes time. Cast-in-place post-tensioned (CIP-PT) concrete has a much shorter lead time compared to precast manufacturing, but the construction schedule cannot be compressed like that of a precast garage. The construction schedule for a CIP-PT garage is sequential. The foundations must be completed before the superstructure of the garage can be started. Concrete for a CIP-PT garage is readily available from the local concrete batch plant suppliers.

Tower cranes can be used to lift forms and rebar and concrete can be pumped into forms. The space requirements and large crawler cranes used in precast parking garage are not needed. The quality and workmanship of a CIP-PT garage is potentially variable. Field curing is subject to onsite weather conditions and temperatures. Field finishing of the concrete is subject to the workmanship abilities of the field labor. This structural system is more sensitive and has more potential effects from weather. There is potential for hot and cold weather concreting of the entire superstructure depending on the location and time of year of construction.

From a durability perspective, CIP-PT is probably the best structural system for a garage. The minimal amount of joints and cracking inherent with this system translates into lower maintenance efforts and costs over time. From a life cycle perspective, this structural system has many benefits over less durable structural systems. Although initial construction costs may be higher, especially in higher labor cost markets, the cost savings over time make this a viable system for most parking garages.

The perceived ceiling height with this type of system in a parking garage is good. The beams spaced at 24 to 28 feet on center allow for a sense of greater vertical space. This helps with lighting distribution as well as with visibility of exit signs and other garage signage.

Vertical expansion of a CIP-PT garage is a fairly straightforward process, assuming it was designed with the capacity to accommodate additional levels. Forming, shoring, rebar, and tendon placement and concrete

FIGURE 11.8
Cast-in-Place Formwork

placement via pumping do not require giant cranes or substantial room around the perimeter.

The architectural expression of a CIP-PT garage can appear very utilitarian. It is not uncommon for the perimeter of a CIP-PT garage to be clad with architectural precast spandrels to provide an enhanced façade to the garage.

Structural Steel in Parking Garages

Hybrid structural systems comprised of structural steel frames (columns and beams) with one of several potential floor systems have been used in parking garages. Some of the floor system options include precast double tees, CIP-PT, and composite metal deck. Steel framed garages can be stand-alone, garage-only structures or part of a mixed-use project with other occupancies.

The steel frames in parking garages need to be protected from corrosion by either being hot dipped galvanized or covered with a high-performance coating. If a fire rating is required on the structure, fireproofing will need to be applied to the steel. If fireproofing is required, a medium-to-high-density cementitious-based fireproofing material should be used. Fireproofing is not a substitute for corrosion protection provisions.

Hybrid steel garages with precast double tee floors often have a higher floor-to-floor height than other structural systems. The depth of the precast double tee plus the depth of the steel beam they bear on can be deeper than other structural system depths. The precast double tees can have daps provided at the ends of the tees to reduce this depth. Daps are notches in the ends of double tee stems that lessen the overall depth of the assembly. With deeper structural depths resulting in higher floor-to-floor heights, the ramps connecting floors need to be steeper or longer to compensate.

FIGURE 11.9
Cast-in-Place Post-tensioned Garage

FIGURE 11.10
Steel Framed Garage

Other floor systems that can be supported on steel frames in parking garages include CIP-PT slabs. The interface between the steel and the concrete flooring systems requires special attention to the connection details.

Composite metal deck with concrete as a floor system in a parking garage can be challenging. The low initial first construction costs without the necessary durability provisions can be tempting. However, if proper precautions are not taken regarding durability, the maintenance and repair costs can be higher and service life of the garage will be shorter than other systems.

Sloped Garage Floors for Drainage

Garage floors are typically sloped to direct water to floor drains. Water is introduced into the garage from rain and snow melt from cars, wind-blown precipitation through openings, spring washdowns to remove road salts brought in during the winter, and potential flooding.

The building code has provided an exception that allows flat floors in garages, but this is generally not a recommended practice. Removal of water increases garage longevity and reduces the potential for freezing and slip-and-fall liability. Drainage is an important durability provision in parking garages. As a rule of thumb, precast parking garages should slope at a minimum of approximately 3/16 inch per foot.

CIP-PT concrete parking garages should slope at 1/4 inch per foot. Washes can help direct water flow toward drains. In precast parking garages, to control tee cracking due to warpage when sloping double tees towards floor drains, limit maximum allowed tee warp per tee to 1–1/2 inch for 10-foot tees, 2 inches for 12-foot tees, and 2–1/2 inches for 15-foot double tees. Set high points in garages at expansion joints and stair towers and slope away from there.

Concrete Durability Provisions for Parking Garages

Salt deteriorates reinforced concrete and should never be used for snow or ice melting on a concrete structure. Concrete cracks. Road salts in snow are carried into garages by cars during the winter or salt air from coastal areas may be another source. Salt water migrates to the steel reinforcement that is embedded in reinforced concrete, causing the steel to corrode. As steel rusts, it expands, creating internal stresses in the concrete that cause it to spall and crack further, accelerating the deterioration process.

Concrete durability is an important factor to help ensure that a parking garage structure realizes a long service life. Premature failure of a garage's concrete can lead to expensive repairs and restoration work.

The building codes, standards and guides require and recommend certain durability provisions based upon the geographical corrosion zone in which a parking structure may be located. ACI 362.1R-12 Guide for the Design of Durable Parking Structures lists five different corrosion zones in the continental United States. Zones I, II, and III divide the country across latitudes from south to north:

FIGURE 11.11
Water in Garage

FIGURE 11.12
Garage Floors Sloped for Drainage

- Zone I includes the most of the southern states as well as the west. These areas rarely experience freezing and road salts are not used.
- Zone II is further north of Zone I, stretching from Virginia and North Carolina in the east across to northeast New Mexico and parts of Colorado. Freezing occurs here but road salts are never or rarely used.
- Zone III is the remainder of the continental United States north of Zone II. Freezing and the use of de-icers are common here. The last two of the five categories pertain to coastal zones.
- CC-1 corrosion zones are those areas located in Zone I areas and are within 5 miles of the ocean.
- CC-2 corrosion zones are those areas located in Zone I & II and are located within a half mile of the ocean.

The requirements and recommendations for durability provisions are a function of what corrosion zone a structure is located within.

Numerous durability provisions can be designed into a parking garage. These include concrete mixes with high strength, low water-to-cement cement ratios, and low permeability. Building codes have minimum requirements for concrete durability. Other available provisions include corrosion inhibitor concrete admixtures, epoxy coated reinforcement, depth of concrete cover over reinforcement, penetrating sealers, elastomeric traffic membranes, floor slopes for drainage, and hose bibs to facilitate spring wash downs of the garage floors to remove salts accumulated over the winter.

Corrosion inhibitor admixtures usually consist of calcium nitrite and can be added to concrete mixes as a method of protecting the reinforcement steel. A protective layer is formed on the rebar that helps resist corrosion. Recommended dosage rates, typically two to six gallons per cubic yard of concrete, vary depending upon the severity of the corrosion environment. Another method of protecting reinforcement is to coat it with an epoxy coating. The epoxy coating is only effective as long as it is continuous. When the epoxy coating is damaged or cut, the effectiveness of the protection is compromised. The depth of concrete cover over embedded reinforcement is another way to improve protection and durability. The farther the reinforcement is from the surface, the more difficult it is for salt water to migrate to the rebar. Finally, materials can be applied to the top of concrete surfaces to repel and prevent salt infiltration into the concrete. Penetrating sealers, such as silanes, siloxanes, silicates, and siliconates, penetrate into the concrete forming a protective barrier against moisture penetration and deicing chemicals. Elastomeric traffic membranes

FIGURE 11.13
Traffic Membrane

also provide a protective waterproof barrier against water infiltration into the concrete. Elastomeric membranes are installed with multiple coats. These membranes have the ability to bridge over cracks and still provide protection.

As discussed previously, sloped floors for drainage allow water to drain away and not puddle. Finally, a hose bib system facilitates regular wash downs of the parking garage as part of a preventative maintenance program. Without a hose bib system, wash downs become harder to do and less likely to occur.

Conclusion

Parking garages are often falsely perceived as very simplistic buildings. They are actually very specialized building types, with their own unique characteristics and challenges. Garages need to accommodate both the movements of vehicles and people. All of the floors in a parking garage are typically sloped for drainage, unlike the level floors in other building types. Finally, exposure to the environment presents challenges for accommodating building movements and concrete durability.

CHAPTER 12

Functional Design

Michael T. App, AIA, LEED AP,
and Todd J. Helmer, PE

What is functional design?

Garages are different than most other buildings in that they have two very different types of occupants: people and cars. The circulation patterns within a garage must account for both to ensure safety and efficiency. Functional design is the physical manifestation of the way a parking facility functions, how it serves its users, how it takes into consideration the needs of the users, and the circulation paths of vehicles and people.

There are a few critical decisions to be made when beginning the functional design phase of a parking garage project. One is whether the garage will meet the building code requirements to be considered an open parking garage, or not meet those requirements and be considered an enclosed parking garage. Another is whether the parking facility will operate as a self-park or a valet-attended facility. An important decision will be whether the vertical transportation by drivers will be by ramping slabs or by vehicle elevators; another will be whether all parking must happen on the slab only or if there will be mechanized parking units (known as stackers). Lastly, it may be necessary to determine if the garage is automated (robotic) and will not have vehicles driven through the structure or parked by people.

What factors should be considered during the functional design phase?

As with most buildings, determining the type of users the garage will serve is critical. Also, the number of users will determine the number of parking stalls the garage must provide. A thorough understanding of the site, including its location in relation to the destinations the parking garage will serve, is required (see more on this in Chapter 10). In addition, recognizing the parameters of the site, including the size of the available building pad, and any height restrictions, will set the restrictions of how large of a facility can be accommodated. It is also important for the operation of the garage that the designer know whether the operator plans to charge motorists for the use of garage or not.

Why is functional design important?

There are several reasons why a thorough understanding of the main considerations is necessary to create a successful functional design. First, a well-thought-out layout will create ease of maneuverability within the parking facility. The efficiency of the layout will ultimately dictate the cost to build the facility. A good layout will also impart a sense of safety in the garage thanks to good sightlines that enhance visibility. Vehicle traffic flow and pedestrian wayfinding will be better and even more inferred in a good functional design. Recognizing the revenue approach can affect the configuration of the garage and that of the entrances and exits. Lastly, a well laid-out functional design for a parking facility will ensure that the garage recognizes and complements the unique needs of the intended user group.

Functional Design Parameters

How does the site affect the functional design?

There are a few places to start the functional design development process, but one of the first would be the analysis of the site. First, local zoning ordinances should be reviewed to confirm that a parking garage is an approved use. If not, the designer may need to apply for a variance. Next, the size of the site should be confirmed to determine if the garage will in fact fit on the buildable pad. The combination of the floor-to-floor height and the parkable/acceptable ramp slope (less than 6.66 percent per the International Building Code, 6 percent or less for general parking industry standards) will determine the length of the ramp. This length, plus the required radius to turn at the end of the ramp, immediately sets one of the dimensions of the garage that can be checked against the length of the building pad. If this distance is not adequate, it might be necessary to design with a steeper ramp (not parkable), or even use a vehicle elevator. Local zoning ordinances will dictate the size of parking stalls and drive aisles, which will govern the width of a single row of parking, and determine if multiple parking rows are feasible for the overall garage width. This width and the length that have been determined are known as the footprint of the garage.

The local zoning ordinance will dictate the overall allowable height of the structure. In conjunction with the floor-to-floor heights of multiple tiers, this restriction will set the number of tiers. With this, the size of the garage will have been set and the number of parking stalls determined to get an initial parking count. This is the first opportunity to check if the garage will provide enough parking to meet the required needs.

FIGURE 12.1
A study of the Surrounding Points-Of-Interest for a Proposed Site.

In addition to the building pad, there are other site factors to consider. Adjacent buildings may be very close to the proposed garage, which may have code implications in terms of fire protection. Existing utilities or easements that cross the site may conflict with the proposed footprint of the garage, possibly requiring relocation. Topography should be studied to determine if it will be detrimental to vehicle circulation.

Another consideration that relates to the site is the surrounding street network. It is important to determine where most vehicle traffic will come from. Will the garage front a major street? Are there major streets or highways nearby that a majority of the motorists will use to come to the garage? Do the surrounding roads have additional capacity to accommodate the concentration of traffic due to the garage? Generally, it is recommended that if in an urban setting, the entry/exit points are away from intersections, and ideally at mid-block. The habits and needs of intended users need to be considered as well. Are there nearby businesses with large populations that might arrive or depart at a certain time of the day? Will there be an intermixing of pay parking (daily or transient) with contract parking (monthly)? If a large number of users arrive at one time, is there an adequate number of reservoir spaces prior to the ticketing machines or valet attendant station to avoid a bottleneck and prevent cars from blocking the street? Similarly, if a large number of users leave at one time, is there adequate queuing space within the garage prior to the exit gates to gradually release traffic to the surrounding streets without causing a backup within the garage? This understanding of entering and exiting may help locate the vehicle entrance and exit points, determine how many are required, and determine their configuration in regard to number of lanes.

How do users affect the functional design?

The perceived size of the garage and its circulation flow are important for the motorist experience. Once the size of the garage and number of tiers have been determined, the correct ramping system should be established. Shorter garages may be best served by a two-way drive aisle, single-helix type of ramp. However, larger or taller garages are likely to be best served by a one-way drive aisle, double-helix type of ramp. These ramp types may also be employed depending on the user group type. For example, at places where users do not visit frequently, like a hospital, the one-way double-helix may be the best solution.

Other considerations for user experience are the proximity and types of surrounding amenities. Are there points of interest near the garage many users would be walking toward after parking, such as retail, restaurants, residences, workplaces, or transit stations? A planner should determine the number of pedestrian entrances/exits and where those should be located based on these destinations.

The users themselves will affect the design. Whether office employees, shoppers, or transit station patrons, the users of a particular destination will affect functional design in numerous ways. How long do they intend to park? Drivers who park for a full day create different conditions than transient parkers who use the facility for an hour and leave. Will there be various user groups in the same garage? Do these users need to be segregated, requiring the garage to be partitioned into separate areas? Parkers who are carrying packages will need larger parking stalls than those parking at their places of employment.

Once users have parked, they no longer experience the garage as motorists but rather as pedestrians. This viewpoint has different criteria for a successful design (see Chapter 11). Patrons who are visiting a healthcare facility may have mobility issues that require different accommodations. Are the paths of travel from parking areas to points of egress an acceptable length? Are stairwells and elevator lobbies adequately sized for the number of people who will be using them? Wayfinding and signage play a large role in helping someone navigate through the garage. If the layout is clear, there should be a sense of inferential

TABLE 12.1 An Analysis of the Varying User Groups and Unique Needs of Each

Use	Sub-Group	Duration	Access	Stall	Ramp/ Drive Aisle	Notes
Corporate	Visitor Employee Executive	Full-day; Daytime	Daily visits—Patrons will be familiar with circulation.	8'-6" 90 degree	Slope is OK; Two-Way or One-Way	Control speed Well lit
Educational	Student Staff Faculty	Half-day; Daytime	Proximity to campus amenities. Daily visits—Patrons will be familiar with circulation.	8'-6" 90 degree	Slope is OK; Two-Way or One-Way	Control speed Well lit Clear line-of-sight
Transit	Short term Long term	Full-day; Daytime	Daily visit for commuter trains—Patrons familiar with circulation. Infrequent visits for airports—Patrons not familiar with circulation.	8'-6"	Slope is OK	Clear signage Well lit
Event		Evening	Incoming and Outgoing Surge. Infrequent visits—Patrons not familiar with circulation.	8'-6"	Slope is OK; One-Way	Well lit
Retail		Hourly; Daytime & Evening	Short walking distances. Patrons may have bags/packages from shopping. Patrons will visit weekly.	9'-0"	Slope is OK, Flat is preferred	Clear signage Well lit Clear line-of-sight
Healthcare	Visitors Staff Doctors	Half-day; Daytime & Evening	Relationship to main entrance, emergency entrance, MOBs. Patrons may have mobility issues. Infrequent visits—Patrons not familiar with circulation.	9'-0" Angled	Flat is preferred; One-Way	Well lit
Hotel		Overnight	Patrons may have suitcases. Infrequent visits—Patrons not familiar with circulation.	9'-0"	Flat is preferred	Well lit
Residential		Overnight	Patrons may have bags/packages from shopping. Daily visits—Patrons will be familiar with circulation.	9'-0" 90 degrees	Flat is preferred; Two-Way	Well lit

wayfinding, where the user knows where to go without having to read the sign. Are the stairwells, elevators, and points of access to the outside easy to find? Once someone returns to the garage, they should be able to easily remember where their car is parked.

A well laid-out parking facility will also give users a sense of safety. In addition to the active forms of security, passive strategies go a long way toward creating a safe-feeling environment, and these passive strategies are rooted in functional design. Long, straight sightlines promote visibility throughout the garage. An efficient layout reduces blind spots or hiding areas. Both of these attributes may be created by the location of the ramp, where the view to the stairs, elevators, and points of egress are not blocked from view. Additional strategies such as glass-backed elevators and stairwells with large openings or windows provide good visibility from the outside to the inside of the garage.

Physical Components of Functional Design

How are these Parameters Addressed with Physical Construction?

The Parking Stall

The parking stall is the basic unit of parking planning. The size of a parking space, or stall, is often determined by the municipal planning agency. A standard stall is typically either 8 feet, 6 inches or 9 feet wide, and 18 feet long. A stall especially designated for compact cars may be as small as 8 feet wide and 16 feet long. Accessible spaces for disabled motorists have additional requirements.

The Drive Aisle

After entering a garage, the drive aisle is the lane that a motorist drives along to get to a parking space. The width of the drive aisle is often set by the municipal planning agency. A drive aisle, designed for two-way traffic, with parking spaces that are oriented at 90 degrees to the aisle, is often required to be 24 feet wide. When the circulation of a parking garage is designed as one-way traffic, the parking spaces along the drive aisle are typically angled, and often the drive aisle becomes narrower based on the amount that the parking spaces are angled.

The Column

The selected structural system will dictate the spacing of columns (see Chapter 11), and that spacing may affect the layout of the parking stalls. This centerline-to-centerline dimension between columns along the drive aisle is known as the bay spacing.

The parking module is the spacing that runs perpendicular to the bay spacing (and therefore perpendicular to the drive aisle), comprised of a standard parking stall length, the drive aisle width, and another parking stall length. This dimension, when reviewed against the available site, will determine the number of parking aisles. A standard structural span will likely locate a column within the drive aisle; long-span structural framing is often used to span the distance of the entire parking module.

The Ramp

One of the first physical manifestations of functional design is the ramp. The location of the ramp or ramps is dependent upon not only the footprint of the garage and the structural system selected but also the motorist and pedestrian needs mentioned above.

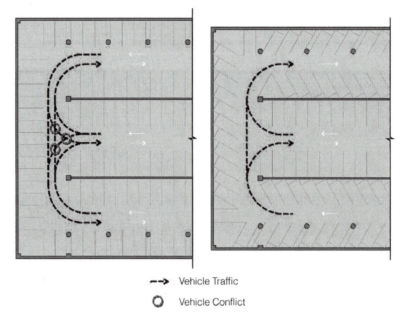

→ Vehicle Traffic

○ Vehicle Conflict

FIGURE 12.2
Left Image: Challenging Layout with Crossing Traffic Patterns. Right Image: Preferred Layout with Simple Traffic Patterns.

The slope of the ramp may be dictated by the horizontal length available and the vertical rise necessary, but will be tempered by the intended user type. There are many types of ramps available to create the circulation of the garage:

- Flat slab. While not technically a ramp, all parking areas have some slope to encourage drainage and respond to topographic conditions on the site. The use of flat slab parking areas is encouraged if the intended users have a higher incidence of mobility issues, such as at a healthcare facility. A designer should keep in mind that any floor surface with a cross-slope over 2 percent is not acceptable as an accessible path, in accordance with the American Disabilities Act.
- Parkable ramp. Any parking areas or drive aisles with a sloping deck that has a grade between 2 percent and 6.66 percent are considered a parkable ramp by the International Building Code. It is generally accepted within the parking industry that the recommended slope for a parkable ramp be between 5 and 6 percent.
- Speed ramp. A sloping deck with a grade greater than 6.66 percent, and transitions less than 6 feet in elevation is considered a speed ramp. By code, parking is not allowed on this sort of ramp, which can only be used as a drive aisle. It is generally accepted by those within the parking industry that the slope for a ramp not exceed 13 percent, while anything over 16 percent is considered a failing ramp slope.
- Express ramp. A sloping deck with a grade greater than 6.66 percent, which transitions more than 6 feet in elevation, is considered an express ramp. In accordance with the International Building Code, parking is not allowed, and therefore this can only be used as a drive aisle.
- Transition ramp. These types of ramps are used to prevent a car from bottoming out when the change in grade is greater than 8 to 10 percent, such as a speed ramp or express ramp. The grade is typically half the grade of the associated speed ramp or express ramp, and it is used at the bottom and top of a speed/express ramp to transition the grade changes.

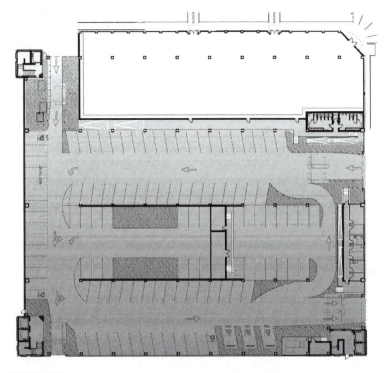

FIGURE 12.3
A Layout of the Ground Floor of a Structured Parking Facility, Showing a Combination of Both One-Way
and Two-Way Drive Aisles. This Garage Also Includes an Infill Office/Retail Area.

The configuration of a combination of ramps will create the circulation type of the garage. In other words, the way in which a driver navigates from the ground level to the top level of the garage and back down to the ground level is a result of how the ramps connect the floor levels of the garage. There are two main types of configurations: single-helix ramp and double-helix ramp. These ramp configuration types are used in different situations, with different parking stall orientations and drive aisle direction.

A single-threaded helix ramp tends to be the most simple ramp configuration and it allows for more driver decisions. The drive aisles tend to be two-way direction with 90-degree parking, which allows drivers to navigate in the direction of their choosing. This is acceptable when the users are familiar with the garage, such as office employees who park in the same garage every day. It is recommended that this ramp configuration only be used when designing a garage that is six tiers or fewer. Because the driver has more freedom to go where they choose, there is also more opportunity for motorists to continuously circle in the garage, and a greater chance of accidents.

A double-threaded helix ramp tends to be a more complicated configuration that limits the driver's decisions and provides a very clear navigation path through the garage. Drive aisles tend to be one-way in direction and employ angled parking. Drivers typically follow the circulation path in and out without endless circling searching for a space. Because there are fewer choices in this ramp configuration, it is a great option when designing a garage for a facility where users are not regular users and will have less familiarity, such as a hospital or an airport. It is also the preferred ramp configuration when a garage is planned to be more than six tiers, as it will reduce the number of turns and distance traveled to the top level.

Signage and Wayfinding

In addition to the hard construction that creates the circulation path, there are other items that aid the motorist in the use of a garage. One example is the signage that encourages wayfinding. These signs, whether wall or ceiling mounted or in the form of markings on pavement, give information in regard to direction of traffic flow and points of egress.

Technology

Another item that is not part of the hard construction is the installed technology, commonly known in the parking industry as parking access and revenue control *(PARCs)*. These items range from access control such as simple gates at the entry and exit points, to license plate recognition (LPR) systems, to parking guidance systems that indicate when the garage is full or where the available spaces are within the garage.

It is important to note that wayfinding and parking guidance technology can change the functional design of a garage even while not changing the physical layout. See Chapter 5 for more on parking technology.

Key Performance Indicators

How Does One Know if the Functional Design was Done Correctly?

There are numerous ways to judge the success of a functional design. As the base upon which the rest of the garage amenities are built, without a good functional design, it is difficult to achieve a successful overall design. A good functional design will go a long way toward a project that is safe, user-friendly, less costly to construct, and more profitable to operate.

With the focus on understanding the needs of the intended users, the ultimate goal is to create a facility that is easy for patrons to use. In addition to being attractive and comfortable, it should make sense. Wayfinding should be simple to understand within the garage, and vehicle entry and exit points should be designed in a way so they are not only easy to find, but set the driver on the path that is most advantageous after leaving the garage. Drive aisles and turning radiuses within the garage should be ample enough to allow ease of maneuvering through the garage. The circulation path should avoid turning conditions that require drivers to cross in front of other motorists. Spaces should be sized so that getting into and out of the car isn't restricted, and pulling in and out avoids damage to the motorist's car, as well as adjacent cars. Stair towers and egress points should be easy to see and give a sense of safety.

This attribute of the vehicle circulation is known as the level of service (LOS). The LOS of a garage is ranked A, B, C, D, or F. An "A" LOS means that a garage is very easy to use, with wide drive aisles, wide parking stalls, and wide turning radiuses; the lower the ranking, the smaller these items become and the less easy to maneuver. A garage that is LOS "F" has failed, and has issues with the functional design that prohibit proper circulation.

The layout should also be efficient for financial reasons. An efficient functional design will ultimately lower construction costs. If the efficiency is good, there should be more car parking spaces provided for the least amount of square footage built. As an example: a garage built for 1,000 cars at 340 square feet average per car would result in a garage that is 340,000 gross square feet. At $68 per square feet, that equates to a construction cost of approximately $23.12 million. In contrast, that same garage, for 1,000 cars, at 320 square feet average per car, would result in a garage that is 320,000 gross square feet. At $68 per square foot, that equates to a construction cost of approximately $21.76 million, or a saving of $1.36 million!

In addition to initial costs, an efficient layout will result in the most users for the least cost. This equates to a profitable operation. For example, a garage that is 320,000 square feet and has an efficiency of 320 square feet per space will provide 1,000 spaces. If the efficiency of that same garage is 340 square feet per space, the result is only 941 spaces, or 59 fewer users. If parking costs $25 per day, that is a difference of $1,475 per day, or $538,375 less revenue per year. Fewer spaces means less opportunity for revenue.

Trends in Functional Design

How is Functional Design Changing?

Advancements in the development of the automobile have always driven advancements in the design of parking structures. Changing real estate needs have constantly moved the centers of activity, requiring new uses to take over the old. These facts are still true today, as we see more people moving from rural areas to urban areas, requiring new modes of transportation. The garage will continue to evolve with these changes.

Integrated Uses and Use Conversion

One of the biggest trends is the integration of multiple building types to create a vibrant mixed-use structure, of which parking is one of the central components. Garages are built as the first wave of the new development and then later surrounded by liner buildings with amenities for the new district. To accommodate these new uses, garages are becoming more sophisticated from a life-safety standpoint, providing necessary fire resistance barriers and points of egress. Also, floor-to-floor heights increase to provide for the conversion of the ground level to a commercial or office use, relegating the parking to the upper levels.

The ultimate objective of this idea is to create a garage whose entire structure converts to another use, such as a residential or office building. This radical change from the initial parking use requires many changes to the layout of the garage, including new locations for

FIGURE 12.4
A Mixed-Use Building with Parking, Retail, and Office Space.

stair and elevator towers, increases in floor-to-floor heights, increased structural capacities, provision for vertical utility runs, and the eventual weather-tight, thermally broken façade system.

Summary

The functional design of a parking facility serves two users—motorists and pedestrians—and good functional design strives to ensure a good experience for both. If the correct decisions are not made, the facility may be inconvenient, unpleasant, unsafe, and underused. However, armed with proper drive aisle dimensions, turning radiuses, ramp slopes, and stall sizes, and with a thorough understanding of the surrounding site and the needs of the uses, the parking planner can design an environment that provides a smooth vehicle circulation path, and a safe and efficient pedestrian pathway. If the facility is efficient, it will also provide a profitable facility for the owner. As the base of the design decisions for the parking facility and the elemental factor for success, it is critical to have a well-trained parking planner to achieve good functional design.

CHAPTER 13

Constructing Parking

Patrick Wells

Once the decision is made to construct a multi-story parking garage, there are a number of considerations an owner should review. A study or needs assessment reveals the site and land selection, car capacity, and possibly even the rapidly changing market for vehicles and technology. When an organization has reached this juncture and is ready to move forward with construction, they often miss a critical piece of the puzzle. When hiring a parking designer and engineer, expenditures are in the thousands of dollars; when an owner approaches construction of a typical multi-level parking structure, expenditures reach into the millions. Creating and designing the best parking structure for the site, users, and budget requires a careful balance of all elements and a logical plan from start to finish.

Owners have been putting more pressure on the architecture/engineering/construction (A/E/C) industry to improve quality, reduce cost, and more importantly, compress the amount of time required to get from concept to completion for both public and private projects. As a result, both owners and industry experts have experimented with various forms of project delivery, with varying degrees of success. The adoption of alternative project delivery methods has added to the challenge of selecting the method most appropriate to the owner's needs and desires, as well as the project's technical requirements.

A host of choices must be made that will affect the final design and cost of the project. Not having the right team in place can cost valuable time, lost revenue, and hundreds of thousands, if not millions, of dollars in cost over-runs. Which team of consultants and builders should be selected? And when building a parking garage, what type of construction makes the most sense? These decisions will have a direct effect on the success of a project.

A group of leading national and regional construction industry associations, including The Associated General Contractors of America (AGC), Construction Management Association of America (CMAA)[1], and the Allied Construction Industries (ACI), maintain that there are really only three fundamental project delivery methods: design/bid/build (DBB), construction management at risk (CMR), and design/build (D/B). While there are a variety of project delivery methods throughout the industry, the current market agrees with the construction industry. Therefore, this chapter will focus on those three categories.

Understand Project Delivery Methods

The selection of a project delivery method defines the relationships between the owner, designer, and constructor. The term "project delivery" refers to all of the contractual relations, roles, and responsibilities of the entities involved in a project. It defines the relationships, roles, and responsibilities of project team members and the sequence of activities required to complete a project. Selecting the best delivery is the cornerstone to a successful project. The decision will affect the project budget, schedule, quality, and the amount of time that will be required by the organization and staff. Finally, the owning organization will live with the team/decision for 12 to 18 months.

While there are delivery methods growing in popularity such as public-private partnerships (P3) and integrated project delivery (IPD), the vast majority of U.S.-based vertical construction is still design-bid-build, CM at risk, and design-build.

Design/Bid/Build—Design and Construction

Also known as plan-and-spec, this method is characterized by a linear process in which one task follows the completion of another, with virtually no overlap. First, the selected designer completes the project plans and specifications based on the program or client's needs. Bids are solicited from general contractors, who then bid the project per the construction documents provided. The lowest bidder is typically awarded the work.

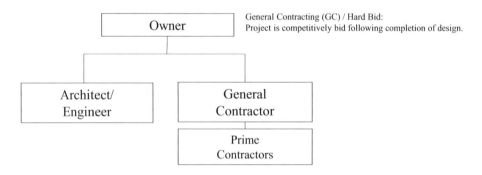

General Contracting (GC) / Hard Bid:
Project is competitively bid following completion of design.

FIGURE 13.1
Design/Bid/Build Design & Construction

Design/Bid/Build Characteristics:

- Most traditional and widely applicable.
- Typically, the longest project duration of any other project delivery method.
- Competitive bidding is used to achieve the lowest price for plans and specifications.
- Final selection of general contractor is often based on price.
- Contract is typically performed on a lump-sum basis.
- No construction input during design phase.
- Firm costs are often not realized until project is bid.
- Owner and architect are responsible for accuracy and completeness of construction documents.
- Owner is financially responsible for cost overruns and conflicts between team members.
- Not very well suited for complicated projects that are sequenced or schedule- or change-sensitive.

Best Suited for:

- Public projects or projects that require a bid award process.
- Projects that are not schedule-sensitive and not subject to significant change.
- Repetitive projects with little design variation.

Construction Management at Risk: Design and Construction

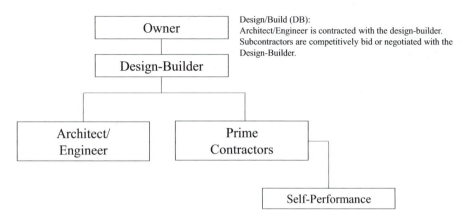

Design/Build (DB):
Architect/Engineer is contracted with the design-builder. Subcontractors are competitively bid or negotiated with the Design-Builder.

FIGURE 13.2
Design/Build Design & Construction

CMR Characteristics:

- Selection of CM based on qualifications, experience, and individual team members.
- Early conflict discovery and resolution.
- Owner contracts separately with designer and contractor.
- Architect provides complete design documents with input from CM on cost, constructability, and value management during design.
- CM provides estimating, value engineering, and estimates of constructability during preconstruction.
- CM provides assistance during design phase for budget, project planning, and value engineering analysis.
- Schedule and continuous budget feedback from CM.
- Commit to guaranteed maximum price (GMP) during design.
- Comprehensive document review for buildability, clarity/completeness, and schedule impact.
- Surprises and significant changes are minimized when construction begins.
- Increased ability to handle changes in design and scope.
- Ideal for fast-track, large scale, and complex projects.
- Need to have completed documents prior to bid.
- Transparency (fees and costs are open-book).
- Criteria documents included in an RFP should be no more than 30 percent complete, decreasing to lower levels as size and complexity of a project increases.
- Provides upfront detailed analysis of systems/products to enhance quality.

Best suited for:

- Owners with qualified staff who can adequately manage the design and construction process.
- Large-scale new or renovation projects that are schedule-sensitive, difficult to define, or subject to potential changes.
- Projects requiring a high level of management due to multiple phases, technical complexity, or multidisciplinary coordination.

The construction management at risk (CMR) method of project delivery allows for a shift of overall project risk to the construction manager (CM) throughout the project. The owner interviews candidates and selects a CM based on qualifications and experience. The CM acts as a consultant to the owner in the development and design phases and as a general contractor during construction. The CM and design team work together to develop and estimate the project. He or she also works with subcontractors to mitigate changes, conflicts, and impacts to the schedule. Because the CM is directly accountable for the cost, the budget is always closely watched.

Design/Build—Design and Construction

Design-build delivery combines architecture/engineering and construction services under a single contract, thereby integrating the roles of designer and constructor. This method is well-suited for the delivery of structured parking facilities. With both design and construction in the hands of a single entity (typically the contractor), there is a single point of responsibility for quality, cost, and schedule. The owner is able to focus on scope and decision-making rather than on coordination between designer and contractor.

The design/build method of project delivery is characterized by a contractual arrangement in which the design/build contractor is retained by the owner to deliver a complete project, inclusive of design services. A guaranteed maximum price (GMP) is provided by the team early in the project, based on preliminary design criteria. The design/build team then develops drawings that fulfill the criteria and complete the design, without exceeding the project budget. Bids are solicited awards made to subcontractors.

There are three basic design/build delivery methods: contractor-led, designer-led, and joint venture/teaming relationships. The majority of design/build work in today's market is contractor-led.

Raising the expertise and experience among staff is a key challenge with any project delivery. However, is this even more critical in the design-build process. Investing in design-build training before attempting to execute your first project is strongly recommended. That training is all-encompassing and should include not only an owner's staff, but also contractors and consultants (architects and engineers). Often, issues arise from a lack of experience with a specific delivery method, and just because a firm is a tenured consultant or contractor doesn't make it an expert in design/build.

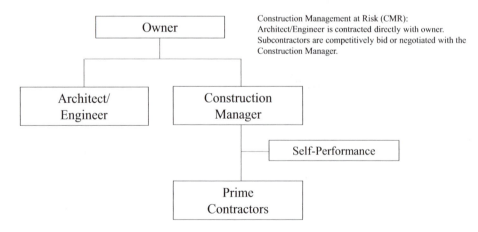

Construction Management at Risk (CMR):
Architect/Engineer is contracted directly with owner.
Subcontractors are competitively bid or negotiated with the Construction Manager.

FIGURE 13.3
Construction Management at Risk (CMR)

Design/Build Characteristics:

- Design/builder has single point of responsibility for design, construction, project completion, and warranty.
- Early knowledge of budgetary constraints.
- Design/build team selection is based on qualifications, experience, and individual team members.
- Early construction input during design, budget, and planning phases (value engineering/constructability review).
- Fastest project delivery (design and construction activities can overlap).
- Enable fast-track delivery because construction can begin (and often does) before design is 100 percent complete.
- Constant feedback from the entire team during programming, design development, and construction documents.
- Change orders are dramatically reduced.
- While the option to self-perform is available and potentially brings several advantages, the majority of the project is competitively bid with prequalified subcontractors.
- Quality of finished product is typically delivered at a very high level.

Best Suited for:

- Construction projects that are highly time and cost sensitive.
- Public or private owners who need an efficient way to manage the design and construction process.

Summary

Every owner should carefully study the risks, costs and benefits associated with each project delivery method in the context of the project under consideration and select the project delivery method that best suits legal, technical, business environment, and staff experience.

Note

1   https://cmaanet.org/owner-resource-center-0 and https://cmaanet.org/sites/default/files/files/Owners%20Guide%20Ver%209-2011.pdf.

CHAPTER 14

Maintenance and Repair[1]

Ryan A. Carris, PE and
Torrey L. Thompson

Introduction

Parking facilities, including parking lots, free-standing parking structures, and parking facilities integrated into mixed-use facilities, are distinct from residential and commercial buildings in that they are exposed to severe conditions throughout their service life. Parking facilities will typically deteriorate more rapidly than other types of built structures because direct exposure to ambient weather conditions, extreme temperature fluctuations, freeze-thaw cycles, ultraviolet radiation, vehicle impact, and deicing salts will, in time, lead to deterioration of the concrete, embedded reinforcing steel, and exposed metal components. Even the best designed and constructed parking facilities will require regular maintenance and repairs to achieve their intended service life.

What Is Maintenance and Repair?

Maintenance is the work required for care and upkeep, and can include the replacement or renewal of existing systems that are nearing the end of their service life. Maintenance is intended to minimize premature deterioration of facilities and benefit their long-term performance. Repair is defined by the International Existing Building Code as the reconstruction or renewal of any part of an existing building for the purpose of maintenance or

TABLE 14.1 Routine Maintenance Checklist

Task	Minimum Frequency
Cleaning/Sweeping	Weekly
Trash Removal	Daily
Wash Down Floors	Bi-Annual
Parking Control Equipment	Weekly
Architectural System and Elements	Monthly
Doors and Hardware	Weekly
Elevators	Monthly
MEP Systems	Yearly
Lighting/Bulbs	Weekly

to correct damage. Repair is typically focused on corrective action to address a current deficiency or damage.

The key elements for a comprehensive maintenance program include routine maintenance, preventive maintenance, and repairs and replacement maintenance.

In this chapter, the discussion of maintenance includes preventive maintenance, and repairs includes the repair and replacement maintenance. Routine maintenance items such as painting, cleaning, snow removal, mechanical equipment servicing, and routine operations within a parking facility are not the subject of this chapter but are important for the long-term maintenance and life cycle of the building; Table 14.1 shares a brief listing of routine maintenance items that should be addressed in general operations.

Common Maintenance and Repair Activities

Maintenance and repairs are required throughout a parking facility's service life to address a number of conditions, including:

- Deterioration of materials with a limited anticipated life, such as joint sealants and traffic-bearing membranes.
- Structural deterioration of materials due to aggressive environmental factors, such as concrete exposed to deicing or airborne salts.
- Distress due to faulty design or construction.
- Physical damage caused by overloading or vehicle impact.

Visible evidence that maintenance or repairs are needed include:

- Unintended water leakage.
- Concrete cracking.
- Concrete delamination/spalling.
- Unusual floor or ceiling deflections.

In parking lots, deterioration may include asphalt cracking, settlement, and potholes.

To gain a better understanding of common maintenance and repair activities, the following images provide a reference to many common maintenance and repairs item.

FIGURE 14.1
Joint Sealant Failure

FIGURE 14.2
Expansion Joints Failure

FIGURE 14.3
Concrete Sealer Application

FIGURE 14.4
Traffic Bearing Membrane Deterioration

FIGURE 14.5
Corroded Precast Connection

FIGURE 14.6
Concrete Scaling

FIGURE 14.7
Concrete Slab Cracking

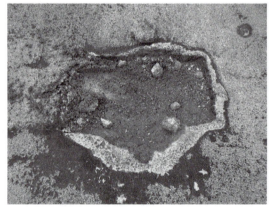

FIGURE 14.8
Concrete Slab Delamination/Spall

FIGURE 14.9
Concrete Ceiling Delamination/Spall

FIGURE 14.11
Column Delamination/Spall

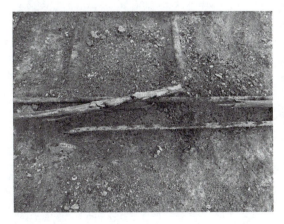

FIGURE 14.13
Slab P-T Tendon Failure

FIGURE 14.10
Beam Delamination/Spall

FIGURE 14.12
Precast Haunch Spall

FIGURE 14.14
Corroded Barrier Strands

FIGURE 14.15
Beam Crack due to Overloading

FIGURE 14.16
Asphalt Cracking

FIGURE 14.17
Asphalt Potholes

The Need for Maintenance and Repairs

The level of maintenance and repairs required for parking facilities will vary based on many factors. While some parking facilities can go decades without requiring significant repair or maintenance, others may require repairs or maintenance within as few as five to seven years. Some factors that determine the need for repairs and maintenance include:

- Geography. The amount of exposure to freeze-thaw cycles and chlorides from deicing salts and natural coastal salts is the largest contributor to the deterioration of parking facilities and the need for preventive maintenance of waterproofing systems. To assess the effect of geography, the American Concrete Institute (ACI) 362 Guide for the Design of Durable Parking Structures[2] divides the country into five exposure zones, which generally increase in severity from the south to the north, with special regions along coastal areas. Zones with the greatest exposure to chlorides will require the most repair and maintenance.
- Construction type. Most parking facilities are designed using cast-in-place concrete construction or precast concrete construction. Understanding the construction type is

important because it can dictate the facility's maintenance and repair needs. For example, a precast parking structure may require frequent replacement of joint sealants throughout its life, while cast-in-place concrete construction may require more repair of delaminated concrete toward the end of the facility's anticipated design life. For parking lots, whether the pavement is concrete or asphalt will be a major factor in the amount of maintenance repairs required.

- Construction timeframe. The age of the facility will affect deterioration expectations. The length of exposure, as well as improvements in design and construction methods since original construction, will affect the rate of deterioration. Newer facilities with improved construction technology will typically require less repair and maintenance than older facilities.
- Size/configuration. A parking facility's configuration will alter the effect of environmental exposure the facility experiences, including UV exposure, expansion and contraction, and load distribution. For example, a single-level large footprint configuration will have more UV exposure than a similarly sized, multi-level garage. This could result in requiring more frequent replacement of joint sealants and other waterproofing elements. The amount of deicing salts used on the floors can also be affected by the parking facility's configuration.
- Use. Parking facilities will have varying levels of turnover and use based on the function they serve. Hospitals, retail, and other high-turnover garages will typically require more maintenance repairs than a corporate facility where less frequent vehicle turnover is expected. This is generally related to vehicles carrying water and deicing salt into the structure.
- Durability design. Not all owners afford the same level of importance to service life during the original design process. The design can achieve a higher level of anticipated service life through the optional use of more durable construction technologies, such as corrosion-inhibiting admixtures in the concrete, stainless steel connections, and other durability enhancing materials. In parking lots, the choice of concrete over asphalt or thicker pavements will lead to longer anticipated life. Durability can also be negatively affected by cost-saving design decisions, such as the elimination or reduction in the number of expansion joints or drains. Higher levels of maintenance repairs should be expected in facilities that were constructed for the lowest initial cost.
- Construction quality. Not all construction is performed at the same level, resulting in varying achievable service life. Factors that impact construction quality include location, labor availability, local material sources, bidding environment, and similar factors.

Why Perform Maintenance and Repairs?

In time, all parking facilities will show evidence of material and structural deterioration, with the rate of deterioration increasing after every year of service. Maintenance and repairs are important to address this deterioration and achieve the facility's desired service life while also maintaining the facility in a safe operating condition.

Parking structures constructed in northern climates during the 1970s and 1980s frequently required significant structural repair programs within 15 to 20 years of initial construction to address corrosion of embedded reinforcement due to the impact of deicing salts on the concrete.

Improvements in construction materials and design practices, combined with a better understanding of the need for proper preventive maintenance, will greatly reduce future repair needs and extend the life of the structure. But eventually, all parking facilities will require some level of repair. Performing this repair in a timely fashion can extend the life of the facility, lower repair costs, and maintain a higher level of user comfort. By not performing regular or preventive maintenance, larger structural repair programs may be required in the future, with the potential for safety concerns and the reduction in useful life.

With timely and proper maintenance and repairs, an asphalt parking lot can have an anticipated design service life of 20 years, and a modern parking structure can have an anticipated design service life of 50 years or more before a major structural repair project is needed.

Maintenance and Repair Program

While some deterioration can be effectively addressed by an owner or parking operator as it develops, the most effective method to minimize premature deterioration and overall repair costs of a parking facility is implementing timely and proper maintenance and repairs using a proactive asset management plan. An asset management plan provides a process for evaluating, repairing, and maintaining a parking facility. These plans are most effective when they are established early in a facility's service life and updated on a regular basis as the goals and needs of the facility change. There are many variations of asset management plans, but they typically include the following stages:

- Planning.
- Construction documents preparation.
- Competitive bidding/contract negotiation.
- Construction.

Planning

Planning is typically the first step in developing an appropriate maintenance and repair program. The asset management plan will define the current condition of the facility, anticipated future maintenance needs, and how the maintenance and repair recommendations are intended to be implemented. This often can be the most challenging aspect of developing an asset management plan, as the plan must consider the owner's timeline for owning the facility, overall maintenance goals, available budgets for repair, available parking for closure during the repairs, site restrictions for noise, potential disruption of site operations, along with other factors. Sometimes, these factors can be contradictory, and a bigger factor in the execution of an asset management plan than deterioration and long-term repair costs. For example, if a parking facility is at 100 percent capacity and there are no spaces that can be closed to allow for repairs to be completed, repairs may need to be deferred and additional repair costs may be incurred until more parking can be secured. Similarly, if repair work will disrupt the facility entrances/exits, the work may have to be performed on nights, weekends, or holidays at extra costs. Identifying these issues up front is important to developing the overall asset management plan.

The next step is gaining an understanding of the facility's current condition and anticipated future maintenance needs. This is often best accomplished by having a Professional Engineer or other Licensed Design Professional (LDP), who is experienced in the repair and restoration of parking facilities, complete a condition assessment of the facility. The condition assessment process involves systematically collecting information that affects the performance of an existing structure and evaluating the collected information to make informed decisions regarding the need for repair or proactive maintenance. Depending on the facility and the owner's goals, the condition assessment may include only the structural and waterproofing elements or it may be more comprehensive and include the lighting, mechanical, parking equipment, etc.

To assist in the completion of a condition assessment, the engineer may refer to industry documents such as ACI 362.2: Guide for Structural Maintenance of Parking Structures,

ACI 364.1 Guide for Evaluation of Concrete Structures before Rehabilitation,[3] ASCE/ SEI 11–99: Guideline for Structural Condition Assessment of Existing Buildings,[4] PCI Maintenance Manual For Precast Parking Structures,[5] and other industry publications. For asphalt and concrete parking lots, the engineer should refer to the PASER Manuals published by the Transportation Information Center at the University of Wisconsin-Madison.[6]

To collect the required information, the engineer will:

- Research to understand the construction and history of the structure. This may include reviewing the original construction drawings, previous condition assessment reports and repair projects, and interviews with on-site maintenance staff.
- Visually observe the facility to identify and quantify conditions such as cracking, delamination/spalling, worn or failed waterproofing, pavement settlement, and other adverse conditions.
- Visually observe the facility to identity facility elements that are prone to wear or anticipated to exceed their design life in the near future.
- Perform testing as required to determine material properties that are not readily obvious through visual observation, such as:

  - Chloride Ion testing of small concrete samples extracted from the floor or other structural elements to determine the levels of chlorides (salt) within the concrete, which can indicate the likelihood of corrosion developing on the embedded reinforcement.
  - Documentation of embedded reinforcement using non-destructive techniques, such as ground-penetrating radar (GPR), to allow comparison to the original design documents or for structural analysis purposes.
  - Pavement cores to determine the pavement thickness and condition of the aggregate sub-base.
  - Petrographic examination of small concrete samples extracted from the floor or other structural elements to determine the concrete quality and potential latent defects within the concrete.
  - Sounding of elevated floor slabs, beams, and columns using chains or hammers to identify concrete delamination that indicates ongoing corrosion of the embedded reinforcement.
  - Testing excavations to observe concealed conditions, such as the condition and configuration of embedded reinforcement or the condition of buried waterproofing membrane concealed beneath a concrete topping slab.

With this information, the engineer can combine knowledge of the owner's maintenance goals, available budgets, and other factors discussed previously to make recommendations to address current deterioration observed within the parking facility, conditions likely to develop in the future, and if there is structural distress in elements that requires additional analysis or immediate attention to address potentially hazardous conditions. It is best if the repair recommendation includes an opinion of probable construction costs for the recommended repairs, an anticipated construction duration, number of spaces that can be taken out of service, any adverse effect on traffic flow, and closures of stairs/elevators/entry/exits during construction.

Once the basic repair program is established, the owner and engineer can collaborate in an iterative process to prioritize the recommended repairs and develop the repair recommendations into a one-, two-, five-, or 10-year capital asset management plan. This will allow the owner to properly plan for and budget the repairs, while also balancing long-term repair costs, yearly available budget, and site disruption, among other considerations.

Construction Documents

Except for minor repairs, implementing condition assessment repair recommendations typically involves engineering design services for the preparation of appropriate construction documents. Construction documents will ensure that all contractors are providing the same desired repair scope, materials, and comparable bids. Construction documents will also provide the legal basis of the contract between the owner and contractor for the proposed work, describing the necessary parameters for the completion and performance of the work.

Construction documents should include:

- Plan drawings that clearly describe the overall project scope, general size and location of required repair items, and appropriate repair details.
- Material specifications that identify products to be used, quality assurance testing, and warranty requirements.
- Construction schedule anticipated by the owner and any special schedule requirements.
- Phasing requirements and closure limitations to keep the parking facility partially open while repairs are in progress, unless the parking facility is being completely closed during the repair project.
- Bid forms for the contractor to use. Often on repair projects, the bid will provide estimated repair quantities for each repair work item and request that the contractor provide unit repair costs.
- Site-specific restrictions and requirements.

Construction documents should be prepared in accordance with local building codes. Depending on the repair scope, some jurisdictions will issue a work permit before repairs commence. Permit requirements vary by jurisdiction. Smaller or more routine maintenance projects may require only a maintenance permit or no construction permit at all, while larger repair projects generally require a permit with construction documents signed and sealed by a professional engineer. The project engineer and contractor can advise on what type of permit is required, if any.

Competitive Bidding/Contract Negotiation

Implementing an asset management plan's construction documents may be bid for or directly negotiated with a contractor. Parking facility maintenance repairs are distinct from new construction and require different skills and techniques to implement; these differ not only in repair materials and methods, but also work phasing and site protection so the parking facility can remain partially operational during repairs. Typically, parking facility repairs are best performed by an experienced waterproofing and concrete restoration contractor. Qualified contractors should be familiar with technical guidelines from parking and repair industrial organizations such as ACI, ICRI, PCI, and SWRI to receive the highest-quality repairs.

The engineer who prepared the construction documents is best equipped to assist with competitive bidding and/or contract negotiation because he or she is familiar with qualified contractors, has detailed knowledge of the site and construction documents and can provide clarification to prospective contractors during the bidding process, can review bids received for conformance to the project scope, and identify items requiring clarification. They can also compare the bid pricing to similar repair projects and make a recommendation for award.

The work can be awarded to the contractor using either industry standard contracts, such as those licensed by AIA or EJCDC, or an owner's standard agreement. It is generally not recommended to use a contractor's provided proposal or contract, because these may not be as comprehensive as the industry standard contracts and may offer the owner limited legal protection. The project engineer can generally assist with the preparation of an industry standard contract.

Construction

After contract award, the next step is construction to implement the repairs. Often, construction begins with a kick-off meeting with all parties involved in the project to review the contract scope, construction schedule, anticipated phasing, routing of traffic, and any other item that will affect the normal operation of the facility.

Although reasonable attempts can be made to minimize disruption to parking facility operations during construction, site operations will be affected: traffic patterns will likely be altered, drive lanes may be reduced, parking spaces will be temporarily closed to provide work areas for construction, and there may be stair/elevator/access disruptions. There is also often loud noise associated with jackhammering concrete or other construction activities. Construction dust frequently drifts onto vehicles parked within the garage, which can be upsetting to garage patrons. Therefore, communication between the parties is vital to a successful project. Prior to beginning construction, the project engineer and contractor should advise the owner of the areas where the garage operations and patrons may be affected. The owner should then provide appropriate notification to garage patrons, alerting them of upcoming activities and changes.

Throughout the project, the contractor must maintain an updated construction schedule and phase plan so that everyone is aware of any changes in the construction progress. With proactive communication, most disruptions can be reduced to a minor nuisance for most patrons.

The contractor is contractually obligated to complete the work in general accordance with the construction documents. However, it is advisable to have periodic onsite observations during the repairs. There may be concealed or unforeseen conditions that require changes to be made to the project scope. This may or may not be obvious to the contractor. The engineer will verify that the existing construction is consistent with the design and advise of any changes in scope, if required. The engineer will also assist in reviewing the contractor's material submittals to ensure quality products are used, track repair quantities, review payment applications, and answer questions throughout construction. Most importantly, the engineer will verify that the construction is in general conformance with the design documents and that appropriate warranties and record documents are provided.

After construction is completed, it is important to develop an updated asset management plan to reflect the recently completed repairs and outline maintenance repairs that will be required in the future. For most parking facilities, it is recommended that this plan be updated a minimum of every five years. In parking facilities that are exhibiting high levels of distress or accelerated deterioration, however, it may be necessary to have condition assessments performed more frequently.

Summary/Conclusion

Planning and implementing a maintenance and repair program is vital to achieving the expected service life for a parking facility and maintaining a safe environment for patrons. It is an ongoing process and needs to be budgeted, scheduled, and managed over time, with condition assessments performed by a licensed design professional on a regular basis and timely performance of the recommended repairs.

Deferring repairs and maintenance on parking facilities can be penny-wise and pound-foolish. Parking facilities are continually exposed to severe conditions. Not repairing deterioration can lead to greater, more expensive repairs. As deterioration is progressive, a facility that does not exhibit deterioration today may be absorbing moisture and chlorides over time, making future deterioration and expensive repairs unavoidable. Deferred maintenance and repairs will lead to decreased customer satisfaction, direct loss of revenue, and increased liability risk for owners.

Notes

1   *International Existing Building Code*, 2018 Edition, International Code Council, Washington, DC, 2018.
2   ACI 362.1R-12 Guide for the Design and Construction of Durable Concrete Parking Structures, American Concrete Institute.
3   ACI 364.1R-07 Guide for Evaluation of Concrete Structures for Rehabilitation, American Concrete Institute.
4   SEI/ASCE 11–99 Guideline for Structural Condition Assessment of Existing Structures, American Society of Civil Engineers, Reston, VA.
5   PCI Maintenance Manual for Precast Parking Structures, 5th Edition, Prestressed Concrete Institute, Chicago, 2004
6   *Asphalt PASER Manual*, Wisconsin Transportation Information Center, University of Wisconsin- Madison, Madison, WI, Revised 2013.

CHAPTER 15

Safety and Security

Alexander Smith, C.M.

Introduction

By our nature, human beings value safety and security. We strive to ensure that our well-being is safe from the outside world and that we are secure from anyone or anything that may cause harm to ourselves or our loved ones. These common principles have transcended time and apply to our daily lives, and they are a priority in the parking industry. The modern world continues to see an ever-changing safety and security threat environment, whether it is complex parking technologies with significant electrical considerations or terrorists who seek to disrupt our way of life. Safety and security are paramount in the parking industry.

Safety

According to the *Merriam-Webster Online Dictionary*, safety is "the condition of being safe from undergoing or causing hurt, injury, or loss."[1] The parking industry has multiple safety disciplines that affect everyone from engineers to parking operators; these include fire, electrical, and life safety.

Fire Safety

Like any residential or commercial structure, parking facilities are constantly under threat from fire. The National Fire Protection Association (NFPA) established formal fire safety standards for parking facilities beginning in 1932 and continuously updates them based on architectural, engineering, and safety matters.[2] The NFPA addresses six different areas of concern for parking facilities:

- Means of egress.
- Construction.
- Building service and fire protection.
- Special hazard protection.
- Housekeeping.
- Special structures.[3]

In practical application, there are two primary areas of fire safety: fire prevention and fire suppression, and both are essential to preventing loss of life or property.

Fire Safety Considerations

- Parking operators and facilities should maintain building evacuation plans and regularly practice emergency egress.
- Smoke detectors and other fire-sensing equipment should be installed throughout a facility. By detecting fire early on, the loss of life and property can be significantly mitigated.
- Parking facilities should be equipped with fire suppression systems that can handle anything from a vehicle fire to an all-out structural fire. These systems can include anything from a fire extinguisher to a sprinkler system.

Electrical Safety

Modern parking technologies have changed the way vehicles are fueled and how facilities are powered. Electrical safety has come to the forefront with the advent of solar panels and electric vehicle charging stations. Both of these valuable resources store a large amount of energy that can cause serious injury or a fatality.

Electrical Safety Considerations

- Solar panels and electric vehicle charging stations are high voltage and must be treated with the utmost care and attention.
- Proper emergency controls for these systems, such as an emergency shutoff, allow instantaneous shutdown in the event of a catastrophic failure or routine maintenance to prevent accidental electrocution.
- Batteries, whether for a vehicle or part of an electrical system, pose the same electrocution hazards as solar panels or electric vehicle charging systems.

Life Safety

Every individual, whether an employee or a visitor, has the right to patronize a facility or business without being exposed to unnecessary hazards that could cause serious bodily injury or death. In addition, extraordinary situations such as an active shooter or a suicide attempt may occur, and parking operators must be ready to respond.

Life Safety Considerations

- Vehicles and pedestrians are regularly in close proximity of one another within a parking facility. The potential always exists for pedestrians to be struck by a vehicle due to a distracted driver, facility blind spot, or from sheer inattentiveness by the pedestrian(s) themselves.
- Parking access revenue control systems (PARCS) have gate arms and other moving parts that can pinch limbs/fingers and cause serious bodily or head injuries.
- During the summer, vehicles can be deadly if animals, children, or the elderly are left unattended without air conditioning and shade.
- First aid equipment should be readily visible and available for use in the event of a life safety event.
  - Automated external defibrillator (AED) and CPR. AEDs are critical in the event an individual goes into cardiac arrest. These devices analyze heartbeat and deliver lifesaving electrical shocks in the event someone is in cardiac arrest.[4] Facilities equipped with AEDs and staff trained in CPR could mean the difference between life and death for someone having a cardiac emergency.

  – First aid kit. First aid kits help organizations take care of minor injuries that may occur at their facilities. Most kits are generally stocked with bandages, disinfectants, and other minor medical supplies.

- Mass casualty incidents are low frequency, high impact events that can occur without warning. These can include active shooters, natural disasters, social/political unrest, or any other activity in which there is a high likelihood of a large number of injuries or fatalities. When incidents occur, having a well-stocked first aid kit and an emergency egress plan can prevent loss of life and help mitigate serious injuries until first responders can arrive on the scene.
- During times of despair, depression, or hopelessness, some individuals decide to take their own lives and in some instances, decide to do so at a parking facility. Many steps can be taken to prevent such a tragedy from occurring. Parking operators can build physical barriers to prevent falls, provide resources such as signage for suicide prevention hotlines, and have systems in place to detect individuals who may be attempting to jump.[5] Together, tools like these can help prevent tragedy from occurring during someone's darkest hours.[6]

Emergency Planning

While having knowledge of hazards that may exist within a location or facility is beneficial, having a plan to mitigate them is another story. In the most simple form, emergency planning consists of having a plan of action to prevent, mitigate, and recover from an incident that is detrimental to life and/or property. These plans can be used for a multitude of situations, from local events to national disasters. In times of crisis, parking operators and facilities must be ready to react to the worst, and assist local, state, and federal agencies in their operations.

Emergency Planning Concepts: ICS and NIMS

Organization is key when responding to incidents. The Incident Command System (ICS) and the National Incident Management System (NIMS) are tools used by federal, state, and local governments, private businesses, and other involved stakeholders to manage incidents of various sizes and scale.

ICS

- ICS was developed after massive wildfires that ravaged California during the 1970s.[7] Those involved with the fires concluded that a lack of proper incident management may have contributed to the massive losses of property and life throughout the area of operations. Today, ICS enables organizations participating in small- to large-scale incidents to have standardization and a command structure to ensure a streamlined response and subsequent recovery.[8]

NIMS

- Developed by the U.S. Department of Homeland Security, the National Incident Management System was designed as to provide a common approach to incident management to all levels of jurisdiction.[9] NIMS was designed as a functional support tool to assist incident command during an event in whatever capacity is needed. Furthermore, during times of national crisis, it allows for the seamless integration of resources into the National Response Framework, established by the federal government.[10]

Facility Emergency Plans

Each parking facility should develop and regularly exercise an emergency plan. A facility emergency plan has a very basic outline that defines the hazards within a facility, actions that should be taken during an emergency, and usually an outline of some sort of response structure. Many government organizations such as FEMA provide templates to business to develop their own specific plans.

Security

Since the terrorist attacks of September 11, 2001, security in the transportation industry has become a top priority for the traveling public. Airports, transit stations, and even parking facilities have been, and continue to be, targets for these acts. Parking professionals need to be ready to act at a moment's notice when something seems out of place, maintain relationships with law enforcement partners, continuously plan for the worst, and remain vigilant.

Threats

Terrorists and criminals are constantly looking for a way to disrupt normal, everyday life, whether to achieve a goal of terror or financial gain. The below analyses are just a brief overview of what threats currently exist in our world.

Terrorism

There are currently two different facets of terrorism that exist in the U.S. Both use terror and destruction to bring about their way of thinking.

- Violent foreign extremists. On a global scale, violent foreign extremists implement their ideologies by creating terror among citizens around the world. One attempt happened in 1993 within the World Trade Center's underground parking garage in New York City. Ramzi Yousef and his criminal conspirators detonated a vehicle bomb in the building's garage, killing six people and creating massive path of destruction.[11]
- Homegrown terrorists. At home, homegrown terrorists want attention for their cause or seek to show their disdain for the federal government. In the case of the 1995 Oklahoma City bombing, Timothy McVeigh and Terry Nichols detonated a bomb made of 2,000 pounds of fertilizer inside a parking area at the Alfred P. Murrah Federal Building.[12]

Crime

Crime is an everyday experience. Parking facilities are scenes of a significant amount of crime, both violent and property related.[13] From 2004 to 2008, the Bureau of Justice Statistics (BJS) conducted a survey detailing the places in which violent and property crime occur. The survey found that 7.3 percent of all violent crime victimizations and 11.2 percent of all property crime victimizations occurred in parking facilities.[14] Crimes included within the survey were everything from rape, robbery, and aggravated assault to motor vehicle theft, burglary, and property theft.[15] Parking facilities are attractive areas for crime, as many are not always under surveillance, have a lack of activity at certain hours of the day, and have the potential to have high-value items in and around them.[16]

Developing a Facility Emergency Plan

An effective facility emergency plan requires many parts. Some of those include:

- Incident command structure. An incident command structure should be designed following ICS and NIMS principles. Generally, an incident command structure will have an incident commander who has overall authority over an event and delineates the various command functions of other responders.
- Operational considerations. Each parking facility is unique and has its own operational considerations. For example, parking structures in Arizona may be more susceptible to electrical fires from solar panels than those in Minnesota. Therefore, an Arizona parking facility may put a greater emphasis on electrical and fire hazards than another location.
- Functional annexes. While a facility emergency plan generalizes responsibilities and looks at emergency response in a holistic way, functional annexes in the plan specifically dictate roles and procedures for specific events. Example:
    - Functional annex 1: facility fire.
- Fire department.
    - Assume incident command.
    - Conduct firefighting and life-saving operations.
- Parking management company.
    - Assist with emergency egress of staff and customers.
    - Make notifications to facility owner and corporate safety/security.

Security Considerations for Parking Facilities

Balancing customer service and security is one of the biggest issues facing parking operators. On the one hand, facilities must be protected from those who wish to do harm, but at the same time operators must balance the needs of the customer, ensure they have a pleasant experience, and respect their rights.

- Threat reporting and mitigation. One of the first ways to prevent the worst from happening is through threat reporting. The Michigan State Police developed a framework called The Seven Signs of Terrorism they use to teach law enforcement and the public about warning signs that someone may be planning a terrorist attack. Many federal, state, and local law enforcement agencies have hotlines or web portals through which information regarding threats can be disseminated for investigation. Based upon these tips, law enforcement such as the FBI and the Joint Terrorism Task Force (JTTF) can investigate leads and act upon them if necessary.
    - In addition to law enforcement campaigns, corporate security initiatives can help raise awareness of specific issues that may plague an area and offer incentives for reporting security tips.
- Employees. Employees are on the front lines each day and have a wide range of responsibilities, from customer service to handling deposits of revenue. Vetting employees' criminal background for the previous 10 years and motor vehicle records for the last 36 months can put customers at ease. In addition, background screening can help ensure regulatory compliance and prevent potential internal fraud or theft of company resources.

- Access control. Controlling who has access to a facility gives an operator the upper hand in combating security vulnerabilities. PARCS equipment that has proximity card or ALPR-only access allows individual vehicles into a facility that have been accounted for in some capacity; for example, an employee who has been entered into a database and issued a card or had their license plate number recorded. The same holds true for access controls for pedestrians using a facility. By having physical access controls in place, only those vetted in a system and who hold access media can gain entry into a facility.

  - Tying into the access control system can be emergency call boxes or panic buttons. Both of these interfaces enable someone in need of emergency assistance to trigger a response either from site security or law enforcement.

- Surveillance. Having complete situation awareness of a location is essential. Closed-circuit television (CCTV) camera systems allow for continuous facility monitoring and can alert operators when noise or motion triggers are alarmed, triggering response from staff, security, or law enforcement.

  - Regular facility security and appearance patrols by staff allow for immediate corrective action to a situation and act as a deterrent for criminal activity.

Facility Security Plan

Much like the facility emergency plan, parking operators should develop a facility security plan to delineate a response to various security-related scenarios. While many security incidents may fall under a facility emergency plan, there may be specific nuances that must be documented separately from an emergency plan.

- Incident command. As with a facility emergency plan, a facility security plan should follow the same design principles incorporating ICS and NIMS for incident command. One point to remember is not to let either plan conflict with one another in delineating an incident command.
- Operational considerations. In the case of security, the way a facility is designed can significantly affect the way a plan is executed. For example, if a facility only has one ingress/egress point to a certain location, law enforcement may have to alter their tactics in the event an active shooter occurs in that area.
- Functional annexes. The functional annexes, as with the facility emergency plan, detail specific procedures for a response to specific incidents.

Considerations for Parking Professionals

Safety and security are vital components of any job for parking professionals. There are three levels in which safety and security principals are exercised in any parking organization.

- Executive level. Organizational management—directors, CEOs, COOs, etc. Executive-level staff have the exclusive responsibility of running an organization. This is facilitated through outlining business objectives, providing strategic direction, and implementing sound business practices. With regards to safety and security, executives provide overall goals for the organization to be ready for anything and delegate the planning and implementation to the professional level.
- Professional level. Administrative staff such as procurement officers, accountants, IT personnel, operations managers, etc. With direction provided by organizational executives, professional-level staff work to develop, implement, analyze, and improve safety and security practices and policies for their organization. This may include

creating a parking security plan, investigating incidents, or developing best practices to prevent theft of funds during the counting of cash from parking equipment.

- Operational level. Parking enforcement officers, lot attendants, valets, etc. Staff on the operational level will be the ones to use organizational safety and security practices on a daily basis within their facilities or area of responsibility. If an incident were to occur, these staff members would be the ones to implement an emergency plan and take corrective action to address the situation.

The International Parking Institute's *Emergency Preparedness Manual* is a valuable resource for all levels of parking professionals. It provides individuals at each level a thorough, "to-the-point" breakdown of what they should be taking into consideration with their roles.[17]

Conclusion

Books, articles, journals, and hundreds of thousands of other publications have been written trying to define the best ways to keep people safe and secure. The elephant in the room is that no matter how much we plan and prepare for the worst, incidents will continue to happen. As Murphy's law states, "anything that can go wrong, will go wrong." While there may never be a way to prevent the unthinkable from happening; the best we can do is mitigate the problem so that our customers and stakeholders have a safe and secure parking environment.

Notes

1 "Safety," Merriam-Webster, www.merriam-webster.com/dictionary/safety.
2 National Fire Protection Association, NFPA 88A—Standard for Parking Structures (Massachusetts: 2015), *www.nfpa.org/codes-and-standards/all-codes-and standards/list-of-codes-and standards?mode=code&code=88a&tab=about.*
3 Ibid.
4 "Learn About Automated External Defibrillators," American Red Cross www.redcross.org/prepare/location/workplace/easy-as-aed.
5 Larry Cohen, "Saving Lives," The Parking Professional, August 2015, 34–37.
6 For additional information, reference *Suicide in Parking Facilities: Prevention, Response & Recovery* at parking.org.
7 "ICS Review Material," Federal Emergency Management Agency, last modified May 2008, https://training.fema.gov/emiweb/is/icsresource/assets/reviewmaterials.pdf.
8 Ibid.
9 "NIMS: Frequently Asked Questions," Federal Emergency Management Agency, accessed April 24, 2017, www.fema.gov/pdf/emergency/nims/nimsfaqs.pdf.
10 Ibid.
11 "FBI 100, First Strike: Global Terror in America," Federal Bureau of Investigation, last modified February 2008, https://archives.fbi.gov/archives/news/stories/2008/february/tradebom_022608.
12 "Oklahoma City Bombing," Federal Bureau of Investigation, accessed April 30, 2017, www.fbi.gov/history/famous-cases/oklahoma-city-bombing.
13 "Location," Bureau of Justice Statistics, last modified May 2016, www.bjs.gov/index.cfm?ty=tp&tid=44.
14 "Location," Bureau of Justice Statistics, last modified May 2016.
15 Ibid.
16 For greater information about designing for increased security, reference Crime Prevention Through Environmental De. http://cpted.net/
17 *IPI Emergency Preparedness Manual.* Alexandria, VA: International Parking Institute. Accessed January 10, 2018. www.parking.org/wp-content/uploads/2016/10/IPI_Emergency_Preparedness_Manual.pdf.

CHAPTER 16

Marketing, Communications, and Public Relations

Vanessa Solesbee, CAPP and
Gary Means, CAPP

Introduction

The chapters in this publication have addressed parking design, maintenance, studies, operations, and even finance. However, a comprehensive communications, marketing, and public relations strategy can take those efforts, and a parking or transportation operation, to the next level. Mastering the art and science of communication can mean the difference between success and failure for any business, and parking and transportation organizations are no exception. Whether a parking program is budgeting for dollars, staff time, and/or resources, investing in branding, promotion, and public education may be viewed as ancillary or extra rather than of critical importance. But thinking strategically about the ways a parking program is communicating with its customers and the community can support every other aspect of a parking program's operations.

Parking and transportation professionals confront countless challenges every day: dwindling parking spaces, combating disability placard abuse, protecting public safety, the political implications of a proposed parking rate increase, and/or the introduction of new technology. By harnessing the power of communications channels and tools together in a comprehensive plan, they can drive traffic, boost sales, educate customers, improve perceptions, and boost their programs and their bottom lines. Absent a thoughtful communications program, other voices (i.e., the media, competitors and/or advocacy groups) have the opportunity to tell their own story—one that may not be accurate or complete, and that could ultimately cause damage to a parking organization or program's reputation.

Communications Planning: A Four-Step Approach

The best marketing and communications programs share a common framework: a simple, four-step process that includes research, planning, implementation, and evaluation. Each step is critical, informing the next one and offering a complete picture of where a program is today, where it could be tomorrow, and the variety of paths available to get from one to the other.

Step One: Research

While only some organizations have the ability to conduct costly marketing research and stakeholder outreach efforts, every organization—even those on small budgets—can take steps to better understand their current environment, including attitudes and perceptions of current and future customers. Research can be as simple as gathering existing articles, studies, and information that help create the foundation for an effective communications plan. Often, a parking and transportation organization can identify key issues, audiences, sensitivities, competitive products, and/or policies that might affect its future communications and marketing efforts.

More sophisticated approaches to research (commonly referred to as "market research") are generally divided into two major categories: quantitative and qualitative. Quantitative research is broader in scale and can be used to generate data and usable statistics. An online survey or poll of stakeholders (i.e., current and/or potential customers) is considered quantitative research. Quantitative research activities can provide an important benchmark that helps define what a customer, patron, or community partner currently knows or believes about a parking or transportation organization's offerings, programs, and/or function.

Qualitative research is more exploratory and can help identify the underlying reasons, attitudes, perceptions, and language used by people when discussing a problem, program, or issue. Hosting one-on-one interviews or a series of small focus groups with stakeholders are both examples of qualitative research.

Step Two: Planning

The exercise of developing a written communications, marketing, and/or public relations plan cannot be underestimated. A plan will discipline thinking, allow an organization to grow and mature, help achieve buy-in from organizational leadership, and define an actionable work plan for staff to follow.

A communications plan generally includes:

- **Goals.** These are a simple and concise outline of what success looks like. Goals can be stated broadly and be visionary or aspirational.
- **Objectives.** These include specific accomplishments and/or milestones that are ideally stated in a measurable way.
- **Audience(s).** While every unique communication effort doesn't have to be tailored to meet a specific stakeholder group's needs, it is important to keep in mind that communication—especially during tense or challenging times—isn't a one-size-fits-all solution. Audience identification can help a parking program know when additional communication or an explanation of a situation might be needed. It also helps prevent overwhelming customers with irrelevant or too much information. The more parking professionals understand their audiences—what is important to them, what they read, how they process information, who influences them—the more tailored a communications and/or marketing effort can ultimately be.
- **Key Messages.** The foundation for creating content and tone for marketing and customer education efforts. Messaging for a parking and/or transportation organization should focus heavily on how the program will work to align parking and mobility policies and activities with the community's strategic development and growth goals. When crafting key messaging for public education and communication about a parking or transportation program's operational and customer service enhancements, it is important to carefully consider the tone of the messaging and how various messages will be perceived by the general public. In an arena as technical and complicated as parking management, it is a common pitfall to attempt to convey too much information at once, or communication with heavy jargon or technical instructions that will not resonate with the intended audience. See Figure 16.1 on the next page for sample messaging.

FIGURE 16.1
Have You Fed Your Meter?

The three key elements to effective messaging are:

1) Consistency: Developing and keeping a similar tone or feeling throughout communications.
2) Frequency: The driving force—keeping the message in front of the audience as often as possible and appropriate. It is important that messages focus on more than essential information about construction, special events and programs, but also on updates that reinforce the goals of the organization.
3) Anchoring: Messaging that provides a compelling call to action. Memorable, high-impact language and visual presentation that talks to the patron, not at the patron.

Tactics and tools. This includes specific actions and deliverables that will be produced or accomplished by the plan. A high-level sampling includes:

- **Organizational branding.** In the parking and transportation industry, branding is much more than just a logo, a sign on the door, or even the color and condition of employee uniforms. Branding is the image that customers have of an organization; it is an unspoken promise of quality and service customers can expect when interacting with an organization.
- **Digital marketing.** Digital marketing is a general term to describe online marketing and includes websites, email marketing, mobile apps, and paid advertising. In any marketing effort, a website should be considered the most tangible public-facing representation of a company, and one of the most important. An organization's website must be easy to find and regularly maintained to keep content fresh and new. Users returning to the site and finding nothing new are likely to stop using it as a resource. In addition to hosting

static content, the site should include tools to allow users to select how they want to communicate with the organization; how they'll receive information about upcoming changes that will affect parking in the downtown area, for example. Websites should be design to be mobile-responsive for viewing on different mobile devices.

- **Social media.** Social media has changed the way people communicate, how stories are told, and how information gets distributed. However, as many industries are noticing, social/new media strategies are only as effective as the consistency of the staff, intern, or volunteer time that is spent to maintain them. Using social media effectively means making a commitment to keeping it updated and fresh with content. The most successful parking programs and organizations using social media are creative in their messaging and approach, using the site not just for information, but also for contests and fun interactions. They also make good use of all three categories of social media: owned (their own pages or feeds), earned (reposts, retweets, or mentions on other people's feeds or in media feeds), and paid (advertising on social platforms). Social media gives the brand a personable and down-to-earth accessibility that gives users a continuous reason to keep coming back.

- **Customer programs.** Airports have readily adapted customer loyalty programs in response to increased competition from improved transit and shuttle services. Municipalities are using loyalty programs to incentive parking patrons to use under-utilized facilities. This provides the customer with financial incentive and opens more convenient, higher-demand parking facilities up to those willing to pay a premium.

- **Multimedia campaigns.** Telling an organization's story consistently across a variety of media and materials (i.e., videos, infographics, print, and digital) is a hallmark of successful parking and transportation marketing programs. Gone are the days when a simple brochure or public service announcement would be sufficient. More video content is uploaded to the internet every 30 days than the major television networks created in the past 30 years (https://www.wordstream.com/blog/ws/2017/03/08/video-marketing-statistics).

- **Community relations.** Developing goodwill in the community can benefit an organization on multiple levels. The main principle of community relations is accepting roles and responsibilities as a good neighbor and good corporate citizen who listens and cares about the well-being of community. Community involvement can encompass everything from sponsoring local charities or school sports teams to rewarding employees for volunteering with local groups. Incorporating social responsibility as part of communications planning is an essential part of good business.

- **Special events.** Sponsoring a community program or fundraiser, launching a donations-for-citations program, or hosting a parking meter art contest are all examples of special events that can be components of a communications plan. Special events can work on many levels to achieve positive visibility for an organization by reaching a far broader audience than just event attendees—and in some cases creating news and photo opportunities that translate to positive media coverage.

- **Crisis communications.** Preparing for a crisis is a critical element of any organization's public relations planning. It is important to be prepared with a plan that includes clearly-defined protocols and coordinated statements, and often a pre-identified, trained spokesperson. The three most important rules in a crisis are to know the facts, tell the truth, and tell it fast. Crisis communications experts used to always talk about the golden hour—that first hour after a crisis before the media start calling. Today, that hour is a millisecond because chances are someone already knows about the incident and has tweeted it, posted it on Facebook, or sent out a video. By telling the truth and telling it fast, a parking professional can get ahead of the crisis, display openness and transparency, and protect the organization's reputation.

- **Partnerships and alliances.** The use of strategic partnerships, alliances, joint programs, or endorsements with companies, brands, or organizations that share or are relevant to an organization's mission can often be a way to reach your target audiences effectively. The distribution of messages or materials through a partner can be an outstanding (and most affordable!) path to achieving an organization's communication goals.

Step 3: Implementation

Once there is a plan, the task of carrying it out begins! As parking professionals know, as people begin to delve into any project, it is inevitable that course corrections and adaptations may need to be made. As a plan unfolds, new opportunities and/or challenges will likely arise, and the plan should be flexible enough to take new developments (or areas of organizational focus) in stride. A plan may include the development of an organizational brand, which might lead to the need for a new logo or visual presence, an updated website and supporting visual materials ranging from brochures to enforcement vehicle wraps. It is in the implementation phase that tasks may be assigned to specific staff or contracted vendors, a timeline is created, and plans are transitioned into actual work plans with defined roles and budgets.

Some communications and marketing efforts can be accomplished on a shoestring budget, making use of existing staff and community partner resources. Others will require a larger investment that might include hiring outside marketing expertise, graphic design, printing or video production, advertising, spokesperson training, and/or special event expenses. Budgeting for communications and marketing work—from research to implementation—should be done annually as part of a parking and/or transportation program's annual budget process.

Step 4: Evaluation

It is impossible to know whether a program is a success or failure without measuring its effectiveness. It is helpful to use Key Performance Indicators (KPIs) that can be applied across organizations and program types.

Examples of the type of performance indicator that might help a parking and/or transportation organization track the progress and/or success of a communications plan include:

- Research (follow-up or post-wave research is often conducted to see if target audiences have changed attitudes or perceptions).
- Increase in desired behavior (i.e., more parking customers in a previously underused facility).
- Decrease in undesirable behavior (i.e., fewer neighborhood permit citations).
- Accurate and timely press coverage of an event, facility closure or new program.
- Impact to consumer perceptions (i.e., tracked through a decrease in complaint calls and/or via customer satisfaction survey).
- Website traffic, media impressions, and/or social media views/shares.
- Downloads of a new mobile app.

Performance indicators and evaluation criteria should be determined during the research phase (Step 1) so baseline data can be gathered. If one waits until the implementation phase to consider what benchmark might be appropriate to track the success of your communications plan, it will be impossible to determine how the investment in various strategies affected meeting goals and objectives.

Public and Media Relations

Organizations can manage their reputations and build credibility and trust among key audiences with a carefully curated public and media relations plan. Customers are sophisticated, and they look for credible information and candid—often instantaneous—communications. Smart companies invest in public relations because it allows them to build trust with key audiences. Public relations can give a parking organization a solid strategic direction and facilitate the development of relationships that achieve strategic and business goals.

Public Relations

At its most basic level, public relations is the practice of managing the communications and information flow between an organization and its publics. The practice involved far more than issuing a news release or publishing a newsletter article. It is strategic: it engages and informs key audiences, builds important relationships and brings vital information back to the organization for analysis and action. When done properly, public relations has a real, measurable effect on the ability of an organization to achieve its strategic goals.

Public Relations vs. Advertising

There are important distinctions between advertising and public relations. Advertising is paid media, while public relations is earned media. In placing an advertisement, the organization has complete control over the message, but the audience understands that the ad has been purchased. For this reason, positive media stories about an organization can be perceived as more credible than paid advertisements. When coverage is favorable, an organization gains content they can share with customers and the public, which can then be leveraged in sales materials and on websites (with the appropriate copyright permissions).

Media Relations

Media relations includes interactions with newspapers, radio, television, and web-based media as well as developing relationships with the reporters, journalists, news directors and editors who work at these outlets. Many organizations have one person who is the media relation specialist, and some chose to hire a media relations firm to assist with the creation and control of their messaging. The goal is to work with and not against the media to create positive impressions and perceptions of the parking organization. Communicating to the media effectively requires both technical savvy and the ability to communicate in a relatable and clear way. Relationship-building can be slow, however there are a few strategic first steps that can be taken to begin developing productive relationships with local media organizations:

- **Identify and train an organizational spokesperson or spokespeople.** One of the biggest missteps that an organization can make when interacting with the media is to send a spokesperson who is unprepared or not equipped to adequately answer questions.
- **Be out in front of stories.** Staff should meet regularly to discuss potential public relations issues and make a joint and informed decision about what communication is needed and the best angle to take. Outreach to media organizations should be done in advance of a crisis.

- **Feed information to media.** This may run counter to the operating norm for parking programs that try to fly under the media's radar, but it is particularly effective when a crisis hits, and the organization hopes to be a primary source to reporters.
- **Ramp up communication during times of transition.** People and organizations often stop communicating during times of transition (i.e., construction, program building, and introduction of new technologies) because they feel they "aren't there yet" and need to have everything completed before bringing their constituencies along. This is exactly the opposite of what should be done; parking and transportation changes and/or "inconveniences" can lead to intense customer frustration and fuel complaint volumes. During times of transition, communication should be clear and understandable, tailored to key audiences, repetitive, and simple.

Communications, Marketing, and Public Relations in Action

Whatever an organization's marketing and communications challenges might be, it is likely that other parking and transportation professionals have had to address similar issues. Industry trade publications, summaries of marketing competition awards winners, websites, conferences, and online communities are excellent resources for drawing inspiration from colleagues and learning about programs that have achieved success. Here are just a few examples:

Bi-lingual Campaign Uses Straight Talk to Reduce Distracted Driving (Montgomery County, MD)

Montgomery County officials were startled to discover that pedestrian collisions in parking lots and garages were about the same as what occurred on county roads and the numbers

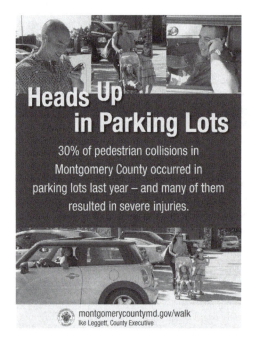

FIGURE 16.2
This Montgomery County, Md., Campaign to Reduce Parking Lot Accidents Won a Communications Award

were increasing. Using an edgy message in both English and Spanish—"Heads Up in Parking Lots: Don't Run Over People. Don't Get Run Over"—the campaign featured photographs of people in parking lots who were distracted with cell phones and otherwise inattentive to their surroundings. Employing no-cost and low-cost techniques, including in-house artwork and digital marketing, the campaign used multimedia education such as posters and pavement decals at partner shopping centers, bus and bus shelter ads, downloadable materials on the county's website, a press conference and public service announcements on YouTube and the county's cable television channel. The results? A 30 percent decrease in parking lot pedestrian collisions.

Innovative Campaign Highlights Campus Bike and Pedestrian Safety . . . Literally! (Texas A&M University, College Station, Texas)

In 2016, Texas A&M University Transportation Services embarked on a multi-year campaign to improve bike and pedestrian safety. The effort included construction of the nation's first green solar luminescent (glow-in-the-dark) protected bike pathways, designed to store solar energy by day and increase visibility at night; the first glow-in-the-dark paint to receive Federal Highway Administration approval. The Transportation Services Marketing & Communications

FIGURE 16.3
Texas A&M University Launched a Communications Campaign to Spark Interest in and Knowledge of its Green Bike Lane

team relied on creative resources using its website and cost-effective design elements such as electronic infographics, interactive marketing clings designed to stick to cement, digital advertising, an online and printed FAQ page, and social media. Google Analytics revealed more than 24,000 page views augmented by 6,900 shares on Facebook, and national and international media interest, including pick-up by a Netherlands Reddit forum and metro-area public transportation blogs.

"Food for Fines" Program Goes Primetime (Lexington Parking Authority, Lexington, Kentucky)

The Lexington Parking Authority (LPA) developed a food donation program with an uncommon twist. In the weeks before Christmas, LPA published a carefully crafted press release to promote its first-ever "Food for Fines" canned food drive that invited citizens to pay for each of their parking meter fines with a donation of 10 cans of food. The campaign resulted more than 5,000 meals for hungry Fayette County families. "Food for Fines" created a local and national media relations buzz, including in *The Washington Post*, *USA Today* and live interviews on MSNBC. Locally the LPA is able to get booked on noon shows and many of the local reporters from TV and print media schedule interviews due to relationships built between LPA and the local media.

"Finding Your Hot Spot" with Spring Break Express Parking (Dallas/Fort Worth International Airport, Dallas, Texas)

During a busy Spring Break travel season, Dallas/Fort Worth International Airport officials wanted to maximize revenues with increased parking at on-site lots while ensuring customers could easily find a parking spot. Its "Spring Break Express Parking: Find Your Hot Spot," campaign promoted Express Parking and encouraged travelers to upgrade from the less expensive Remote Parking lots. It incorporated traditional advertising (print and radio ads in English and Spanish), digital (online banner ads, e-newsletter), guerilla marketing (ski roamers who met travelers on the shuttle bus and distributed promotional items, surfboard pop up stands, vouchers) and social media (shareable viral photos with travelers).

CHAPTER 17

Integrating Parking with Transportation Demand Management (TDM)

*Isaiah Mouw, CAPP, LEED GA
and Brian Shaw, CAPP*

Introduction

While parking may seem unrelated to—and perhaps the exact opposite of—non-driving choices, in fact parking is now integrated and a complement to solving transportation challenges. Parking is an integral part of transportation demand management (TDM), the all-encompassing term for non-drive-alone modal choices.

Transportation Demand Management

- TDM includes programs, policies, and services that help the traveling public make use of alternatives to driving in single-occupancy vehicles (SOVs) and reduce demand for roadway travel. It includes public transit, intermodal connections, shuttles, and other alternative methods of transportation.
- Improving connectivity to public transit routes through the use of sidewalks, walkways, transit layover locations, well-placed bus stops, and last-mile shuttle routes.
- Modifying and/or extending transit routes to directly serve destinations.
- Providing incentives to use transit, carpooling, and other alternative commuting methods to increase commuter choice and make alternate transportation methods more affordable for commuters.
- Offering disincentives to driving alone such as incurring higher parking fees, remote parking, limiting eligibility for parking to certain cohorts, and ensuring robust parking enforcement.

History of TDM: The Origin

In the U.S., TDM began during World War II (WWII) with efforts by the federal government to reduce the public's use of materials needed for the war effort. Rubber, gas, and steel were needed for the troops, which meant people back home needed to conserve. Convincing folks to minimize the use of their cars to conserve gasoline, ride public transit, and/or carpool as much as possible were part of an awareness campaign. Public transit ridership saw its highest per-capita use in the nation's history during WWII.

History of TDM After WWII

After WWII, the federal government began to support the use of the automobile through the building of interstate highways. While intended for national defense to speed the movement of troops and supplies, the interstate program also helped put people to work by expanding the roadway infrastructure. However, the policies and spending that focused on automobile transportation, along with the growth of suburbia, led to the decline in the use of transit, and increased dependency on automobiles for travel needs.

The use of transit emerged once again in the 1970s. In 1973, during the first Arab oil embargo (a result of the United States' support of Israel in the Arab-Israeli war), a shortage of gasoline led corporations to develop what we now know as vanpools to help their employees get to work. It also led to the development of the first computerized ride-matching system and reinvestment by the federal government into public transit systems. A second oil crisis in 1979 led to the creation of regional ride-matching programs, the expansion of public transit, and deployment of high-occupancy vehicle (HOV) lanes and express buses on the nation's highways.

The 1980s saw the creation of the U.S.-based organization called the Association for Commuter Transportation (ACT)), which was the result of merging two groups created during the 1970s oil crises: The Association of Ridesharing Professionals and the National Association of Van Pool Operators. ACT helped promote TDM strategies in federal legislation in the early 1990s. A funding program known as Congestion Mitigation and Air Quality (CMAQ) allocated federal transportation resources toward TDM programs such as vanpools, transit services, ride matching, and transportation management associations (TMAs). CMAQ continues to be available for TDM purposes in federal transportation authorization legislation.

Tax Policies

In the late 1980s, transit and vanpools were included in the commuter tax benefit. Parking costs had long been allowed to be a tax-free expense. However, parking had been given a higher monthly limit than transit or vanpools for the majority of the time the benefit was available. In 2016, the federal government passed legislation that brought parity to the commuter tax benefit, which became $260 per month. This means that commuters can be provided tax-free and/or allowed to use pre-tax salary to pay for parking as well as transit or vanpool fares. However, the tax reform act passed at the end of 2017 removed the ability for employers to deduct the costs of providing transportation benefits such as commuter shuttles, transit passes, and vanpool fares from their corporate taxes.

Overall Benefits of TDM

There are numerous benefits to TDM, ranging from reducing air emissions and traffic congestion and the accompanying public and health benefits, to reducing the need for new and increased road and parking infrastructure.

Having more travel options can translate to fewer cars on the roads. Fewer cars results in less traffic congestion. By reducing traffic congestion, fewer street mitigation measures are needed and resources are not needed to widen streets, improve intersections, or upgrade traffic controls to accommodate increased numbers of travelers.

Health and Safety

Health and safety benefits result both from reducing traffic and enabling and encouraging more people to bike and walk. This may even lower healthcare costs for the campus or private business that implements the TDM measures. Additionally, creating spaces that are free of cars as a result of a TDM program can eliminate conflicts between pedestrians and vehicles, increasing safety and producing more walkable, bikeable areas. Finally, with more people walking or biking, TDM can encourage healthy, vibrant streets with significant foot traffic and social interaction.

Parking Benefits

Parking problems can be mitigated with TDM solutions. Municipal parking rules and regulations are often changed as a result of congestion and increased parking demand. For example, a commercial real estate development may be limited in how much parking it is allowed. TDM can help reduce parking demand and allow the development to succeed with fewer parking and traffic impacts. Parking garages and lots are land-intensive uses and can be expensive to build, operate, and maintain. TDM helps reduce parking demand and less parking needs to be developed, freeing up land for other needs.

Integrating Alternative Transportation

The first public garage was constructed in Chicago in 1898. Since then, parking facilities have evolved from monolithic singular-purpose structures to multi-modal facilities with an integrated vision of enabling more varied and sustainable means of integrating TDM strategies. By integrating alternative transportation modes such as ride sharing, bicycle storage, and bicycle sharing, parking facilities can help decrease the need for people to use single-occupancy vehicles, and lead to a reduction of pollution and land developmental impacts.

Ridesharing

Ridesharing encompasses everything from traditional carpooling and vanpooling to real-time ridesharing services that arrange one-time car sharing on demand. With a goal of filling empty seats in vehicles, ridesharing helps address congestion problems, emissions, and fossil fuel dependency by reducing the number of vehicles on the roads. If the average vehicle carried just one additional person on their commute, the U.S. could save 33 million gallons of gas every day. [1]

Parking facilities can offer reserved or premium parking spaces to ridesharing vehicles and even offer discounted parking for such vehicles to encourage customers to carpool. Simple accommodations like these can assist a building to earn points toward LEED certification. Accommodating ridesharing vehicles can earn points toward LEED certification for eligible buildings.[2] Ride-share also factors into the Parksmart[3] garage certification program.

Car Sharing

Car sharing is a service that provides members the ability to rent a car for short periods, usually by the hour. Car-share program members can reserve a vehicle, and are then charged for the time or distance of use. Even scooter sharing is growing in popularity in certain markets. The key to a successful car or scooter sharing service is having access to vehicles across a network of convenient locations. This is where parking facilities can contribute. Parking facilities often serve as great car sharing hubs in municipal and university sectors due to the convenient locations, lighting, safety, and covered shelters. A report from the University of California, Berkeley, estimated that one car share vehicle removes between nine and 13 vehicles from the road.[4] In addition to removing vehicles from the road, other benefits include encouraging people to use other forms of transportation, such as public transit, walking, and cycling.

The Parksmart[5] certification program encourages parking facilities to create car sharing hubs by partnering with an existing private or nonprofit car share program, purchasing at least two vehicles and creating a local car share program, or partnering with businesses or community organizations to develop a car share program.

Bicycle Storage

Parking facilities often serve as prime locations for bicycle storage due to their convenient locations near end destinations. When bicycle storage is installed in a safe, attractive, and convenient way, parking facilities can attract customers who prefer to cycle to work some days and drive to work on others. In addition, increasing bicycle use reduces emissions, congestion, and the resources needed to build automobiles. *Sustainable Parking Design & Management: A Practitioner's Handbook* offers standards on how much bicycle storage to add and what type of racks and other design considerations to consider when installing bicycle storage in a parking facility.

Installing bicycle storage is just the beginning when integrating parking facilities with cycling. Cyclists may often arrive at their end destination dirty or sweaty. Parking facilities should consider providing users with secure rooms with lockers and showers and a place to change clothes. Parking operations can also offer air compressors for filling bicycle tires and bicycle tool stations for repairs.

Bicycle storage also factors into the Parksmart certification program, which offers two tiers for this particular measure, and can also contribute to LEED certification for eligible buildings.

Bicycle Sharing

Bicycle sharing is a service that allows customers to rent bicycles through an automated kiosk on a temporary basis, encouraging customers to use bicycles on short errands and allowing people to travel to their end destination when mass transit fails to get them close enough. Bicycle sharing was first established in 1965 in Amsterdam, but has only recently grown significantly, due in large part to the technology and phone apps that have improved bike sharing communications and tracking.

One key to a successful bicycle sharing program is having strategically located bicycle hubs in convenient areas. Similar to car sharing, parking facilities often serve as convenient locations for bicycle sharing hubs; this program also contributes to Parksmart certification. Bicycle sharing reduces emissions, noise, and traffic congestion while improving public health through exercise.

Integrating with Transit

Mass Transit

As discussed in the chapters on planning, design, and sustainability. Environmental effects should be kept in mind during the site selection phase and design phase when developing parking facilities. Locating a parking structure within a half-mile radius of mass transit, as encouraged by both LEED and Parksmart, allows customers greater mobility choices. If the facility also participates in a bicycle-sharing program, customers can take mass transit and then bike to complete the last mile of their trip, further advancing their mobility options.

While one of the goals of mass transit is to reduce the reliance on the automobile, some parking facilities have been designed and created solely to support mass transit hubs.

Take for instance the Massachusetts Bay Transportation Authority, which has a total of 101 parking facilities (10 garages and 91 surface lots) with more than 44,000 parking spaces, making it one of the nation's largest parking operations. These parking structures are an important part of reducing automobile use even though an abundance of parking is needed. Customers drive a short distance from their homes, park their vehicles, and then proceed to take the transit system to get to work.

Shuttles, Taxis, Limos, and Ridesharing Apps

Parking facilities can also integrate with transit by accommodating shuttle services, limos and other ridesharing companies such as Uber and Lyft. Many corporate shuttles make limited stops and only pick up the employees of specific companies. Taxis, limos, and ridesharing apps are often used to take riders to and from work or to the mass transit system. Parking facilities can accommodate parking for these shuttles, taxis, limos, and ridesharing companies, or create convenient sheltered pick-up and drop-off hubs in the parking facility.

TDM Benefits—Recruitment

Under certain circumstances and in some locations, TDM can be used to assist organizations with talent recruitment and retention. The job commute is a very real consideration for an employee when considering accepting or even leaving a job. TDM can help improve commute options and minimize the effects of challenging commutes. Offering an employee options that incur less wear and tear on the employee's vehicle is also a positive. A recommended approach is to inform new employees during interviewing or orientation of their commute options before their commute habits have been formed.

The Future of TDM

Technology has and will continue to change the travel options and services made available to the traveling public. It is hard to predict with certainty the long-term effects of autonomous (self-driving) vehicles, alternative transportation services such as Uber or Lyft, the role that ride-matching services such as Scoop will play in influencing carpooling, or how people will choose to travel when they can use Mobility as a Service (MaaS) tools. What if one could monitor commuter behavior real-time and issue rewards for reducing driving and charge higher parking rates for frequent drivers? Sounds like science fiction, but technology exists today or will very soon to make this possible.

The Trends of TDM and Millennials

The transportation network companies (TNCs), Uber and Lyft, continue to impact millennial-generation members' car use. Abandoning car ownership is a real option for a growing number of urbanites. As the millennial generation moves out into the work force and lives on their own, they are choosing at an increasing rate to forgo vehicle ownership. They are using TNCs because they are cost effective and simpler than owning and operating a vehicle in an urban environment. By combining their use of TNCs with car-sharing, some members of this group are able to live car-free, or at least car-lite. A portion of these millennials will continue to rely on TDM programs to support their chosen lifestyle and will likely choose to live and work where they can do so without owning a vehicle, at least for a period of years. What they may need is not a parking space, but rather pick-up/drop-off points for a TNC ride, access to public transit, and support for biking/walking. In addition, the advent of the autonomous vehicle will certainly have impacts on TDM strategies and planning, and these impacts remain unknown at this time.

Scoop and LPR

Sharing the ride to work has traditionally involved having to find or be matched with someone who has a similar commute to yours, then committing to riding with them most of the time. However, new apps, such as Scoop will match you each day for each leg of your commute based on who also either needs a ride or can provide one. Fees are collected to offset the costs for the driver and paid by the rider, administered by the app. By using technologies such as license-plate recognition (LPR) to monitor parking usage, data from the carpool matching apps can be combined with parking management database information to approve the use of carpool parking spaces by recently formed, app-based carpools. This will allow commuters to form carpools on an as-needed basis and to be able to park in a carpool parking space without needing to register in advance. This will also allow for more flexible and fluid commute options and reward those who can carpool occasionally.

TDM Integration Software

Gathering mode split information has usually meant conducting surveys and doing traffic, parking, and ridership counts. Currently, there are software programs that can tap into parking management systems, travel, and fitness apps, as well as carpool matching apps to compile commute data. The system, known as a TDM integration system, allows parking and transportation managers to understand the commute behavior of their customers. By having this information available, new reward or incentive programs can be instituted to encourage overall desired travel and commute behavior. Conversely, frequent drivers can be charged more for parking above certain frequency thresholds or in highly used locations.

Transportation Network Companies (TNC) — Uber and Lyft

The development and adoption of on-demand ride hailing apps such as Uber and Lyft has changed mobility choices. These services use smartphone apps to allow users to request a ride, which is paid for via the app. Drivers are paid as independent contractors with fares allowed to surge when the demand for rides exceeds the supply of drivers. TNCs have resulted in decreases in taxi use, increases in traffic, double parking, and a decline in use of transit in some cities. The ability to request a ride at an affordable rate will allow more commuters to feel comfortable leaving their own cars at home. TNCs are also becoming the preferred way to provide emergency rides home. It remains to be seen if these services can pool their rides so they are not creating more traffic and taking up valuable curb space.

Mobility as a Service

Imagine that you can use an app to determine how to get from your location to your destination considering all modes of transportation, from taxis to rental cars, public transport, and bike share. The app would give you options based on travel time, cost, and availability, and let you pay directly from the app for the service you choose. This is MaaS, and as this book is published, it is being tested in Helsinki, Finland with an app called Whim, which allows users to pay a subscription fee for mobility solutions for all modes of transport.

MaaS will take some testing before coming to the U.S. due to the various transportations and service entities that must be involved, but it is an important concept to understand and be aware of moving forward. The emerging area of MaaS will help to bring TDM to the masses and bring real time transportation choices at any time.

Summary

TDM can and should be an integral aspect of every parking operation. TDM can be effective at mitigating parking demand, reducing traffic impacts, and contribute to an organization's sustainability practices. While TDM has been around for more than 70 years, technology will ensure it continues to evolve and adapt to the ever-changing ways that we travel.

Notes

1   www.ridetowork.org/transportation-fact-sheet.
2   Review the USGBC requirements for LEED; stand-alone garages generally are ineligible for LEEd certification, but garages containing mixed-use space may qualify.
3   For more information on Parksmart, refer to the chapter on sustainability, and www.gbci. parksmart.org
4   http://its.berkeley.edu.
5   For details on certification, refer to the Parksmart Certification Standard.

CHAPTER 18

Adaptive Reuse of Parking Structures

Dave Albersman, Casey Leedom, PE and Sanjay Pandya, PE

Introduction

There have been many conversations among parking professionals, owners, urban planners, transportation engineers, and architects regarding the current and future effects of technological, mobility, and societal changes, such as growing numbers of people choosing to drive less; migration of suburbanites to urban centers; the adoption of transportation network companies (TNCs) such as Uber, Lyft, and Wingz; and the introduction of autonomous vehicles. These changes will likely have a direct effect on the built environment—most notably on structured parking.

Because parking structures are typically in service for more than 60 years, it is worth considering the potential of adaptive reuse of this building type during its service life. Although the demand for parking may decline as a result of the aforementioned societal and technological changes, there is not a known timeline for that shift. That said, it is unlikely to occur in the immediate future. Parking is not the primary element of any development or community, but many community planners and developers recognize that parking, executed properly, is key to realizing their vision for a successful development and an active and vibrant community.

The question of whether a parking structure can be designed today and later adapted into a different mix of uses takes on a new significance. Thinking critically from an operational and design perspective, two key concepts emerge related to forward-thinking parking planning: developing strategies that promote maximum operational flexibility in a short- to mid-term time frame, and designing future parking infrastructure that can be adapted and re-used should projections related to changing parking and mobility needs prove to be on-target. Accordingly, consideration should be given for parking structures to be multi-functional and/or adaptable to changing parking and community needs in the future.

Historically, it has been common to see buildings converted to other uses when their original, intended use becomes outmoded. Existing parking structures cannot be easily converted to other uses because of design and technical issues unique to them: one notable issue is that floor-to-floor heights and floor-loading requirements differ from other uses such as office, residential, etc.

Of course, not all projects will lend themselves to implementing design enhancements to facilitate future adaptive reuse, but for some projects and certain owners, it may be beneficial to investigate the possibilities during project planning and design development. The economic decision to proceed in this manner will need to be considered by community leaders and owners to determine the feasibility of such an investment for our environment and communities. Key elements of this discussion include defining adaptive reuse, required design modifications, cost, site location, and size.

Defining Adaptive Reuse

Structured parking garages are most often located where parking demand is high, but the availability of land (for surface parking) is low or density is desired. These structures are built as short-term storage buildings for self-parked automobiles and require a large building volume. Parking structures are fairly expensive to build and are typically located in downtowns, mixed-use developments, airports, universities, and healthcare campuses. Because of the typical locations of these parking structures, it is anticipated that retail, office, or residential is the most likely future use for a portion or all of these buildings.

Adaptive reuse means to convert part or all of an existing building to a different use in the future while maintaining a significant portion of the skeletal bones of the structure. For example, conversion of an old warehouse or factory building into loft apartments or office space is considered adaptive reuse. Adaptive reuse of a parking structure includes a range of options, depending on the pace of reductions in parking demand as well as the future need of that space. This range of adaptation, as opposed to complete conversion, will allow an owner to get the most out of a building in time. The level of anticipated conversion or adaptation should be evaluated early on as the decisions made during initial design affect how readily the structure can be changed in the future. Some options to adapt an existing parking structure include:

- Accommodating automated and connected vehicles by removing the self-parking component of the facility through improved infrastructure to better house driverless vehicles, which may be able to more efficiently use the same space.
- Accommodating more drop-off and pick-up loading zones for shared-use services such as Uber and Lyft, or for transit uses such as a bus depot.
- Conversion of the ground floor of the facility to commercial space such as retail or office while the upper floors remain for parking.
- Conversion of the top level of the garage to another use, such as assembly areas or green roofs, while the lower floors are used for covered parking.
- Conversion of one or more floors of the parking garage to a different use, such as office or residential, while still having some floors for parking.
- Conversion of the entire structure to another use altogether, which could be a combination of office, residential, retail, or other storage uses.

Horizontal parking expansions, vertical parking expansions, and wrapping a parking structure with another use—such as residential towers—each have an effect on the building but were not considered here as adaptive reuse since the general use of the parking structure remains unchanged.

Key Design Modifications to Facilitate Adaptive Reuse

Parking structures are unique building structures. They are often open to the environment, are designed to be storage facilities (Group S occupancy per the building code), and are not considered occupied spaces, even though people use the various levels and stair/elevators are provided. They are typically more horizontal than vertical in configuration. The primary focus of parking structure design is to efficiently store and move cars in, through, and out of the structure; in other kinds of buildings, the design focus is making the occupied space safe, habitable, appealing, and accessible for people.

A number of design features of a typical parking structure do not lend themselves to non-parking uses. These include story heights; sloped floors for vehicular circulation and drainage; design floor loading; size, number and layout of stair and elevator cores; non-existent or insufficient HVAC and fire protection systems; lack of exterior enclosure; and modest architectural treatment. So, what can be done differently when planning for and designing the parking structure of the future to compensate?

- Increase floor-to-floor heights so the height of the first level is 15+ feet and the height of a typical upper level is 12+ feet. These heights are more suitable to provide higher clear heights of approximately 12 feet for ground-level, small, commercial/retail use, and approximately nine feet for office or residential use. If sufficient site length is not available to provide a parked-on ramp with these story heights or a larger flat floor area is desired, then non-parked on express ramps (with slope of more than 6.67 percent) can be provided. These ramps can be situated near ends of the floor plate or along its side to provide for more flat floor area.
- Design the floor framing to allow for the sloped parking bay to be more readily demolished. One way of accomplishing this is providing a double row of columns along the bay with the ramp and expansion/construction joints at the top and bottom of each floor-to-floor ramp segment. This would likely result in needing to provide additional framing elements for lateral load resistance and detailing to facilitate load transfer and accommodate building movement at the expansion/construction joints.
- Design floor framing for additional load carrying capacity by including provisions for adding columns and beams to reduce beam and slab spans or supplementing conventional and post-tensioned slab and beam reinforcement to carry additional floor loads. This additional load-carrying capacity could accommodate a topping slab to level out the floor drainage slope. Building columns and walls could be designed to accept vertical expansion and an added podium level for a public plaza recreational space or a one- or two-story light framed (wood construction) building structure.
- Include a 25- to 30-foot-wide light well between parking bays to provide space for construction of additional elevator and stair cores within the interior of the floor plate. Foundations for these future pedestrian circulation elements could be constructed as

FIGURE 18.1
Plan Before and After Adaptive Reuse

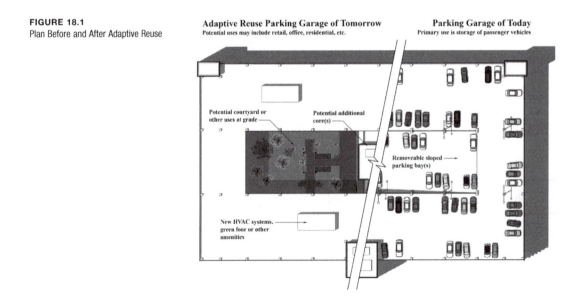

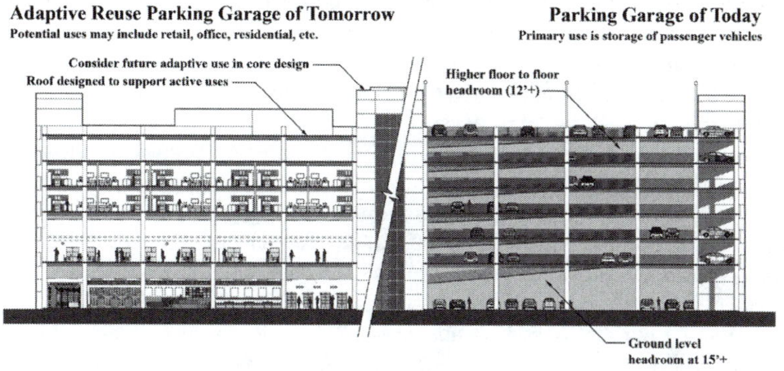

Adaptive Reuse Parking Garage of Tomorrow
Potential uses may include retail, office, residential, etc.

Parking Garage of Today
Primary use is storage of passenger vehicles

FIGURE 18.2
Elevation Plan-Before and After
Adaptive Resuse

Consider future adaptive use in core design
Roof designed to support active uses

Higher floor to floor
headroom (12'+)

Ground level
headroom at 15'+

part of the initial construction. The perimeter stair and elevator cores that serve the parking structure could be located outboard to the floor plate. This will allow easier demolition of these elements if they don't adequately serve the alternate use.

- Design for either the removal of perimeter vehicle and pedestrian guard rails or detail connection points to accept future installation of building façade elements (e.g. curtain wall/store front system, panelized EIFS, or stucco wall system, etc.), including doors and windows to fully enclose the perimeter of the structure.
- Provide additional capacity in the electrical service, sanitary sewer, and fire protection systems. Include provisions for electrical and mechanical chases to accommodate duct work and cabling and rooms for fans for a building HVAC system and additional space for electrical service and fire-protection equipment (e.g., fire pumps and emergency generators).

Additional structural and architectural considerations may need to be identified based on whether the parking structure is of cast-in-place concrete, precast concrete, or steel construction (see Chapter 11 for more on this).

Building Code Considerations

When considering the design of a parking structure for adaptive reuse, it is also important to take into consideration the differences in building code requirements for various occupancy types. A change in occupancy will trigger additional code requirements due to changes in design floor loading, design lateral loading, ventilation requirements, fire suppression system requirements, mechanical and plumbing fixture requirements, means of egress, and accessibility.

Parking structures are required to be designed for a live load of 40 pounds per square foot (psf), which is generally less than that required for office buildings, retail use, residential, and roof level assembly uses (e.g. athletic field or gardens). The parking structure can be initially designed to support a higher live load, or retrofitted to provide the additional load carrying strength. A change in occupancy classification could also affect lateral loads from seismic or wind forces. The risk category of the building has the potential to change, which would affect the seismic importance factor, and therefore seismic story forces, diaphragm design forces, and allowable story drift. This would also affect the basic wind speed and wind pressures used in design for wind loads. Maintaining a constant risk category when changing the occupancy of the building would lessen the need for significant design changes due to increased lateral loads.

In general, parking structures are initially designed with less stringent requirements for structural fire rating and fire protection systems than office buildings, residential, or other uses. Because most other feasible occupancies would require a fire sprinkler system, it would be prudent to design the original parking structure with an automatic fire sprinkler system, providing an easier transition to a new occupancy in the future. Other types of occupancies may also require additional fire rating or vertical and horizontal separations. Several occupancies also require a fire alarm system to be installed.

A change in occupancy to part or all of the parking structure may require an increase in the overall egress width and the number of points of egress provided. Parking structures can have different occupant loads and longer maximum allowable travel distances to exits than other kinds of buildings. If a full building occupancy conversion were to occur, it's likely that additional stairs would need to be added to accommodate new occupant load and egress requirements. Future uses will likely also trigger additional accessibility requirements, as the accessible design for parking structures can often be confined to one or two levels of the structure where accessible parking is located. An occupied building, however, requires that many more floors and areas be accessible.

Financial Considerations and Initial Cost Implications

Few adaptive reuse parking garages have been constructed in the U.S. to date, so there is not enough construction cost data to evaluate the actual cost of designing for adaptive reuse. A few limited studies have suggested the premium may be an additional 30 to 40 percent. The uncertainty of accurately evaluating premium cost, combined with the unknown pace of the decline of automobile use, makes it hard to answer the question, "Is the additional cost worth it?"

Each project must be evaluated on a case-by-case basis. The key question is when a need for adaptive reuse may occur.

One framework for analyzing an individual project is to consider the present value of the investment in adaptive reuse. In simple terms, present value is the value in today's dollars of a future revenue stream. By analyzing the future revenue stream, it is possible to judge whether or not an investment in adaptive reuse is financially justifiable.

A present value analysis requires judgements on several variables, including:

- The additional cost of adaptive reuse relative to a conventional design.
- Anticipated future parking demand and potential revenue.
- Estimated revenue streams from alternative use and the timing of the conversion.
- The costs of the conversion at the time it is needed.
- Rate of return required for the investor.

The answer to these questions will undoubtedly be speculative but necessary to determine whether or not to invest in an adaptive reuse parking structure. Sometimes the answer may be to invest in an adaptive-use garage. Conversely it may be prudent to build a conventional garage that will be partially or completely removed before the end of its useful life to make way for redevelopment in a conventional sense.

CHAPTER 19

Trends in Parking: Future Thinking

Richard W. Willson, PhD, FAICP

$\mathbf{P}$arking will undoubtedly be different in the future. Everything is changing—factors that affect the amount of parking used, the way it is accessed, the design of parking facilities, and parking management tools such as dynamic pricing. This is a time of rapid disruption in city management, transportation, and parking. Because there is uncertainty about how trends will play out and interact, parking professionals must be adaptive and creative. It is vital for the parking industry to be ready for a range of future conditions.

Seemingly daily media accounts discuss the development of autonomous vehicles, transportation and parking apps, and the sharing economy. As well, parking tools for integrated data collection, facility management, payment alternatives, and financial management are rapidly advancing. One thing is certain: changes in technology will help us use parking more efficiently.

More broadly, consumer trends favor experiences over ownership. Those trends are likely to apply to both transportation services and parking. Shared mobility services are responding to those preferences by providing mobility without private vehicle ownership. Similarly, arrangements for parking use are shifting, with parking use no longer bundled with rent in some instances. This will leave parking to justify itself as an independent economic enterprise. Some residents, for example, may choose not to own a vehicle when facing a separate cost for parking. In the retail sector, malls are struggling and congested urban places are prospering, calling into question the old model that plentiful, free parking is the key to retail success.

While some trends are clear, others are uncertain. Demographers inform us about an aging society, marked by members of the large baby boom group who will stop driving in the coming decades. While at least some of the millennial group seek urban communities that are less reliant on private vehicles, the delayed entry of some members of this generation into job and housing markets creates uncertainty about whether they will adopt living and commuting patterns as their parents did. They may.

An important question for the future of parking is this: will people own their vehicles in the future or will they prefer to use mobility services as needed? If they choose the latter, this will reduce the amount of parking used in cities and suburbs. It is likely that these preferences will differ between urban and suburban areas, with urban areas experiencing the largest decreases.

There is no crystal ball to answer these questions. There are many scenarios and contingencies, but most of them involve less parking per unit of development. Fast-growing communities may continue to add parking, albeit at a slower rate, while status quo or slow growth ones may be able to reduce parking supply. This chapter summarizes a key point: parking will play a smaller role in cities and suburbs in the future. The primary shift will be to emphasize efficient management of parking over new parking construction.

Peak Parking?

Predicting how the various forces described above will translate into parking practices is difficult, but taken together they raise the question: Will there be less parking use per unit of development in the future? As noted above, signs point toward yes. Here are some of the reasons.

Changes in planning and policy are reducing reliance on private vehicles.

- Local and regional transportation plans are calling for a more balanced multimodal transportation system. They include better transit and active transportation modes, such as walking and bicycling. This may enable lower household vehicle owner-ship and/or use of other travel modes for some trips. Road expansion will not keep pace with population or economic growth and although dynamic road pricing will squeeze more efficiency from existing roadway networks, the travel time costs of driving alone will increase in many places. At the same time, management tools, such as real-time transit arrival information, will increase the desirability of alternative travel modes.
- Local and regional land-use plans are supporting infill development, increased density, and mixed-use development. These changes are associated with lower vehicle ownership and will reduce the amount of parking occupied per unit of development. Plans may restrict or discourage the continued outward sprawl of cities. Some regulations, such as parking maximums or prohibition on freestanding parking, will limit parking construction.
- Resiliency and adaptability are watchwords for planning. Given uncertainty about the future, from technology changes to environmental conditions, plans for cities will favor designs that can recover from shocks and adapt to changes.

Smart infrastructure is broadening travel options and making private vehicles less necessary.

- Real-time information is increasing travel options. Consumers have access to real-time information concerning traffic levels, options for driving, and transit arrivals, which reduces the uncertainty of modes other than driving alone, e.g., real-time bus arrival apps that reduce the frustration of waiting. As well, just-in-time, real-time ridematching systems will provide commuters with a broader range of options than a traditional, fixed carpool. Rather than commute the same way each day, commuters will use multiple modes in a trip and will vary modes by daily activity and quality of service.
- Rail and rapid bus transit are expanding, as is attention to last-mile transportation services that connect the traveler from the stop to the final destination.
- Bike lanes and improved pedestrian facilities are increasing the suitability of these modes for replacing private vehicle trips, and making other modes such as transit more competitive by providing last-mile connections.

Smart growth is favoring alternative travel modes and land use efficiency.

- Developers are providing more options for housing in transit-rich areas, in built-up, mixed-use areas, and new suburban clusters, all of which offer the possibility of reducing private vehicle ownership. The higher cost of structured parking is discourag-ing excess parking construction.

- The changing nature of work is reducing commuting, with an increased role of work-at-home, growth in the service economy, and more "gig" activities. Traditional workplaces, with regular hours are being replaced by a wider variety of work arrangements, are reducing the traditional, consistent commute to work.
- Cities are seeking to use scarce land resources more efficiently by pursuing shared parking arrangements, remote parking, or smaller space sizes.

Technology is providing alternatives to private vehicle ownership, and substitution for trips.

- Alternatives to vehicle ownership are expanding—these include short-term vehicle rental, peer-to-peer vehicle sharing, shared mobility services, and shuttles. Car makers are aggressively moving into these markets.
- Autonomous vehicle technology is advancing quickly. Once rolled out, the key question is whether consumers will choose to own autonomous vehicles or simply use shared autonomous vehicle when they need to get around. If the latter occurs, personal vehicle ownership will decline and the remaining vehicles may be parked for a smaller proportion of the time.
- Telecommunication is substituting for physical travel for some work, shopping, and social trips. This reduces parking use at some locations and may reduce vehicle ownership.

Demographics and culture suggest less driving and parking.

- An aging population is reducing household vehicle ownership, yielding reductions in parking use. The availability of autonomous vehicles may balance this somewhat.
- Some members of younger generations are seeking car-free lifestyles.

Quality of life priorities are working against private vehicle ownership.

- Public awareness of the health effects of sedentary automobile commuting lifestyles is growing.
- Public concern about pollution and climate change is spurring consideration of alternative travel modes. Balancing this trend is increased vehicle fuel economy, low carbon fuels, and elective and hydrogen vehicles that can be powered with renewable energy.
- The stress and time waste of traffic congestion is growing in many communities. This is a disincentive to commuting by private automobile. Road capacity is not being expanded commensurate with vehicle miles traveled. People are more aware of the health effects of sedentary commuting in a private vehicle.

Energy policy and carbon taxes may discourage private vehicle ownership.

- Energy may be costlier in the future. Currently, gas prices are lower than expected due in innovations in oil extraction techniques, but these techniques are controversial and may not be environmentally sustainable.
- The future may involve carbon taxes on fuel use. While practices vary across states and national government, the urgency of climate change effects may lead to taxes or other disincentives to use carbon, disincentivizing private vehicle use.

All of the factors described above suggest less vehicle ownership at the household level, and lower vehicle use for the most types of trips. Two factors, however, could lead to an increase in parking use per unit of development:

- New office work arrangements are in some cases increasing employee density; these include shared workspaces instead of private offices in technology companies and collaborative workspaces.
- Some communities are not building enough housing to keep up with supply. Crowding in individual residential units, such as two families in a house or extended family members sharing a residential unit, may increase parking use per unit.

Listing these trends, one-by-one, doesn't give enough attention to their synergistic effects. For example, when the consumer considers vehicle ownership, that decision is affected by transit, walk/bicycle options, shared mobility services, and real-time ridematching apps. These provide a portfolio of travel options that are more compelling than one single option, such as driving or using transit every day. This can convince a person they can get along without a private vehicle. Long-time parking industry professionals will note many false alarms about systematic changes in transportation systems that have been predicted in the past, as witnessed by the 1970s energy crisis, recent concerns over rising energy prices, or the first iteration of electric vehicles. This time, despite a turbulent regulatory situation at the federal level, the changes are real. As evidence, consider the level of investment by technology and automobile companies in this new era of mobility.

Overall, the factors suggesting lower vehicle ownership and parking use far outweigh those that suggest increases. Thus the question: does the current period represent "peak parking," the highest level of vehicle ownership that we will observe? Does it represent the highest level of parking occupancy we will observe? Will parking use decline in the future, in absolute terms?

The strength of these trends in urban areas may be able to decrease the total parking supply going forward, creating opportunities to redevelop surface parking lots, and resulting in parking-free new developments that rely on shared parking pools. It may also facilitate the repurposing of curb parking for bus lanes, bike lanes, wider sidewalks, parklets, and other benefit uses. Of course, this will not happen without shared parking and effective parking management.

Except for the fastest growing communities, the total current parking supply may accommodate future growth if it is properly managed. Does this mean the end of the parking industry? Most certainly not. These trends signal a transformation in the parking industry, from an early focus on parking supply with limited management required, to parking being a high-value, managed element of the transportation network. More often than overseeing new parking construction, parking professionals will manage parking use with sophisticated management concepts, pricing, and technology.

Parking Facilities

In the past, parking facilities were designed for one purpose only: to park vehicles. While surface lots are often deployed in anticipation of future development on a site, most parking structures and underground facilities are a long-term bet on one use. Now, however, parking developers are aware that the factors described in the previous section may reduce future parking use. Some of them are designing flexible parking facilities that can be repurposed to other uses, should parking use decline in the future (see Chapter 18 for more on this).

The other important facility issue is how parking will be used with the advent of self-parking and autonomous vehicles. For example, if drivers drop a vehicle at a parking facility for self-parking, areas for this drop-off and pick-up area should be allocated. The cars then can park themselves at higher density, in narrower spaces (no need for door clearance), and with queuing in aisles. If autonomous vehicles become commonplace, people who own their vehicles will be dropped off at the front door of the destination and then the vehicle will proceed to park. Many commuters may choose instead to consume mobility services in an autonomous shared vehicle that serves many users throughout the day, much as a current taxi operates. Personal vehicle parking may decline, but these taxibots will need temporary storage when demand is low. This parking can occur in peripheral areas, freeing up centrally located parking for other uses, or they could line up in centrally located structures, first-in, first-out, perhaps doubling the density of parked vehicles.

Surface parking can be repurposed to other land uses, and new layouts may be as simple as restriping. Because there is no such thing as a historically significant surface parking lot, they can be easily built upon. The reuse or redesign of structures or underground parking, on the other hand, depends on their configuration and design. Sloping-floor, low-clearance structures are difficult to repurpose to anything but storage, as is underground parking. In above-grade facilities, short-span structures can lock in space configurations and widths that might not fit the greater vehicle density possible with self-parking vehicles or alternative uses.

The most adaptable structures are those that are built with level floors, enough floor clearance, and sufficient structural load capacity. The concept of adaptive reuse is applicable to a variety of land uses, depending on local needs, should future parking demand be lower. Those uses can range from temporary uses such as entertainment venues or seasonal urban food production in raised beds on surface lots, to permanent repurposing as residential and commercial uses. While these structures cost more and are likely less efficient because of external ramps, the benefit of future flexibility may pay for those added capital costs. Other design issues may come to play, including acceptable levels of vibration, natural light, and stairway/elevator locations (internal versus external). If the structure is wrapped with land uses, then repurposing the inner core of parking may also be problematic.

The design concept for new parking facilities sees them as multimodal transportation hubs, perhaps hosting areas for patron self-parking, automated parking, shared-mobility vehicles, electric recharging stations, bicycle parking, and close links with transit and shuttles. The structures can be made more sustainable with payment systems that do not require gate arms or attendants, thereby reducing idling time while cars queue. Space availability information will reduce cruising for parking, and solar panels (and perhaps wind) will provide energy.

High-cost areas are seeing innovation in automated and mechanical parking. These systems improve efficiency by reducing aisle space and increasing the density of parking. Parking developers are designing parking facilities either with these features at the outset, or so they can be efficiently retrofitted.

Curb parking is likely to be under pressure from other competing uses of curb area. Those uses include space for:

- Drop-off/pick-up space for transportation network companies.
- Transit boarding and alighting for additional transit service and bus rapid transit.
- Deliveries associated with online shopping.
- Bicycle parking in bike corrals.
- Bicycle lanes.
- Parklets and sidewalk widening.
- Bus priority lanes.

Future-oriented parking developers should think through what their project would be used for should parking demand diminish in the future. Managers of curb parking should reconsider the privileged place it has traditionally held in the public right-of-way and develop tools for better management, including management strategies for displaced curb parking.

Parking Equipment and Technology

Technological advances permit more efficient use of parking and a rapid decrease in the equipment and labor required to manage parking. Those changes include:

- Automated parking garages or automated vehicle storage and retrieval systems (AVSRS) reducing the space needed per parked car.
- Electronic payment replacing cash, and alternatives to credit cards are changing methods for electronic payment.
- Parking apps reducing the transaction costs between parking suppliers and parkers, for facilities and at an individual level.
- Parking apps facilitating shared parking arrangements.
- Parking apps providing pricing and guidance advice, reducing cruising.
- Data aggregation permitting better parking management and transportation/parking system integration.

Geo-gating technology or camera systems can provide information on space availability, guide the parker to a space, charge the parker via an app for the time parked, and then know when the space again becomes available. This is possible without gate arms, cashiers, parking fee collection equipment, or attendants. Parking personnel can be rededicated to customer service and security. Previous chapters reviewed the details of these systems. While it is not possible to determine the development and uptake of new technologies, their logic in terms of customer satisfaction and cost reduction will be compelling.

Dynamic Parking Pricing

Perhaps the most exciting change in parking practices is the growth of dynamic pricing systems to manage parking use. Already used in San Francisco, Los Angeles, Washington D.C., and other cities, dynamic parking pricing is the future. The concept is to vary parking price dynamically to achieve a desired blockface or off-street parking capacity. While these systems may affect total parking use, their main impact is to induce a small number of people to switch parking locations. For example, someone visiting a business district for a short period would benefit from being able to park near the building they need to access. They would pay a higher price than for a space a block or two away, but only for a short time. A person parking longer would seek a space a block or two away, or walk or bike the rest of the way to save on their daily parking.

The principle of dynamic parking pricing is to differentiate price based on the time of day parked, the facility, and location. For example, the recent dynamic pricing demonstration projects in San Francisco and Los Angeles set prices at the blockface and facility level for three time periods throughout the day. The way prices are set involves incremental adjustments—prices are nudged up when parking occupancies are high and nudged down when they are low. Occupancies are measured with sensors. These prices are adjusted every month to two months, based on an adjustment algorithm that seeks the "just right" price for each blockface. These pilot projects show promise but have faced issues with nonpayment, stemming from disabled placard laws in California, sensor reliability, and caps on price changes. Nonetheless, the use of dynamic pricing is expanding, in simpler forms, as in Seattle, and with new occupancy technology, as in Washington D.C. There is no doubt that the days of a uniform price, seldom-adjusted, are over.

Conclusion

The future that has been imagined for decades is almost here. The parking experience in the future will be quite different, as will the way in which parking resources are managed.

New management systems, new information systems, new payment systems, and a different parker experience will be the norm. The parking industry is at a mid-point in this revolution in practices.

While the future cannot be predicted, what is sure is that we are at a point of rapid change. Parking professionals will benefit from monitoring broader social and economic trends, tracking the diffusion of technology into the parking industry, and proactively testing and adopting new technologies and techniques.

Glossary

Abandoned vehicle. A motor vehicle left behind whose owner does not intend to keep or maintain ownership. In some jurisdictions, regulations may be established to restrict parking a vehicle for an excessive period of time without moving. Criteria may differ by jurisdiction, such as, 48-hour limits or 72-hour limits.

Authority. A special-purpose governmental entity that may function autonomously from the governmental authority that established it; has its own governing body and may have decision-making capabilities normally reserved for government. Its responsibilities and purpose are narrowly defined.

Access and Revenue Control Systems (ARCS). Technology that manages access verification of a parking area and the calculation of fees based on specific parking activities. This can include gates, tickets spitters, payment kiosks, and cashier stations. These systems issue access credentials or read electronic credentials to grant access; common examples are multi-space or single-space meters and automated payment systems.

Adaptive reuse. To convert part or all of an existing building use to a different use while maintaining a significant portion of the skeletal bones of the structure.

Allied Construction Industries (ACI). Established in 1929, ACI is comprised of approximately 500 member companies throughout the Greater Cincinnati, Ohio, area. Members include general contractors, subcontractors, architects, engineers, developers, and suppliers to the commercial construction industry.

Analytics and reporting technology. Solutions that collect data from operating software and field technologies, and analyze it to help managers make informed decisions or identify new trends. This includes graphical reporting, demand prediction engines, budgeting and forecasting, pricing analytics, etc.

Architectural balance. A term used to describe the architecture of a building through visual weight, symmetry, and asymmetry.

Asset management program. A systematic approach to maintaining a facility.

Associated General Contractors of America (AGC). An association for the construction industry. AGC represents more than 26,000 firms including 6,500 of America's leading general contractors.

Audience identification. A successful communication strategy starts with identification of the audience(s). Audience identification can help one know when additional communication or explanation of a situation might be needed. It also helps prevent overwhelming customers with irrelevant or too much communication and can assist with making choices about which communication tools will be most effective for a particular audience.

Automatic vehicle identification (AVI). A system that enables automatic identification of a vehicle when it enters a parking facility so it can be authorized and permitted to enter and exit. AVI access methods include RFID, LPR, and Proximity cards.

Automated parking garages. See automated vehicle storage and retrieval systems; also called automated parking systems (APS) and automated parking facility (APF).

Automated vehicle storage and retrieval systems (AVSRS). Mechanical equipment that places a vehicle in a parking space, usually in a stacked configuration; designed to reduce the area or volume required to store vehicles.

Autonomous vehicles. Also known as driverless or self-driving cars, vehicles that can guide themselves with varying degrees of independence from action by a human driver.

Bay spacing. The centerline-to-centerline dimension between columns along the drive aisle in a parking garage.

Bicycle sharing/Bike sharing. A service that allows customers to rent bicycles, usually from large racks, hubs, or geo-fenced areas, on a temporary basis. Usually, rentals are arranged through smartphone apps or at automated kiosks.

Blockface. The curb space along a street between intersections.

Blue roof. A roof designed to capture and store water, usually rainfall or stormwater.

Bond. A type of loan in which the lender borrows from bond holders instead of from a conventional bank. Government bonds fund transportation, schools, libraries, commercial development, and parking infrastructure.

Branding. Branding is the image customers have of an organization, which is carefully crafted and implemented throughout all marketing and communication.

Building pad. The buildable area on a site. It is often the area remaining after taking into account property lines, setbacks, and easements.

Capture rate. The number of unique citations divided by the number of unique violations.

Car sharing. A service that offers members car rentals for short periods of time, usually by the hour. Members reserve vehicles and are charged for time or distance of use.

Cast-in-place, pre-tensioned concrete. A long-span structural system that consists of concrete poured into field forms with post-tension strands or tendons.

Commuter tax benefit. A federal program that lets commuters pay a portion of fees for parking, carpool, or vanpool with pre-tax dollars.

Concession. A long-term lease where public parking assets are converted to a private enterprise and turned over to a private owner and a concessionaire in exchange for a single lump sum of money.

Condition assessment. The process of investigating by systematically collecting information that affects the performance of an existing structure; evaluating the collected information to make informed decisions regarding the need for repair or rehabilitation; detailing of findings as conclusions and reporting recommendations for the examined structure.

Congestion Mitigation and Air Quality (CMAQ). A federal program in the U.S. that allocates federal transportation resources toward transportation demand management programs.

Constructability. Defines the ease, efficiency, or difficulty with which structures can be built. The more constructible a structure is, the more economical it will be.

Construction Management Association of America (CMAA). An association that promotes the profession of construction management. The CMAA has more than 16,000 members, including construction management practitioners, corporate members, and owners in the public and private sectors, along with academic members.

Contractor-managed parking. A management model in which all facets of parking operations are outsourced to an outside party.

Core competency. A skill needed to be successful at a job or other activity.

Credential. Also referred to as a permit, allows access to a facility or to park in a certain on-street area (i.e. residential parking pass) and references access control systems.

Damage. A condition causing a building element to not function as intended due to faulty design, construction, or external influence such as vehicle impact.

Deferred repairs. Preventive maintenance or required repairs recommended by the asset management program but not implemented within the recommended time period.

Design service life. The period of time after installation or repair during which the performance satisfies the specified requirements if routinely maintained but without being subjected to an overload or extreme event.

Deterioration. Physical manifestation of material failure caused by environmental exposure or decomposition of material during exposure to service.

Distress. A condition causing a building element to not function as intended due to deterioration or damage.

Drive aisle. The lane a motorist drives in to get to and from a parking space.

Dynamic pricing. Also known as performance-based pricing or variable pricing, a form of parking pricing that alters the price by time and space to affect parking behavior and demand.

Earned media. Usually media coverage, social media coverage, or uncompensated reviews, these are stories, posts, etc., that spread the word about an organization but that the organization does not own or pay for.

Edge devices. Field devices that are on the front edge of data collection and at the furthest point from centralized data management systems.

Effective capacity. The occupancy level at which a parking system begins to exhibit capacity issues. This varies by user type and knowledge of the system, but is generally considered to be 85 to 95 percent of the total capacity of a facility or system. When occupancies begin to exceed this threshold, the system operates less efficiently, and patrons can experience challenges finding available spaces.

Electrical safety. Standards, best practices, and behaviors that are expected to mitigate the dangers of electricity.

Emergency planning. The process by which an organization or individual develops a set of procedures or standards in order to react, respond, and recover from an incident.

EMV (Europay, MasterCard, and Visa). A global standard for inter-operation of integrated circuit cards (IC cards or chip cards) and IC card-capable point of sale (POS) terminals and automated teller machines (ATMs), for authenticating credit and debit card transactions. EMV chip cards contain embedded microprocessors that provide strong transaction security features not possible with magnetic stripe cards.

Encryption. The placement of data into a coded format that can only be read with an encryption "key" or formula that translates the data into a readable format.

Façade. A term used to describe the vertical front, side, or back of a building.

Facility emergency plan. A site-specific guide with standard operating procedures for an organization to react, respond, and recover from various types of emergencies that are specific to the facility environment.

Field technology. This includes the hardware (meters, gates, etc.) and software found physically on-site used to collect information about the environment (video, space sensors, loops) and to interact with customers and onsite personnel (handhelds, ticket dispensers, signs, intercoms, apps).

Fire safety. Standards, best practices, and behaviors that are expected to mitigate and stop the threat of fire.

FLSA Duties Test. The Department of Labor has issued a series of tests employers can use to identify which job roles are exempt from overtime and which roles are non-exempt. Based on the job category, the employer selects and completes the applicable duties test to make this determination.

Frontline associates. Industry positions that interface directly with customers and include attendant, cashier, enforcement patroller, and valet. All frontline associates have two main responsibilities: ensure vehicles park safely and efficiently.

Functional design. The physical manifestation of how a parking facility functions, serves its users, considers the needs of different users, and the circulation path of vehicles and people.

Geo-gating technology. Systems that provide spatial recognition of parking spaces or facilities, enabling parking guidance, occupancy information, access control, and parking payment without gates/arms or parking cashiers.

Green roof. Also known as a living roof, a building roof that is partially or totally covered by plants, usually in soil laid over a waterproof membrane, which may include irrigation systems.

Guaranteed maximum price (GMP). Essentially, a cost-plus agreement with a cap on the owner's liability for the costs of the construction project.

Guiding principles, values, goals, and objectives. Guiding principles are more of the "why" or the rules; values are more of the "what" or the importance; goals are the destination or where managers want a business to be; and objectives are progress markers along the way to the goal achievement.

Handheld ticketwriter. A computer that is small enough to be held in one's hand; used to write electronic parking citations.

Hiring manager. The individual directly responsible for either an individual or collective group of employees' life cycle; i.e., is expected to hire, train and develop, coach, and make decisions that directly affect the terms of his/her direct reports' employment status.

Idle reduction payment systems. Payment systems that reduce vehicle idling at parking facility entrances, payment areas, and exits. Most are designed to speed entry and exit so cars aren't waiting in line.

Infrastructure technology. The hardware, software, and data/voice bandwidth to connect the facility with the world. The technology includes communication services (T1 lines, cable) plus the necessary hardware devices to manage network security and system integrations. Infrastructure technologies are common, are widely available, and are used in many solutions in other industries.

Integrated project delivery (IPD). A project delivery method that integrates people, systems, business structures, and practices into a process that collaboratively harnesses the talents and insights of all participants to optimize project results, increase value to the owner, reduce waste, and maximize efficiency through all phases of design, fabrication, and construction.

Internally vs. Externally managed. Facilities are either managed internally by an entity such as a university or municipality or outsourced to a third-party management group (externally).

Internet of Things (IoT). A network of field devices, vehicles, and other things embedded with sensors, software, electronics, and network connectivity that lets them collect and share data.

Key Performance Indicator (KPI). A measurable value that demonstrates how effectively an organization is meeting goals. High-level KPIs focus on the overall performance of the organization and low-level KPIs focus on processes in individual departments.

Latent demand. An unexpressed demand, such as a localized deficit, usually attributed to a specific user or land use, that indicates demand cannot be met for that user or land use by the surrounding parking supply, either due to capacity issues or restrictions.

Learning objective. A statement establishing a measurable behavioral outcome, used as an advanced organizer to indicate how the learner's acquisition of skills and knowledge is being measured. Obtained from www.td.org.

Lease agreement. A legal contract whereby a land owner agrees to lease a parking facility or lot to an operator for a set period and in return receives a monthly fee. In exchange, the parking operator is responsible for remitting all expenses and receives all the parking revenues.

LEED. Leadership in Energy and Environmental Design, a sustainable rating system for buildings devised by the United States Green Building Council (USBGC). Most standalone parking garages do not qualify for LEED certification, facilities with ancillary occupied spaces and mixed-use buildings can qualify for certification.

Level of Service (LOS). The grading system that expresses how easy it is to maneuver through a parking garage. The system grades a garage as either A (best), B, C, or D (worst). Garages that do not fall within these grading levels are typically considered failures in terms of layout and are anticipated to have maneuverability issues.

License plate inventory (LPI). A process that uses license plate recognition or the manual collection of license plate information via handheld devices to count and keep track of vehicle license plates. It can be used in both controlled access and open facility environments to keep track of vehicles accessing a facility.

License plate recognition (LPR). A vehicle identification technology that uses cameras to take pictures of license plates, read the images via character recognition software, and convert the images into text that a computer can use. LPR is common in access control, enforcement, tolling, and stolen vehicle detection applications. Sometimes called ANPR (automatic number plate recognition).

Licensed design professional. An engineer or architect who is licensed to practice engineering design as defined by the statutory requirements of the professional licensing laws of a state or jurisdiction.

Life safety. Standards, best practices, and behaviors that are expected to prevent serious bodily harm or death.

Location Manager. While this job title can vary, the main role for this position is centered around the ability to manage the daily activities of the parking facility.

Long span. A structural system that spans the full length of the parking garage structural bay. This long span provides a clear span that is uninterrupted by additional intermediate columns.

Magnetic stripe. A strip of magnetic media usually found on a credential such as a credit card, hotel key, etc. The term is sometimes shortened to mag-stripe. The magnetic stripe can store a small amount of data.

Maintenance. The work required for care and upkeep; can include the replacement or renewal of existing systems that are nearing the end of their service life. Maintenance is intended to minimize premature deterioration of the facilities and benefit the long-term performance.

> Routine maintenance includes periodic and corrective tasks, housekeeping tasks, and safety checks for effective day-to-day operation of a facility.

> Preventive maintenance includes tasks performed as needed to avoid future repairs and protect an owner's capital investment.

Repairs and replacement maintenance include actions performed to repair elements when possible or economical, or to replace them when they have reached the end of their service lives.

Management agreement. A legal contract whereby an asset owner (or an agent on his behalf) hires a parking operator to manage his/her parking facility and remits a management fee for the operator's services.

Mechanical parking. Parking facilities in which automated or manual mechanized devices stack cars in vertical or horizontal space, either above-ground or in underground parking facilities.

Mechanized parking units. The pieces of equipment commonly known as stackers, which lift cars into parking spaces that are commonly stacked in a rack on top of each other.

Messaging. A messaging strategy is the foundation for all of an organization's marketing efforts. A messaging strategy tells an audience why they should visit an organization, what they will find when they do, and why they should care. For a brand to resonate with its customers and partners, the messaging strategy needs to inspire confidence that the organization understands its patrons' and partners' needs and has something relevant and unique to offer.

Minimum parking requirements. Requirements established in zoning codes for a certain number of parking spaces to be provided per unit of development (based on square footage, number of residential units or bedrooms, or other measure).

Mission. A statement that defines what an organization is, why it exists, and its reason for being.

Mobility as a Service (MaaS). A system that lets travelers plot routes to destinations considering and using all modes of transportation, and allows users to choose and/or reserve travel based on travel time, cost, and availability.

Occupancy rate. The number of hours a space is occupied divided by the total number of space hours.

Off-street parking. All parking not on/along the curbs of streets; includes private and public lots, garages, driveways, etc.

On-street (curb) parking. All parking on/along the curb of streets.

Operating software technology. Solutions that interact with field technology to control access to a facility, process parking and enforcement transactions, process financial transactions, enable customer service support, or interact with third-party systems to enable customer conveniences such as mobile payment, prepayments, reservations, and transportation.

Needs assessment. A process used by organizations to determine priorities and allocate appropriate resources. It involves determining immediate, intermediate, and long-term needs for a particular project.

Node. A place where paths within a network cross or meet, or a momentary stopping point on a journey or trip.

Owned media. The marketing/PR/media channels an organization has complete control over. Examples are an organization's website, mobile apps, newsletters, catalogs, electronic publications, annual reports, videos, and blogs. Also refers to an organization's own social media posts.

Paid media. Messaging that is paid for; advertising.

Parking apps. Programs, generally available on handheld devices, that provide information on parking location, rules and regulations, routing to parking spaces, pricing, payment, and occupancy and use information.

Parking authority. A governmental entity that is only involved with parking and is typically responsible for all facets of public parking in its jurisdiction, including land acquisition, funding, and managing parking.

Parking guidance systems. Used to convey parking space availability to a driver prior to arriving at the parking space. Systems observe entrances and exits at various points in a facility, compute occupancy or use counts, and distribute that information via apps or signage.

Parking demand. Commonly referred to as the number of parking spaces needed within an area. This is often attributed to specific land uses and communicated as spaces per thousand square feet, spaces per dwelling unit, and so on. Economists note that demand is a level of use observed at a particular price, and because most parking is free, the number of spaces "needed" is inflated by that subsidy. Others use the term "parking use" to reflect that distinction.

Parking duration. The time a car is parked. This is often portrayed as an average per parking facility (surface lot, structured parking facility, block face) for the observed period of data collection.

Parking-free new developments. Real estate projects built without any on-site parking.

Parking generation rates. The metric used to define parking demand generation for land use. This is often expressed as X spaces per thousand square feet or residential unit. National guidelines define typical parking generation rates but are criticized for not being responsive to local context. Using local data to calibrate rates is the preferred method for defining generation characteristics.

Parking improvement district. Also known as business improvement district or areas, publicly sanctioned, privately directed, quasi-public organizations that supplement public service to improve shared outdoor public spaces and promote economic and community development goals. Sometimes given direct management responsibility for parking facilities and efforts that influence the delivery of parking services.

Parking management. A group of methods that results in more efficient use of parking facilities by affecting parking behavior, demand, and location.

Parking model. A tool used to define parking demand for existing or future conditions. The tool uses land use mixture and parking generation rates to predict parking demand, then compares against parking supply to define the surplus or deficit for the area. A good model defines existing and future needs and is flexible enough to predict how incremental changes will affect the parking system and community development capability.

Parking occupancy. The percentage of spaces in a facility that are occupied. Rules can be set to limit the number of parked vehicles based on a schedule.

Parking supply. The number of parking spaces within a system. Often categorized by location (on- or off-street), type of parking (surface lot or structure), and ownership (public or private).

Parksmart. A sustainability rating system for parking garages, administered by Green Building Certification, Inc. (GBCI), the certification arm of the USGBC.

Partially self-managed parking. A management model in which a private entity outside of the facility or system owner provides some management functions.

Payment-in-lieu of parking. These programs offer a developer the option to pay a fee for each parking space deficiency in a proposed development application in lieu of providing the number of parking spaces required by local land-use regulations. Fees are collected and held by a municipality or parking authority until they can be used to construct a parking facility in the community.

Pedestrian wayfinding. The collection of signage and other physical items that directs a person who is on foot from one location to a destination.

Placemaking. An approach to planning, designing, and managing public spaces to create spaces that promote public health and happiness. Community participation and consideration of a community's assets and potential play large roles in placemaking.

Point-to-Point Encryption (P2PE). A credit card encryption method approved by PCI in a specific standard (PCI-P2PE). Point-to-point encryption, which differs from end-to-end encryption (not PCI certified as P2PE), is a payment security solution that instantaneously converts confidential credit card data and information into indecipherable code at the swipe of the card to prevent hacking and fraud.

Precast concrete parking garage. A garage that is comprised of individual precast elements that are manufactured offsite before being transported to and installed in a garage with a large crane. Individual pieces are connected via a variety of methods to create a single structure.

Programmatic design. Identifies the types and number of spaces within a building.

Programming. Architectural programming is a structured research and problem-solving process used to identify, examine, and elaborate upon the various needs underlying a design project. The architectural program is the foundation for a creative, meaningful, and—ultimately—useful architectural solution.

Public-private partnership (P3). A contractual arrangement between a public agency (federal, state, or local) and a private-sector entity. Through this agreement, the skills and assets of each sector (public and private) are shared in delivering a service or facility for the use of the general public.

Queuing spaces. The areas required for outbound cars within a parking lot or garage prior to the car driving through the access gates. They are often required to prevent cars in the drive aisle from blocking cars that are trying to back out of the parking stall.

Ramps.

>Double-threaded helix ramp. A ramp with two circular vehicle paths.

>Express ramp. An express ramp's slope exceeds 6.66 percent and the ramp rises in elevation more than six feet.

>Parkable ramp. A ramp on which parking is allowed when the slope of the ramp does not exceed 6.66 percent.

>Single-threaded helix ramp. A ramp with one circular vehicle path.

>Speed ramp. A speed ramp has a slope exceeding 6.66 percent and rises in elevation six feet or less.

>Transition ramp. A ramp with a slope that helps make the transition from one surface to another surface, when the difference between the surfaces is a change of eight to 10 percent, such as a speed or express ramp.

Relationship structure. The specific contractual arrangement between an owner of a parking asset and the provider of outsourced parking management services (contractor).

Repair. The reconstruction or renewal of any part of an existing building for the purpose of its maintenance or to correct damage.

Reservoir spaces. The areas required for inbound cars within a parking lot or garage prior to the car driving through the access gates. They are often required to prevent cars from backing up and blocking the public street.

Residential parking permit (RPP). A parking permit provided for residents in a designated zone to allow parking outside established posted regulations.

Ride-matching. A service that supports sharing rides in private vehicles on a regular or episodic basis to reduce vehicle trips, parking demand, and pollution.

Ride-sharing. A service that matches riders with drivers. This encompasses everything from carpools and vanpools to one-time car sharing on-demand through transportation network companies.

Right-sizing. Building only what is necessary based on accurate supply/demand studies.

Scale. The proportion, size, length, distance, or area used to describe a point-by-point relationship between two objects.

Scofflaw. Most often refers to vehicle owners or drivers with outstanding unpaid parking violations.

Self-managed parking. A management model in which daily decision-making resides with the owner of a parking facility, program or service.

Shared parking. Common in mixed-use shopping facilities, where uses (such as an office and a movie theater) can share parking spaces because their peak conditions occur at differing times. Special care should be taken to understand the impacts of restricted or permitted parking spaces and their inability to share with other users. These require legal shared parking arrangements, which ensure all users share as intended.

Short span. A structural system that uses four columns with short spans in between in the structure of a parking garage. They are often used in mixed-use properties where there is retail, residential, or office space above the garage.

S.M.A.R.T. Goal: A goal that is specific, measurable, achievable, results-focused, and time-bound.

Space sensor. A piece of hardware installed either at or above grade or on or inside a post that monitors the presence of a vehicle in a specific area or space. Sensors transmit this information in real-time or near-real-time to a web-based software application where the data is stored for analytical or enforcement purposes.

Surplus/deficit. Parking demand minus parking supply; defines the availability of spaces within the system (or subset). A positive value indicates a surplus of spaces. A negative value indicates a deficit.

Surveillance. A practice by which an individual or organization utilizes digital or physical means to monitor an area or item of interest in an overt or covert manner.

Transportation demand management (TDM). Programs, policies, and services that help the traveling public use alternatives to driving in single-occupancy vehicles. Includes public transit, intermodal connections, shuttles, ride- and bike-share, and other alternative methods of transportation, and improves connectivity through use of sidewalks, walkways, transit stations and layover locations, bus stops, and last-mile shuttle routes. Provides incentives to use alternate transportation and commuting methods.

Transportation network companies (TNCs). These organization use mobile apps and websites to pair passengers with drivers who provide rides for hire. TNCs include Uber and Lyft.

Triple bottom line. A framework for sustainability, the concept of balancing people, planet, and profit.

Turnover. The number of times a parking space is used by different vehicles throughout the day. This metric is calculated per block face or facility and is the number of cars observed divided by the number of spaces on that block face or facility.

Vehicle traffic flow. The circulation pattern of a car as it drives through a garage.

Vertical transportation. The way cars move from floor to floor in a parking garage, normally either on ramps or elevators.

Violation rate. The number of space hours in violation divided by the total number of space hours.

Vision. This statement should be very aspirational and speak to the organization's ultimate point of success.

Wayfinding. In parking, a system that orients drivers and pedestrians to where they are and where they want to go. Encompasses signage, lighting, color schemes, and sometimes mobile apps or other technologies.

Index

Page numbers in *italics* refer to figures. Page numbers in **bold** refer to tables.